AF378381

GAUGUIN AND THE IMPRESSIONISTS

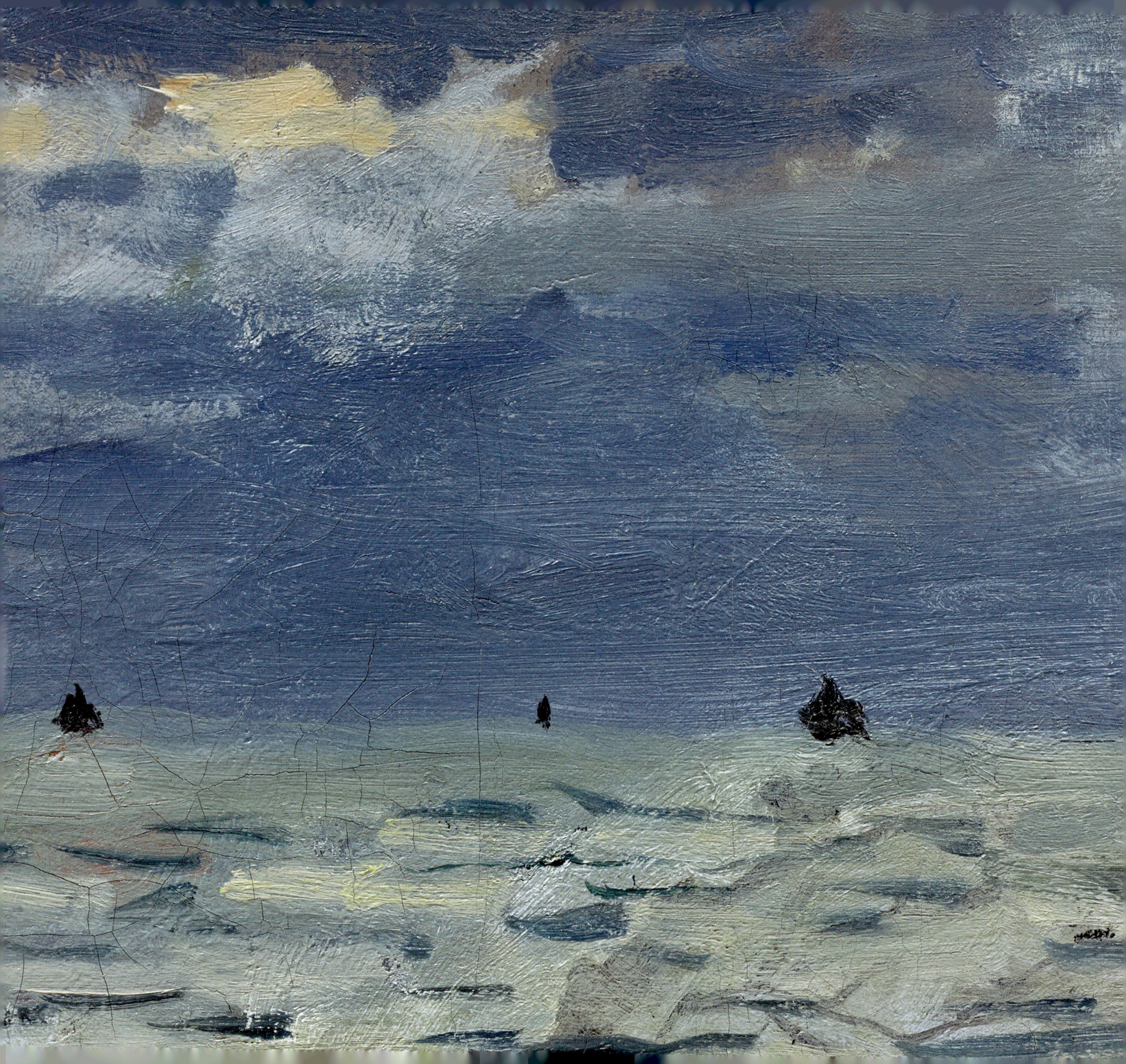

GAUGUIN AND THE IMPRESSIONISTS

THE ORDRUPGAARD COLLECTION

ROYAL ACADEMY OF ARTS

First published on the occasion of the exhibition
'Gauguin and the Impressionists: Masterpieces
from the Ordrupgaard Collection'

Royal Academy of Arts, London
29 March – 14 June 2020

Exhibition organised by Ordrupgaard, Copenhagen,
and the Royal Academy of Arts, London

This exhibition has been made possible as a result of the Government
Indemnity Scheme. The Royal Academy of Arts would like to thank
HM Government for providing indemnity and the Department for
Digital, Culture, Media and Sport and Arts Council England for
arranging the indemnity.

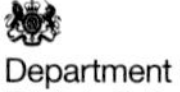
Department for
Digital, Culture,
Media & Sport

SECRETARY AND CHIEF EXECUTIVE, ROYAL ACADEMY OF ARTS
Axel Rüger

DIRECTOR, ORDRUPGAARD
Anne-Birgitte Fonsmark

EXHIBITION CURATORS
Royal Academy of Arts   *Ordrupgaard*
Anna Ferrari   Anne-Birgitte Fonsmark
with Rose Thompson
and Lucy Chiswell

EXHIBITION ORGANISATION
Royal Academy of Arts   *Ordrupgaard*
Elana Woodgate   Malene Anthon
with Lucy Davis

PHOTOGRAPHIC AND COPYRIGHT CO-ORDINATION
Susana Vázquez Fernández

EXHIBITION CATALOGUE
Royal Academy Publications
Florence Dassonville, Production Co-ordinator
Rosie Hore, Project Editor
Carola Krueger, Production Manager
Peter Sawbridge, Editorial Director
Nick Tite, Publisher

Abridgement of original catalogue entries: Tom Neville
Index: Hilary Bird

Design: Maggi Smith
Typeset in Isidora
Colour origination: Gomer Press

Printed in Wales by Gomer Press
Printed on 150gsm Arctic Matt

British Library Cataloguing-in-Publication Data
A catalogue record for this book is available from
the British Library

ISBN 978-1-912520-50-3

Distributed outside the United States and Canada by
ACC Art Books Ltd, Sandy Lane, Old Martlesham,
Woodbridge, Suffolk, IP12 4SD

Distributed in the United States and Canada by
ARTBOOK | D.A.P., 155 Sixth Avenue, New York, NY 10013

EDITORIAL NOTES
All dimensions are given in centimetres, height before width.

Unless otherwise stated, all illustrated works of art are part
of the Ordrupgaard Collection, Copenhagen.

Authorship of the catalogue entries on pages 114–31 is indicated
by the following initials:
BA   Birgitte Anderberg
A-BF   Anne-Birgitte Fonsmark
TL   Thomas Lederballe
ACWI   Anne Cathrine Wolsgaard Iversen

References are given for relevant catalogues raisonnés and
for Ordrupgaard's catalogue of its French collection
(Fonsmark et al. 2011), which lists the full literature for each work.

ILLUSTRATIONS
Page 2: detail of cat. 26   Page 24: detail of cat. 33
Page 7: detail of cat. 48   Pages 32–33: detail of cat. 28
Page 9: detail of cat. 31   Pages 112–13: detail of cat. 36
Pages 10–11: detail of cat. 58   Pages 132–33: detail of cat. 44
Page 12: detail of cat. 39

Contents

President's Foreword

Impressionism took its time to reach Scandinavia, making Wilhelm Hansen and his wife Henny among the first collectors in Copenhagen in the early twentieth century. Wilhelm Hansen discovered Impressionism during business trips to Paris, but it was the outbreak of the First World War that gave him and his fellow Danish collectors the opportunity to acquire collections of outstanding quality. In 1916 Hansen made his first recorded purchases when he bought works by Claude Monet, Camille Pissarro, Pierre-Auguste Renoir and Alfred Sisley. Over the next few years, acquisitions continued apace. Advised by the critic and friend of the Impressionists Théodore Duret, Hansen bought from the most prestigious Parisian dealers including the Galerie Bernheim-Jeune and the Galerie Durand-Ruel, both of which famously promoted Impressionism. Hansen also bought from distinguished private collectors: he acquired works at the sale of Edgar Degas's spectacular collection in 1918 and paintings from the collection of George Viau. In 1922 Hansen's collection was described as one of the best collections of French nineteenth-century painting outside France. Unfortunately, however, the collection was not spared the Hansens' financial difficulties of the early 1920s. When a bank from which Hansen had taken a loan crashed he was forced to sell part of his French art collection, which he later attempted to replace. The collection was, however, changed in character. The Hansens' collection is therefore a reflection of their tastes and circumstances, and of the contemporary fashion for French Impressionism among collectors in northern Europe.

The Royal Academy has a long tradition of exhibiting Impressionism, and we are delighted to present the Ordrupgaard Collection for the first time in the United Kingdom. We would like to thank Tim Marlow, our former Artistic Director, and Andrea Tarsia, our Head of Exhibitions, who programmed this exhibition. We are indebted to Anne-Birgitte Fonsmark, Director of Ordrupgaard, for her generous collaboration and for curating this exhibition with Anna Ferrari, assisted by Rose Thompson and Lucy Chiswell, at the Royal Academy. We are immensely grateful to colleagues across both institutions without whom the exhibition and its catalogue would not have been possible. In particular, we would like to thank Malene Anthon at Ordrupgaard, and Elana Woodgate, assisted by Lucy Davis, and Susana Vázquez Fernández at the Royal Academy. Finally, we extend our thanks to Birgitte Anderberg, Anne-Birgitte Fonsmark, Thomas Lederballe and Anne Cathrine Wolsgaard Iversen for their thoughtful contributions to this catalogue and to Maggi Smith for its elegant design.

Rebecca Salter PRA
President, Royal Academy of Arts

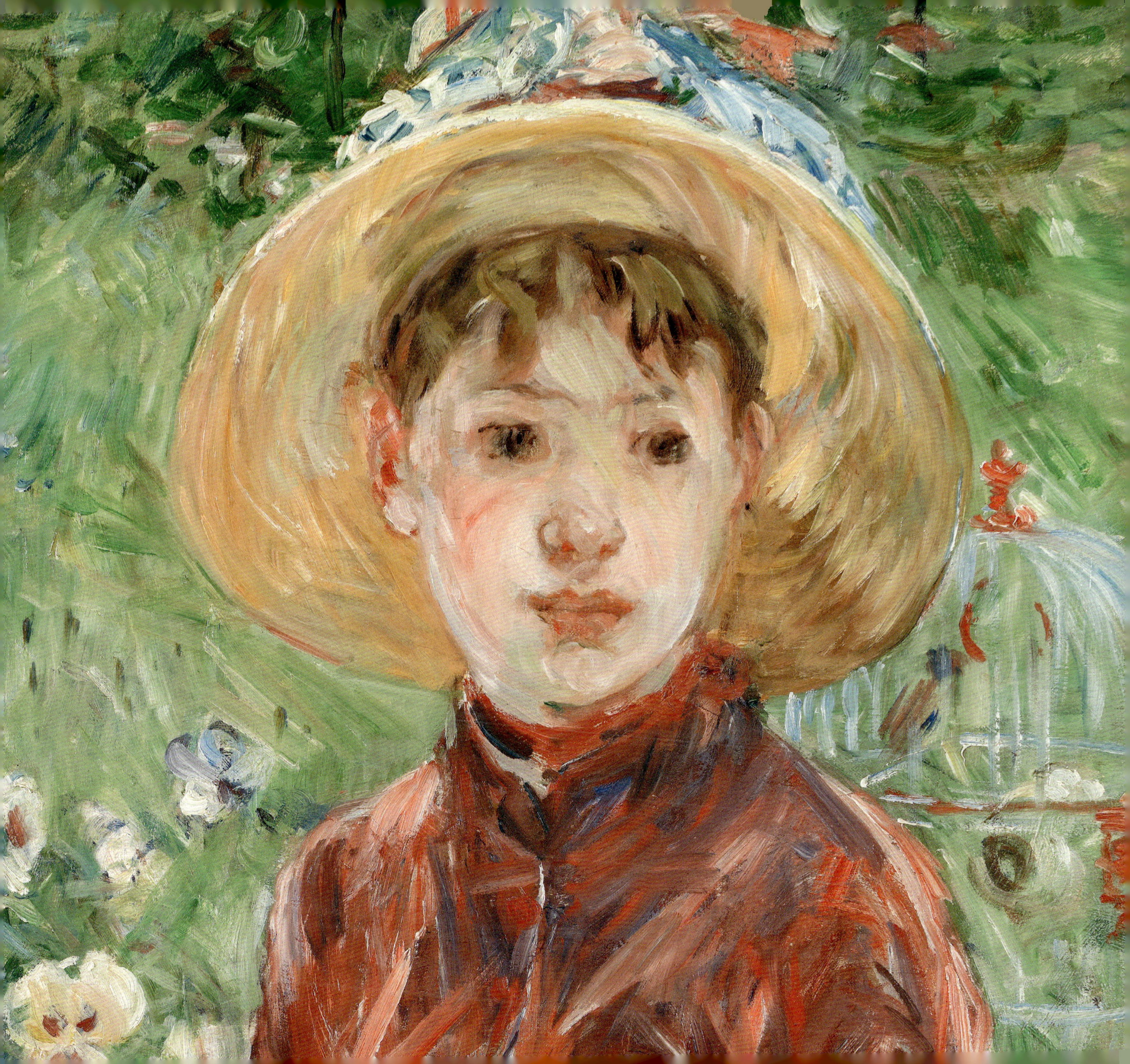

Acknowledgements

The Royal Academy of Arts would like to thank the
following individuals for their invaluable assistance
in the making of this exhibition and its catalogue:

Wayne Daly and Claire Lyon from Daly & Lyon
Ann Dumas
Hanne Faurby
Dorothy Feaver
Ian Gardner
Mari Griffith
Fiona Houston
Tom Johnson from Lightwaves Ltd
Peter Knowles
Adrian Locke
Per Rumberg
Petr Šámal
Nicola von Velsen
Diane Whitehouse

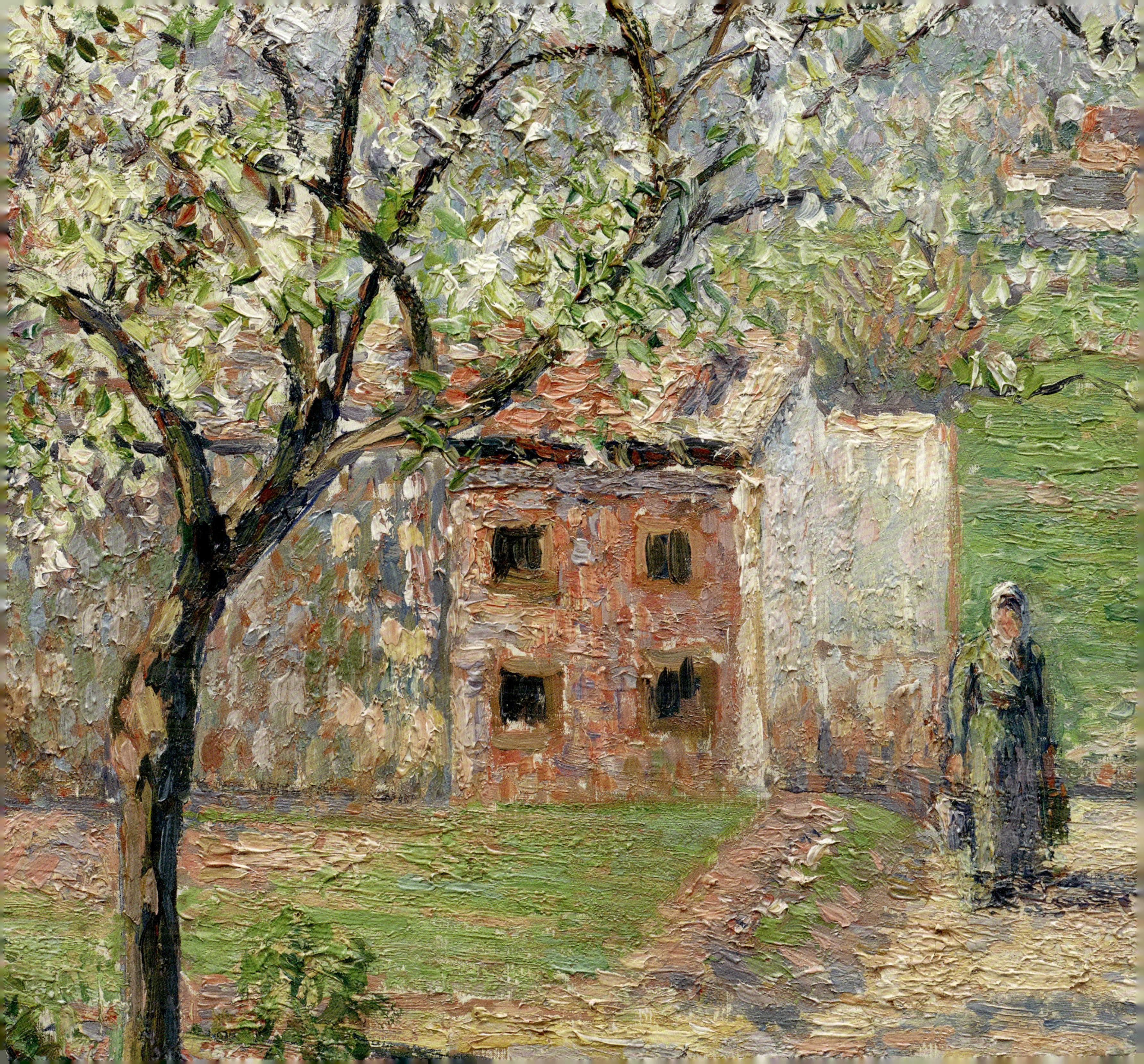

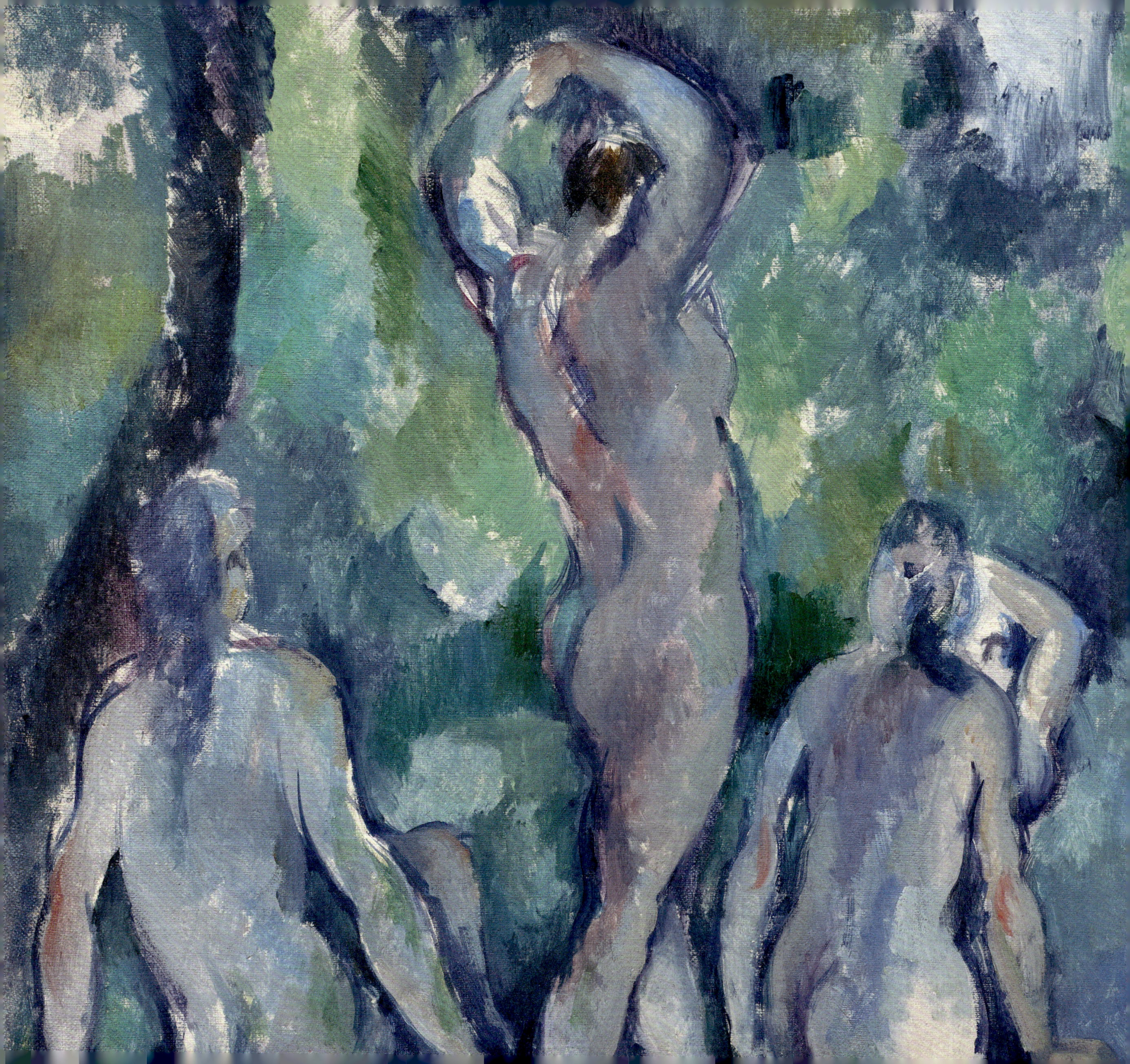

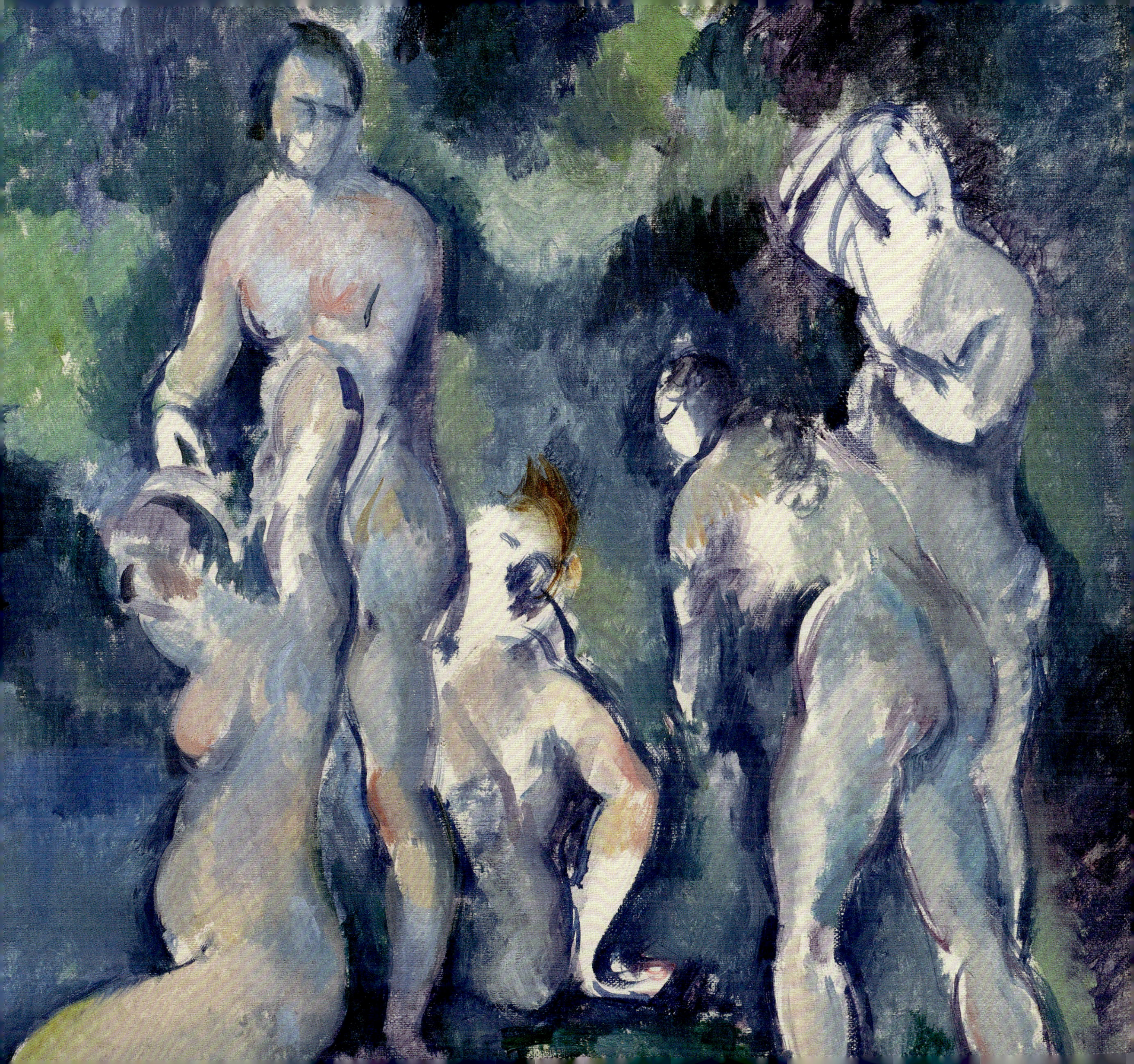

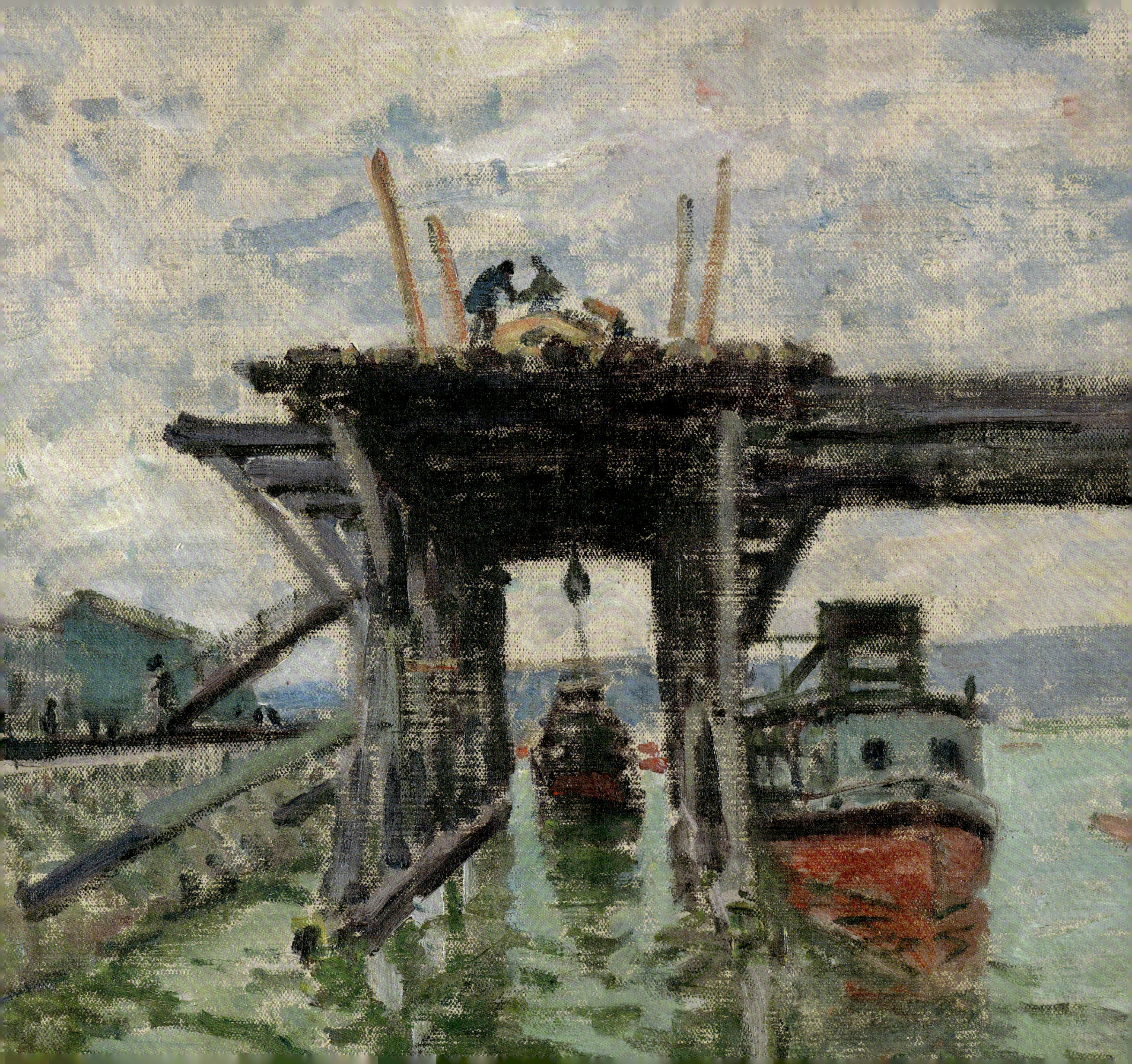

An Introduction to Wilhelm Hansen's Collection of French Art at Ordrupgaard

Although Wilhelm Hansen (1868–1936) came from a modest, middle-class home, it was clear from his early years that he had the ambition and talent to climb the social ladder. In around 1888, aged only twenty, he was given a job by the Copenhagen agency of the British insurance company Gresham's. Three years later, thanks to his initiative and business acumen, he took over the management of the agency during the course of which he became a leader in Danish insurance and one of the most prominent personalities in Copenhagen society – as well as a particularly wealthy man.

From the outset, Hansen's approach to business contained an element of idealism. It seems to have been during a journey to England that, inspired by the English Prudential Insurance Company, he conceived the idea of creating a life-insurance company for the man in the street.[1] He realised his visionary ideas when he founded the Dansk Folkeforsikringsanstalt (Danish People's Insurance Institution) in May 1896: this came to represent his most significant contribution to Danish insurance. He later founded the international life-insurance business Mundus, which he was to merge with Hafnia, one of Denmark's major insurance companies, in 1905, upon becoming a member of the board and administrative director of the latter company. He also helped to found the people's insurance company La Populaire in France in 1902, of which he was director from 1919.

Hansen combined his enormous energy and willpower with a rare enthusiasm. He could be reticent, but behind 'the gruff, often curt and sullen manner that was his mask' there was 'a human warmth and a quiet humour'.[2] His determined expression and a certain wryness can be seen in his portrait by the Danish painter Julius Paulsen (fig. 1).[3] His idealism is also evident in his youthful commitment to the new world language Volapük, which the German priest J. M. Schleyer introduced in 1880 and which had some success, including in Denmark, until it was superseded in 1887 by the less complicated Esperanto. Not content

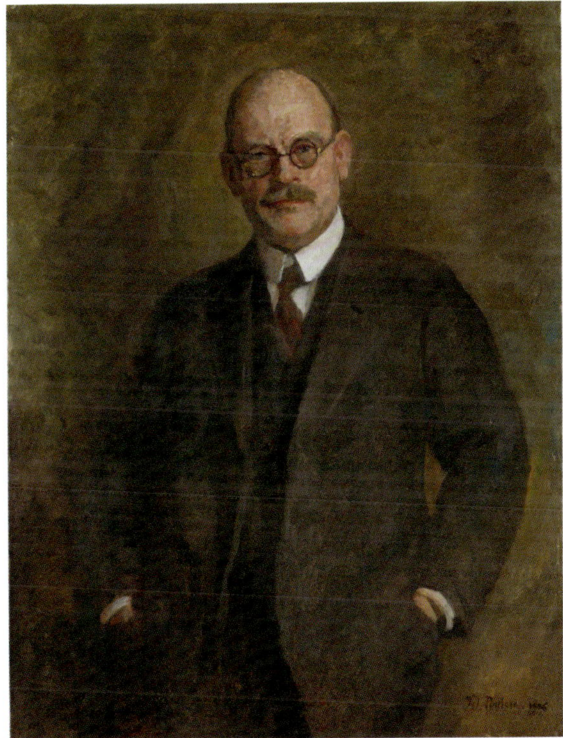

Fig. 1
Julius Paulsen (1860–1940),
Portrait of Wilhelm Hansen, 1926.
Oil on canvas, 105 x 59.5 cm

with simply learning the language, Hansen compiled both a primer and a dictionary to which he attached the motto 'Menad bal – pük bal' ('One mankind – one language'). It was while teaching the language that he met Henny Nathalie Soelberg Jensen (1870–1951), whom he was to marry in 1891. Their love letters were written, of course, in Volapük.

Hansen had no artistic education and came from a home where there was no art. He did, however, take lessons at the Efterslægtskab's school, a philanthropic institution that offered drawing lessons, where he was a contemporary of the Danish painter Peter Hansen (1868–1928), no relation, who not only remained a friend for life but also a good counsellor in questions of art. Wilhelm and Henny Hansen soon began to purchase works of art. They began with pictures from the so-called 'Golden Age' of Danish art, with the Eckersberg School and national Romantic landscapes most prominent.[4] Danish contemporary art was also represented, with works by the major figures of Symbolist Realism, L. A. Ring and Vilhelm Hammershøi. Paintings by the Danish 'Impressionist' Theodor Philipsen were also acquired in abundance, as were those of the 'Funen' painters (an artists' colony established on the Danish island in the late 1880s) including Johannes Larsen and Fritz Syberg, and above all Peter Hansen himself.[5] The Hansens' home in Hambroesgade in Copenhagen was soon filled with pictures and news of their 'famous dining room' started to circulate.[6]

Hansen often travelled as he built up his insurance empire, and his work with La Populaire often took him to Paris. His many letters home to Henny from his first visits to the French capital in 1893 recount his regular visits to the Salon, art galleries and museums, although mention of the art itself is rare.[7] Many years were to pass before Hansen made concrete plans to create a collection of French art. In 1915 he outlined his dream collection to his good friend the Swedish art historian Axel Gauffin.[8] The project was ambitious, his intention to assemble a group of pictures from Corot to Cézanne, comprising twelve paintings by each of the nineteenth-century masters.

His many visits to Paris had given Hansen a solid acquaintance with French art, but his plan may also have been stimulated by other factors. An exhibition of nineteenth-century French painting opened at the Statens Museum for Kunst in Copenhagen in 1914,[9] and was subsequently stranded in the city after the outbreak of the First World War. A second catalyst was the possibility of making favourable purchases at that time of great upheaval. The Paris-based Danish art dealer Tyge Møller advised his customers to be on the lookout for good investment opportunities. In a letter to Hansen's fellow-collector, the then director of the Ny Carlsberg Glyptotek, Helge Jacobsen, Møller wrote: 'Knowledgeable men such as Durand-Ruel, Vollard, Hessel, have declared … that first-class art will become much more expensive after the war.'[10] It was a good time for art investors and Møller did everything he could to tempt his Danish customers: 'As soon as the war ends capital will flow in from America to purchase French art for American galleries, which have already set up a committee with a capital of 50 million – money in other words that is lying there waiting to be converted into works of art.'[11]

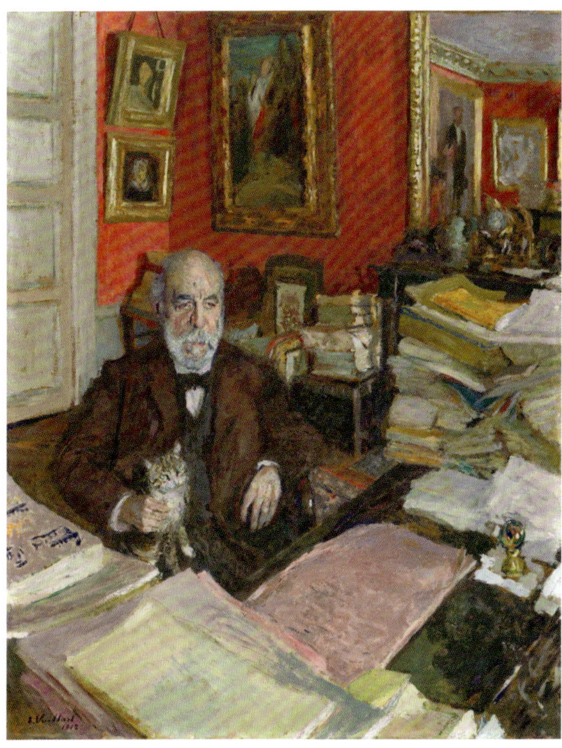

Hansen soon began to realise his plan. He did so very systematically and it was said that he set about it just as purposefully as when he went fishing for pike in the lakes near his summer house. He took only two years, from 1916 to 1918, to attain his target, and present to the public a collection that the Swedish collector Klas Fåhræus described as the 'best Impressionist collection in all the world!'[12]

Hansen made his first purchases in September 1916. He wrote to Henny from Paris: 'I may just as well confess now instead of later that I have been reckless and have made considerable purchases. But I know that I will be forgiven when you see what I have bought; all first-class with stars. I have bought Sisley (2 marvellous landscapes), Pissarro (a fine landscape), and Claude Monet (Rouen Cathedral) – one of his best-known works – and Renoir (Portrait of a Lady).'[13]

He made a number of other purchases at this time, including Renoir's picture of his lover Lise Tréhot (cat. 42) sitting on the grass, and a group of Guillaumins. From Bernheim-Jeune in Paris he acquired in 1916 Monet's *Waterloo Bridge, Overcast* (cat. 28) and Morisot's portrait of Marie Hubbard (cat. 49). From Paul Rosenberg he purchased Sisley's *The River Boat Garage* in 1918 (cat. 39).

He made some purchases outside France during these years, including Gauguin's *The Wine Harvest, Human Misery* (cat. 54), which he bought from the Galerie Arnot in Vienna in 1918. Two years earlier, he had bought Gauguin's *The Little One Is Dreaming, Étude* (cat. 50) from the artist's widow Mette. Another Gauguin, *Portrait of a Young Girl (Vaïte 'Jeanne' Goupil)* (cat. 57), was acquired in 1918 from the picture's original commissioner, the girl's father, Auguste Goupil. Gauguin's *Tahitian Woman* (cat. 55) is another of these early acquisitions.

Although in time the First World War put a stop to Hansen's visits to Paris, his connections in the city meant that he could continue his purchases during the war years. His co-director at La Populaire, Émile Duval-Fleury, helped him with the practical arrangements by spotting works on the market, bidding at auction and looking after storage and dispatch of acquisitions. Hansen, however, doubted Duval-Fleury's 'artistic sense',[14] and chose instead to take advice from one of the leading art critics of the time, Théodore Duret (1838–1927; fig. 2).

When Hansen first came into contact with him, Duret was about 80 and could look back on a long life in which the Impressionists had played a central part. As a young man, he had become a close friend of Manet and a passionate advocate, collector and patron of Impressionist art.[15] As Hansen's advisor, Duret made possible the acquisition of, for example, Manet's late work *Basket of Pears* (cat. 24), writing in 1916: 'I have otherwise no Manet to recommend to you with the exception of the basket with pears that I showed you when you came to visit me. Manets are no longer to be found, they are stuck in museums and private collections.'[16] *Basket of Pears* became one of Hansen's favourite pictures and during dinner at home he is said to have shown it to his guests 'as an extra dessert after the ice cream'.[17]

Duret, too, tracked down and bought an important Delacroix for Hansen in 1917. He emphasised that the 35,000 francs he paid for *Ugolino and His Sons* (cat. 3) was a special 'wartime price', despite the fact that the great Romantic painter's work had 'become extremely rare and ... practically disappeared'. Duret declared that he was prepared to 'wager [his] amour-propre as an old collector in recommending the purchase of this picture'.[18]

From February 1919 Hansen returned to Paris and was able to see Émile Duval-Fleury again, look at paintings, and 'pay a visit to Théodore Duret, Viau, and others...'[19] The dealer Tyge Møller told of the reception Hansen received: 'All the art dealers are waiting for State Councillor Hansen's visit – he is received like a little god. They are all keen to make contact with him and are putting their best things to one side ...'[20]

The art market had changed since the end of the First World War and Hansen noted that prices had risen. He had to withdraw from the bidding at one auction, even though there was 'a fine Gauguin I would really have liked: 58,000 + 10%!'[21] He was to visit Paris a good deal in 1919 and in November he went 'to an art dealer to see Courbet's famous pictures [including *The Artist's Studio*] which are to be purchased by the Louvre. Price 1 million francs...'[22]

To finance his many substantial purchases over an extremely short period, Hansen created a consortium with the collector Herman Heilbuth in 1918. Heilbuth was a strong supporter of the radical left-wing party and press, which he financed for many years, and another passion was art: he became one of the great Danish collectors of the period. The consortium's third partner was the Copenhagen art dealer Winkel and Magnussen. All three parties declared that their aim was the 'purchase and sale of works of art with the aim of bringing good and eminent art to Scandinavia'.[23]

Hansen may have come across such consortia in Paris where, for example, in 1904 the collector André Level established the consortium La Peau de l'Ours ('The Bear Skin') which invested in French modern art and famously sold its collection at a great profit a decade later. Instead of buying one picture after another, a consortium could purchase works in bulk with a view to selecting the finest and selling the remainder. This type of bulk purchasing was financed partially by a loan from what was at the time Denmark's largest private bank, the Danish Landmandsbank, whose board of directors and Bank Council included, respectively, Heilbuth and Hansen.

Heilbuth was an enterprising man and even before the consortium was founded he had bought an entire art collection in Paris that had been put

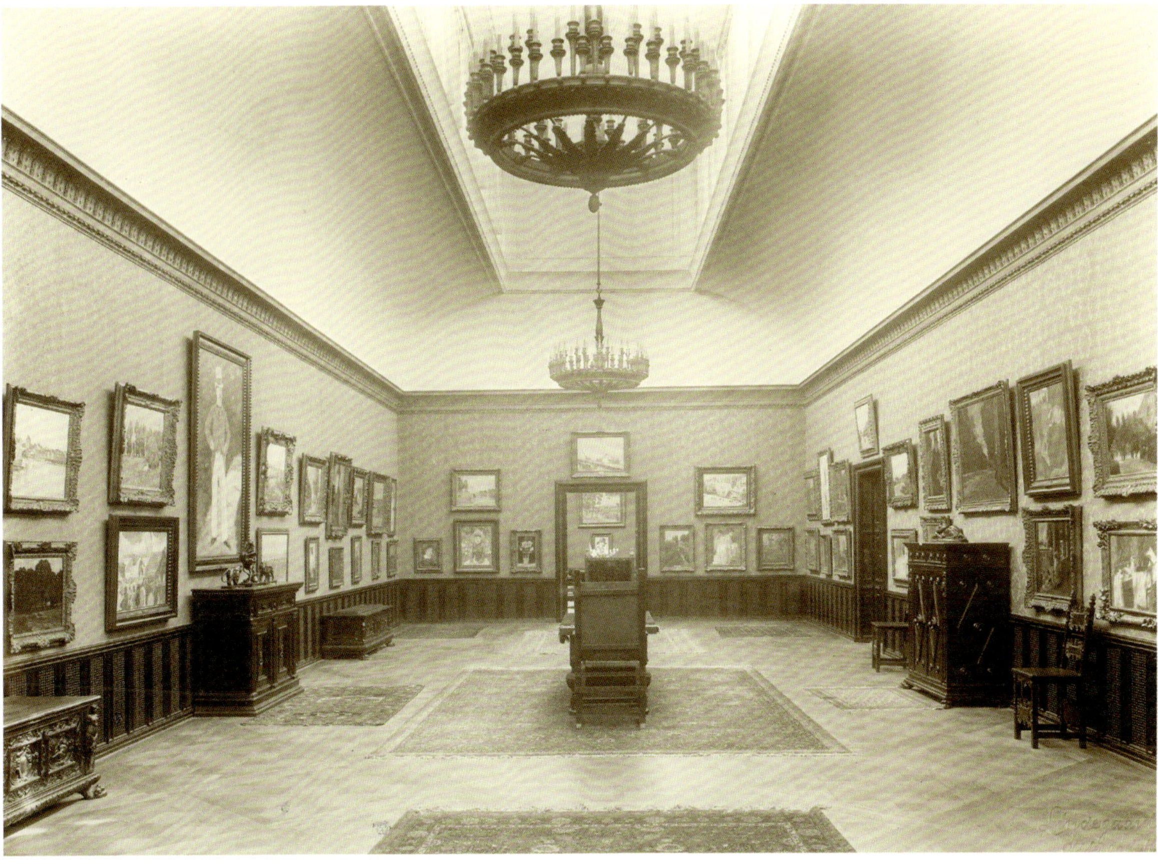

together by Isidore Montaignac, a Parisian art dealer who had originally worked for Georges Petit.[24] The 233 works in this collection were to have been dispersed at an auction in 1917 at the Galerie Georges Petit, but the sale was called off as a result of Heilbuth's private purchase.[25] The same happened with Louis Sarlin's collection, which was slated for auction at the Galerie Georges Petit in March 1918 but instead purchased by Hansen's consortium. The consortium also bought the collection of the Parisian dentist George Viau, some 200 paintings, for 1,371,760 kroner. Many central works in Hansen's collection came from this purchase, including

Gauguin's *Landscape at Pont-Aven* (cat. 51) and *Two Vases with Flowers* (cat. 53) and Morisot's *Young Girl on the Grass* (cat. 48). The consortium also bought from the Durand-Ruel and Tempelaere galleries, including works by Eva Gonzalès and Charles-François Daubigny. Unfortunately, negotiations with the businessman Auguste Pellerin to buy seventy Cézannes for three million francs fell through.

In the spring of 1918 the consortium made a brilliant purchase for over half a million francs at the auction of Degas's estate, during which not only the contents of his studio but also his famous art collection came under the hammer.[26] A sum of

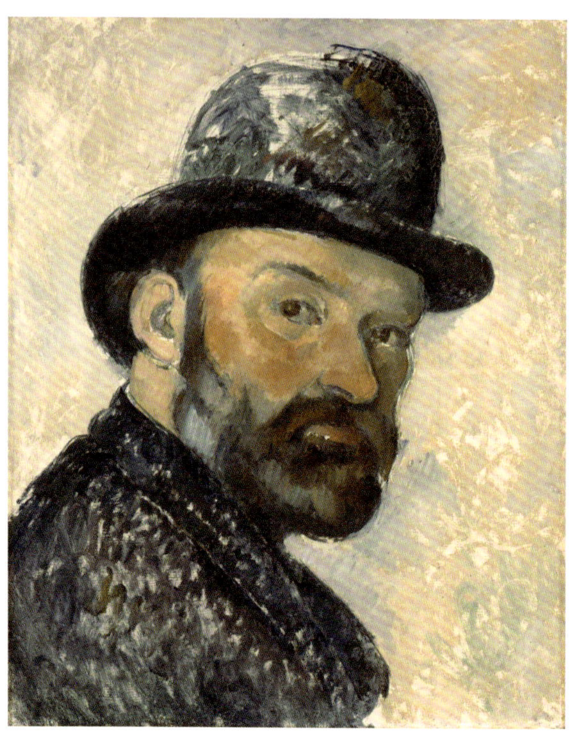

1,500,000 kroner was set aside for bidding for 46 paintings. Subsequent additions to Hansen's collection in 1918 included Delacroix's *Hercules Rescuing Hesione, Sketch* and Sisley's Bougival landscape (cat. 36). In May 1918 the consortium was active at the four auctions of Degas's own paintings. As a result Hansen acquired an oil painting from the painter's stay in New Orleans in 1872–73 (cat. 45). Finally, the consortium spent between 600,000 and 700,000 kroner in 1918 to acquire 28 pictures from Alphonse Kann's famous collection.[27] Hansen's acquisitions included Cézanne's *Women Bathing* (cat. 58), Courbet's *The Cliffs near Étretat* (cat. 8), Gauguin's *Blue Trees (Your Turn Will Come, My Beauty!)* (cat. 52) and *Adam and Eve* (cat. 56), and Matisse's still-life *Flowers and Fruits* (cat. 60).

The consortium's purchases resulted in a unique pool of art from which its members could select works by the key names of French nineteenth-century painting. At the same time Hansen's idealistic openness did not fail to show itself: every Monday the public was admitted free to see his collection, and, in his inaugural speech on 14 September 1918, he promised to present it one day to the state of Denmark. During the opening festivities, the director of the Statens Museum for Kunst, Karl Madsen, described Hansen as an Aladdin who had built up his temple of art with a combination of wealth and intelligence.

While acquiring his French art collection, Hansen had erected a temple of art at Ordrup on the northern edge of Copenhagen in the form of a country house. The building had originally been conceived as an elegant summer house in an estate of 13.6 acres, but it soon became clear that the Hansens' town house in Hambroesgade, already full to bursting point with Danish pictures, could hold no more. So, during construction, plans were amended to turn the summer house into a year-round residence and to provide it with an annexe to house the art collection. A gallery was built by Hansen's architect Gotfred Tvede, who was said to have taken his inspiration from the Swedish collector Klas Fåhræus's art room on the island of Lidingo in Sweden. Hansen's new gallery (fig. 3) was to house his 156 French pictures, ranging from the Neoclassical and Romantic schools, with David and Delacroix as the two main representatives, via Realism, Impressionism and Post-Impressionism, with Cézanne and Gauguin, and to Matisse as the first of the Fauves.

In September 1922, only four years after the opening of Ordrupgaard, however, the Danish Landmandsbank failed. The bank's director Emil

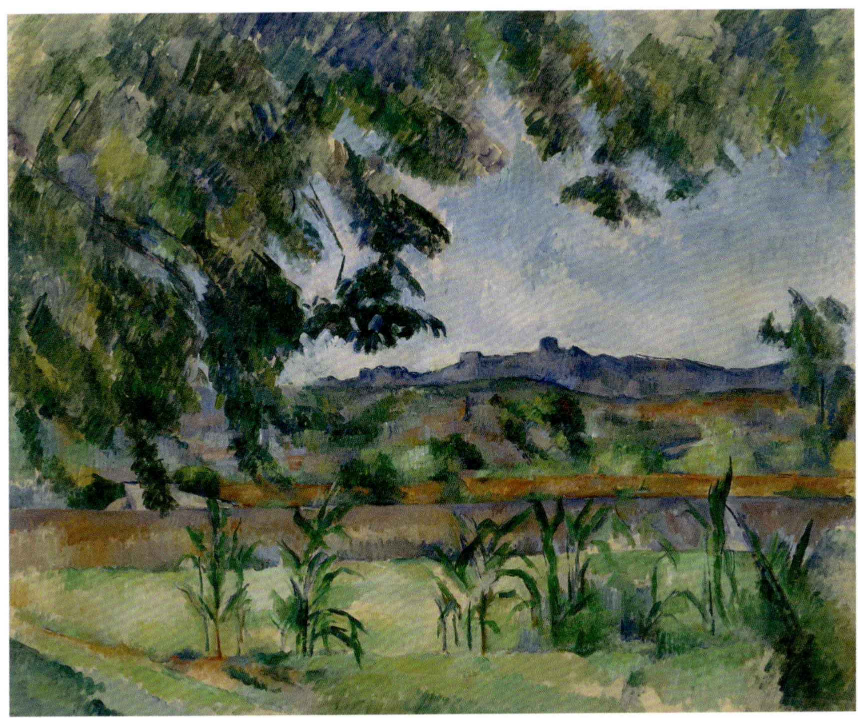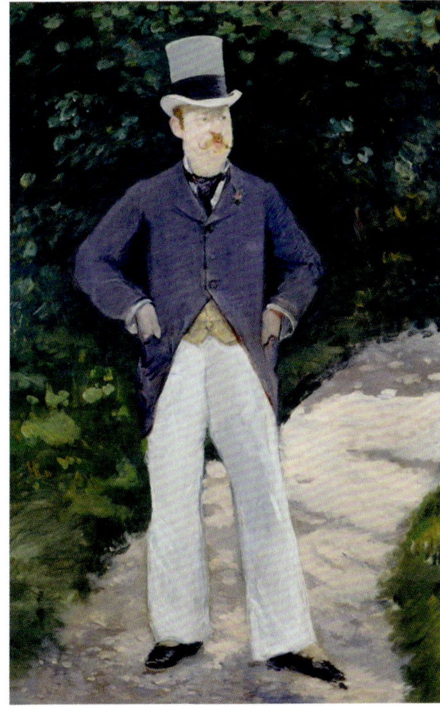

Glückstadt was charged with fraud and a prison term seemed likely, but he died in 1923 before sentencing. One of the bank's dubious commitments was a loan of over 12 million kroner to Herman Heilbuth, with paintings as security.[28] The bank's failure was a blow to Hansen as well, as he had just taken out a loan. He wanted to settle his debt as soon as possible, and made the difficult decision to sell his French pictures, including works by Cézanne (figs 4, 5) and Manet (fig. 6). He acted just as quickly and purposefully as he had done when building up the collection. In the same month as the bank's failure, he travelled to Paris to see the art dealer and gallery owner Henri Barbazanges, who contacted the eccentric American art collector Albert C. Barnes of Philadelphia. Léonce Bénédite, director of both the Musée du Luxembourg and the Musée Rodin, also put Hansen in touch with the Japanese collector Kojiro Matsukata.

The bank failure was a constant worry, and Hansen's daily letters home to Henny at this time reflect the great pressure he felt: 'Barbazanges does say that he will do everything to help me, but can he? I know well enough that I can sell the pictures, but at what price?'[29] They tell of his great anxiety 'with regard to the pictures, as they could certainly only be sold in America and negotiations with the people there are both difficult and slow. To sell them here in France at anything like a respectable price is something I consider impossible, at least at present.'[30]

At a certain point he must have given up on the Americans and decided to deal only with Matsukata. He made only slow progress there, too, and other potential purchasers emerged, including, early in 1923, Oskar Reinhart of Winterthur in Switzerland. Reinhart was the first prospective purchaser to travel to Copenhagen, and he negotiated promptly before

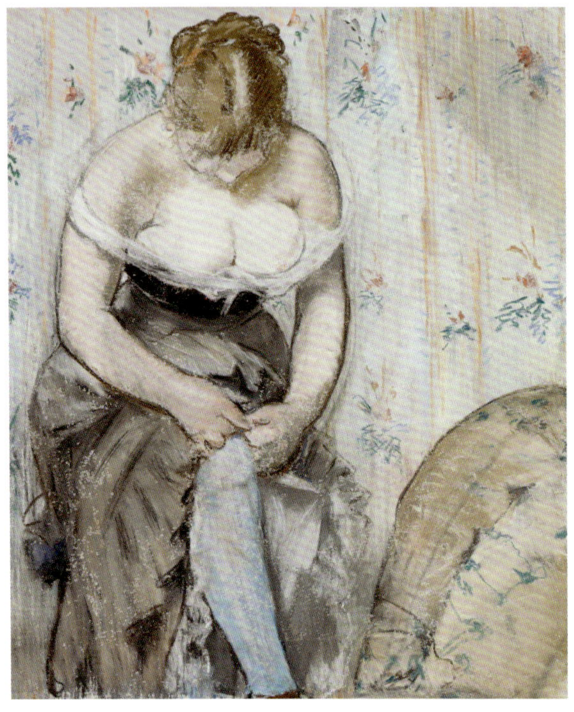

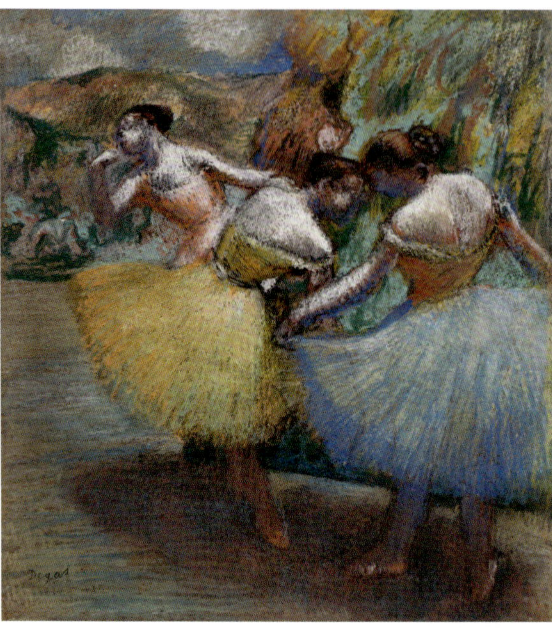

Fig. 7
Édouard Manet (1832–1883),
At the Toilet: Woman Fastening Her Garter, c. 1878–79. Pastel on canvas, 55.5 x 46.5 cm

Fig. 8
Edgar Degas (1834–1917),
Three Dancers, c. 1898.
Pastel on paper, 90 x 85 cm

others had submitted final offers. This enabled Hansen to put pressure on the Ny Carlsbergfond in Copenhagen to negotiate.[31] Matsukata eventually sent an offer on 6 February 1923.[32] At one point Hansen offered the Danish state – to which he intended to bequeath the collection – all his pictures for only one million kroner, only to be promptly turned down. Some years later he remembered with bitterness that he 'was met with an almost hostile coolness'.[33] As a consequence, foreign collectors benefited and most of the works went to Reinhart, apart from the significant purchases made by Matsukata. Reinhart's purchase of twenty-one French pictures enabled him to lay the foundations for an art collection of exquisite quality. Some canvases also found their way onto the walls of the Barnes Foundation in Philadelphia. In April 1923 the sales were concluded and in January 1924 it was announced that Hansen had repaid all his debts.[34]

Having sold a major part of the Ordrupgaard collection, Hansen then undertook to re-create what had been lost, and as soon as his finances allowed, he started to fill some gaps. Some forty works were acquired and the collection reopened on 24 May 1925.[35] Another eight works were added before early 1927,[36] and a few more works joined the collection later on. Hansen was determined, but the market had changed, and it had become more difficult to make such high-quality acquisitions. Nevertheless, he did succeed to some extent in making good the damage suffered by the collection.

It was Hansen's good fortune that Heilbuth wanted to sell works from his collection at this time. Hansen bought from him Corot's *Young Italian Woman Seated near a Lake* (cat. 11) and *Hamlet and the Gravedigger* (cat. 17). From Heilbuth, too, he acquired Delacroix's portrait of George Sand (cat. 2), Monet's

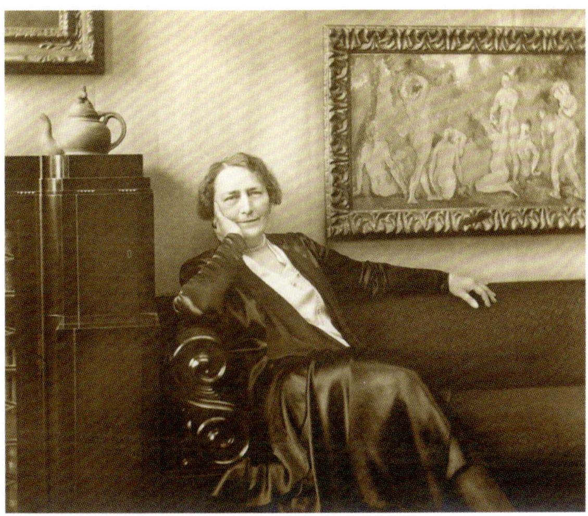

Seascape, Le Havre (cat. 26), Daumier's *The Wrestler* (cat. 6) and Courbet's depiction of roe deer in the snow (cat. 7), this latter work one of Hansen's most prized pictures.

The Galerie Durand-Ruel sold him a number of works around 1923–24, including a pair of beautiful Sisleys (cats 35, 38) and one of Pissarro's late cityscapes (cat. 34). At the Galerie Barbazanges, Hansen found the *Still-life* by Odilon Redon (cat. 59) and perhaps Renoir's sketch for *Le Moulin de la Galette* (cat. 44). Manet's *At the Toilet: Woman Fastening Her Garter* (fig. 7) came from the Pacquement Collection. His purchase of *The Windmill* (cat. 10) did much to restore his holding of Corot. Finally, he made particularly good purchases of works by Degas, including the artist's pastel portrait of his cousin

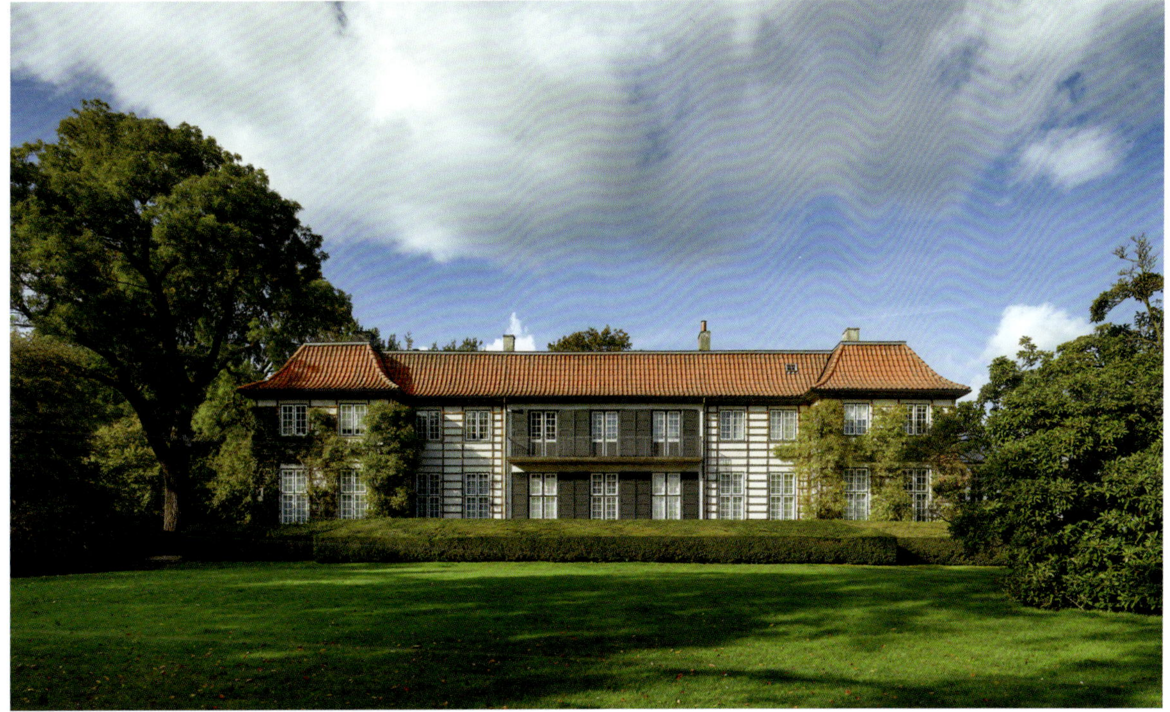

Mathilde Musson Bell, made during his stay with members of his family in New Orleans in 1872–73, and the late pastel *Three Dancers* (fig. 8), which had originally been purchased by the consortium in 1918 from Ambroise Vollard and which is one of the key works in the collection.

One day, in his office at Hafnia, Hansen said to the art historian Haavard Rostrup, a future director of Ordrupgaard: 'Would you like to see what I have bought?' It was Degas's little pastel of a dancer leaning forward to adjust her slipper. The work had previously been owned by Gauguin, who was a great admirer of Degas and had incorporated the pastel into the background of one of his flower pictures.[37] Hansen had purchased the pastel in 1931 from the Danish politician and author Edvard Brandes, who had bought it from his sister-in-law, Mette Gauguin. 'But now I have done with buying,' Hansen added.[38] His collection was complete – but no longer open to the public. His bitterness towards the Danish state led him to leave his pictures to his wife Henny, who ultimately fulfilled his original plan by bequeathing the collection to the state of Denmark.

Since becoming a national museum in 1953, Ordrupgaard has continued to evolve and expand. In August 2005 the collection opened a significant new extension by the prize-winning and internationally acclaimed Iraqi architect Zaha Hadid DBE RA (fig. 11). Hadid was born in Baghdad but trained at the Architectural Association in London, from which she graduated in 1977. When her design won the Danish Ministry of Culture's 2001 competition, the judges commented that although her proposals were the architectural antithesis of the existing building, this brought to both a balancing but contrasting clarity. As in many of her other projects, Hadid worked hard to decode and interpret her new building's surroundings, making it essentially an extension of the landscape. Cast in black lava concrete, which creates surface changes in colour and textural effects according to the weather and wind, the exterior of the building appears both grey or matt and glossy black. Inside, the fluidity of the spaces disguises the transition between galleries and corridors, not to mention floors and ceilings. The rooms relate constantly to the exterior terrain, their ceilings rising and falling as visitors progress through them. Large areas of glass let in daylight and views of the park, reinforcing the building's complete integration with the landscape.

In response to growing space constraints, Ordrupgaard launched an international competition in 2012 and commissioned the Norwegian architectural practice Snøhetta to design five underground exhibition galleries to link Hadid's exhibition spaces to Tvede's original buildings. This intervention will strengthen the character of the site, and connect existing and new gallery spaces seamlessly. Now nearing completion, Snøhetta's design for a steel roof to be integrated into the garden, where it will collect light and play with reflections, and through which visitors can approach the main entrance, has given the project its name: Himmelhaven (Heavenly Garden).

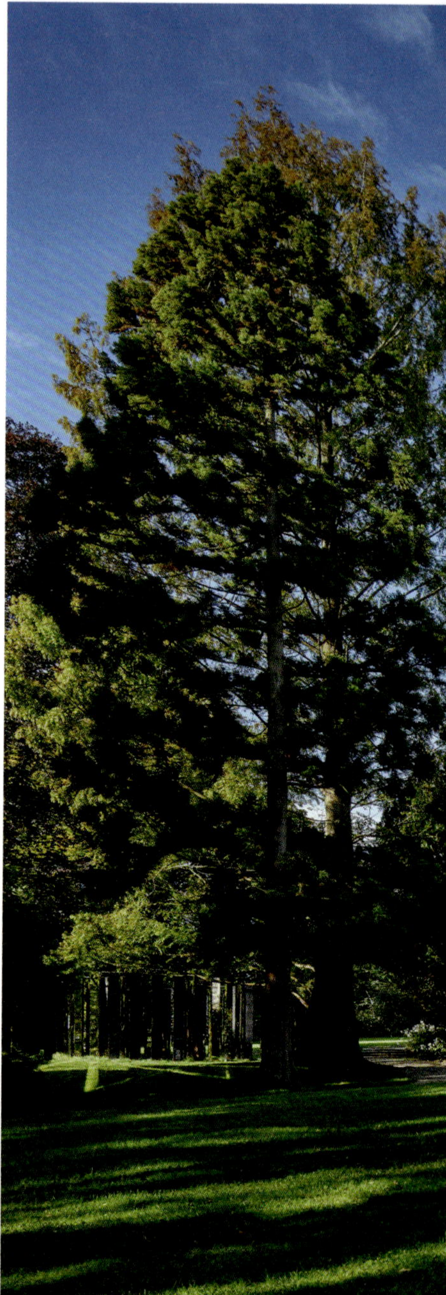

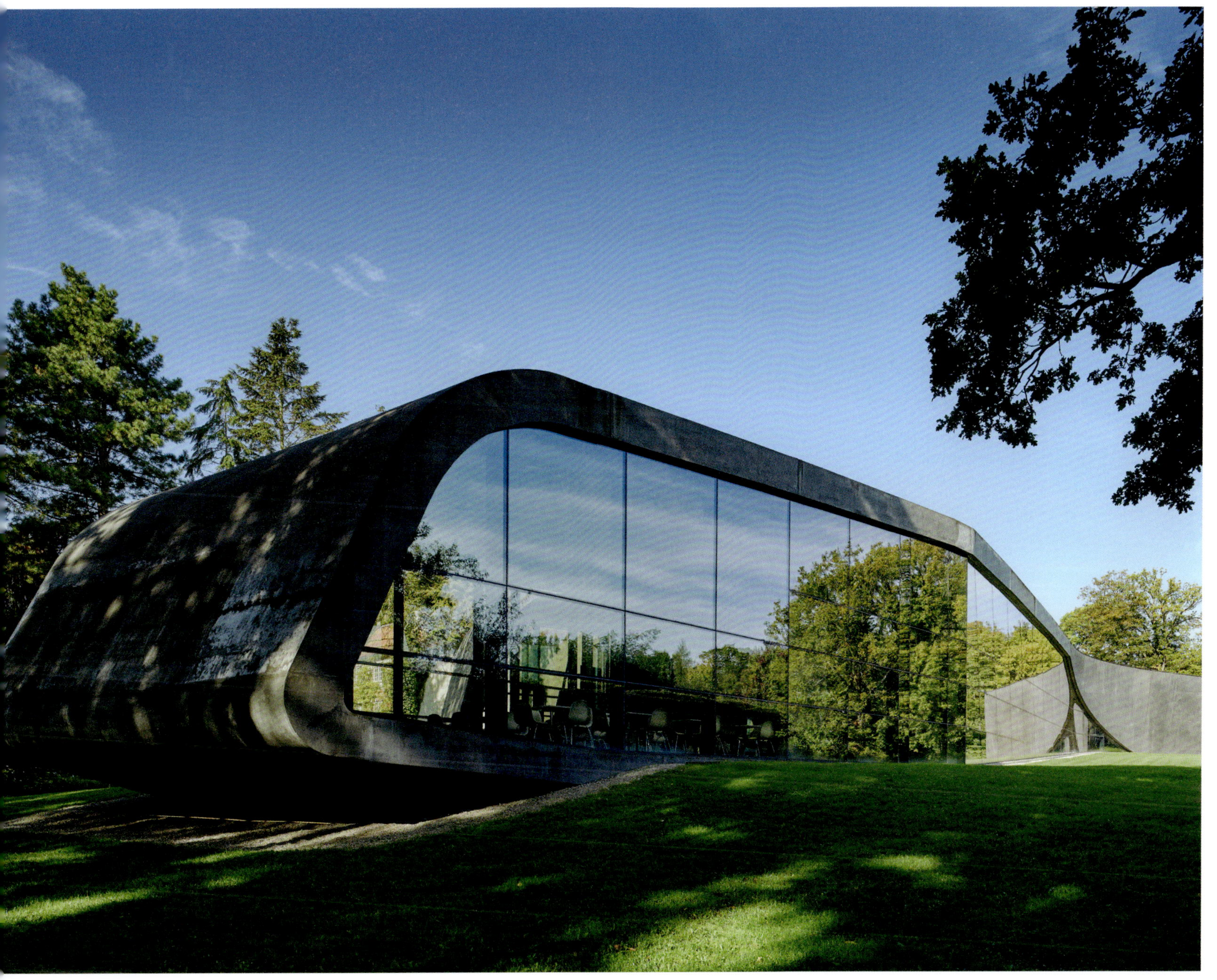

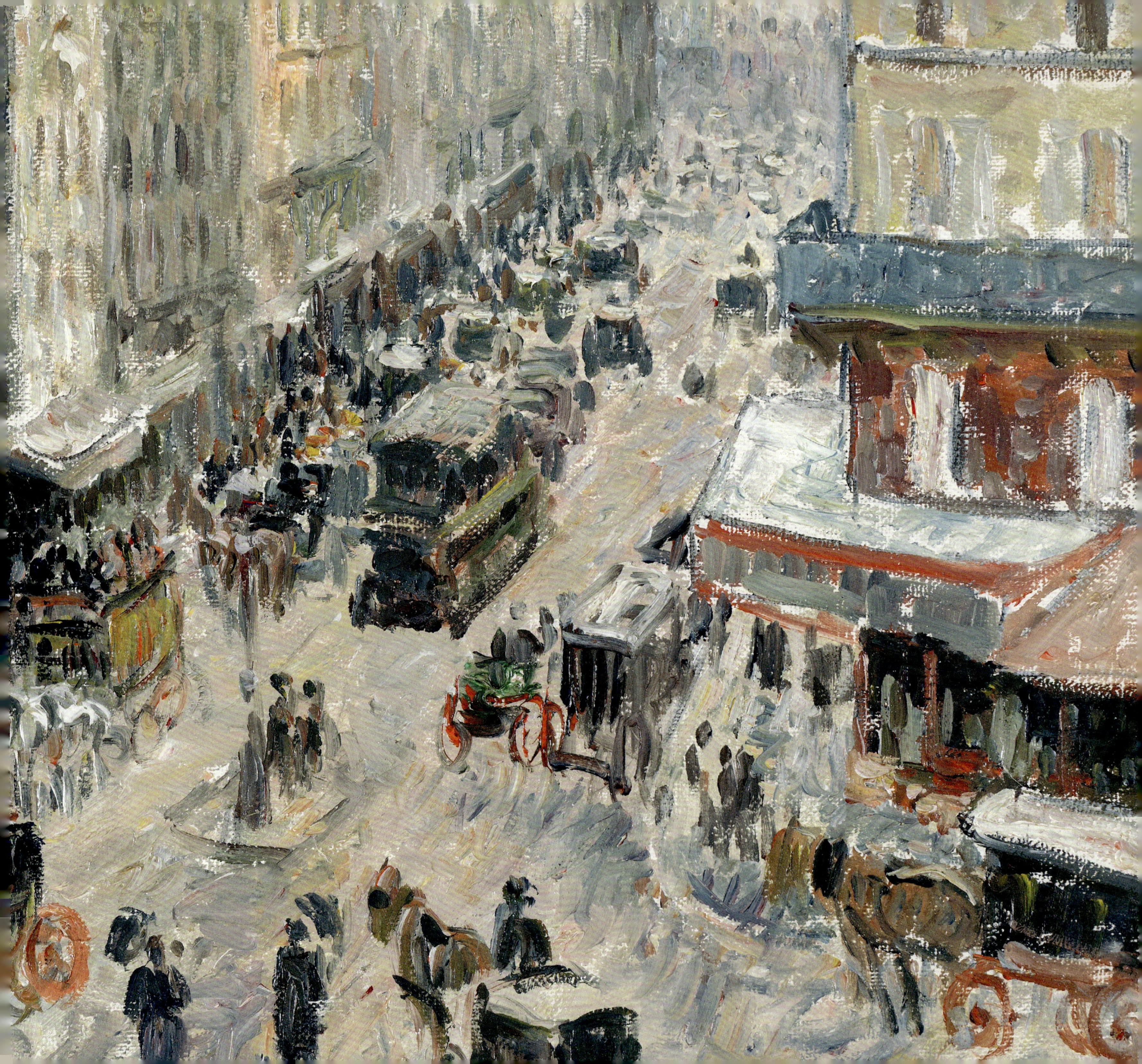

'A wartime price': Collecting French Painting in Copenhagen

Fig. 12
Wilhelm Hansen in the Corot Room
at Ordrupgaard, *c.* 1918

When the Danish insurance director Wilhelm Hansen began collecting French art in 1916, he was 48 years old and had already been collecting nineteenth-century Danish art for half his life. Hansen and his wife Henny ceased to collect Danish works as soon as their interest in French art was aroused and within just a few years they amassed an exceptional collection of works by Corot, Manet, Monet and Sisley as well as sculpture by Rodin. Their collection soon became internationally renowned.[1]

Between the 1890s and the First World War, when the Hansens started collecting, the reputation of Impressionist art shifted considerably. No longer the scorned and ridiculed movement of the 1870s, Impressionism had entered national collections, and publications affirmed the movement's place in the history of art and in the French national narrative.[2] At the same time, prominent international collectors began to vie for works by Impressionist artists, and the first generation of French amateur collectors gave way to newly wealthy industrialists and bankers from Europe, America and Russia.[3] Competition intensified when the Russians Sergei Shchukin and Ivan Morozov started collecting at the turn of the century, rapidly assembling astonishing collections of recent French art.[4] This new competition pushed up prices and, in 1912, Louisine Havemeyer, one of the earliest American collectors of Impressionism, set the record for the highest price paid for a work by a living artist when she acquired Degas's *Dancers Practising at the Barre* (fig. 13) for 435,000 francs.[5] New collectors from America and Europe sustained the competition: in 1904 the Hungarian Marczell von Nemès began his

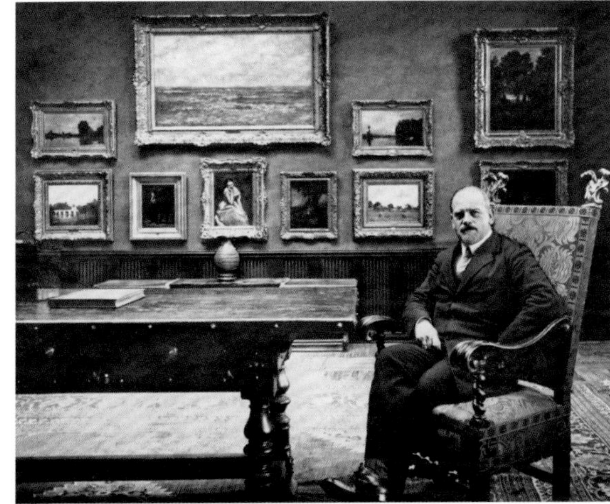

expansive collection, which by 1910 included works by Cézanne, Degas, Manet and Monet; in 1905 the Irish collector Sir Hugh Lane began purchasing Impressionist works; in Switzerland, Georg Reinhart started his collection in 1912 with works by Renoir; while in Philadelphia, Albert C. Barnes already owned 50 works by Renoir and 14 by Cézanne in 1915. As an established collector of Danish art who often travelled to Paris for business, Hansen was likely aware of Impressionism's changing fortunes. Yet it was only around 1916 that he started collecting, when France was at war with Germany, and neutral Denmark offered a favourable climate for collecting. Hansen was undoubtedly passionate about art, but it was the specific Danish context that gave him and his peers the opportunity to collect on such a scale.

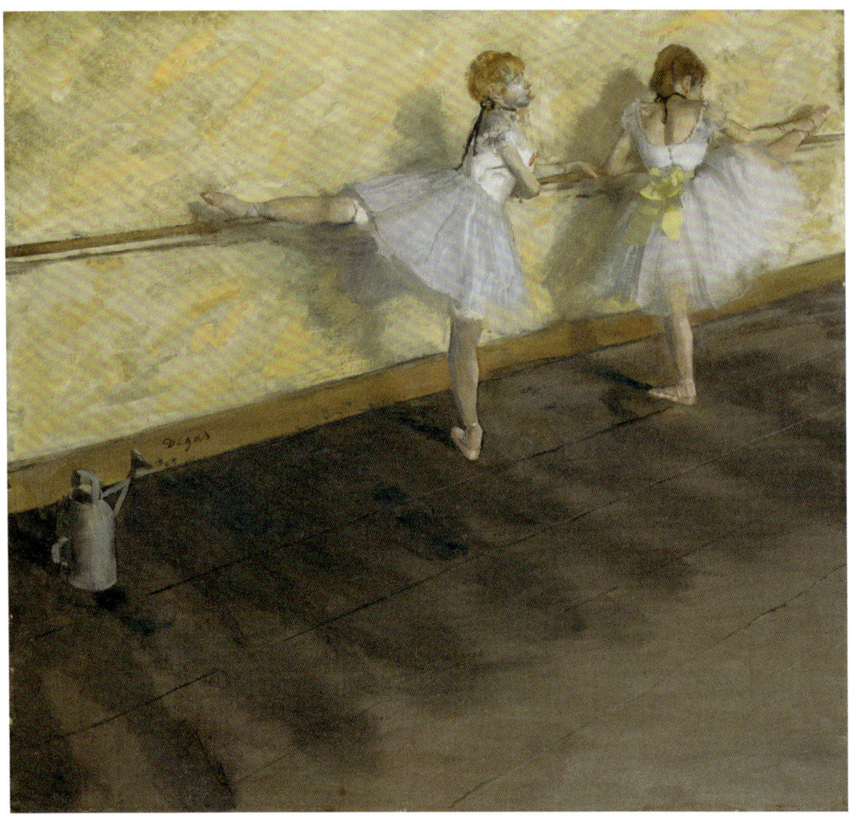

Collecting French art in Denmark

The Hansens were not alone in Denmark in collecting French art and their collection can be better understood as part of a wider context. From the mid-nineteenth century, the Carlsberg brewing dynasty fostered a culture of collecting and philanthropy that inspired the next generation of Danish collectors. The expansion and industrialisation of his family brewery allowed J. C. Jacobsen (1811–1887) to fund the reconstruction of the Danish royal palace, Frederiksborg Castle, which had been ravaged by fire in 1859. His son Carl (1842–1914) became a passionate art collector with a particular taste for antiquities and Danish and French nineteenth-century sculpture, including Rodin's work.[6] He displayed his art in his home, which he opened to the public in 1882, before giving his collection to the Danish nation in 1888 and opening the Ny Carlsberg Glyptotek in 1897.

A champion of academic art, Carl Jacobsen despised Impressionism, writing to his secretary in 1888: 'I would rather do without that kind of art, which is beyond my understanding and a nuisance.'[7] Impressionism was relatively little known in Scandinavia at the time although a few paintings were presented in exhibitions there in the 1880s and 1890s.[8] Gauguin's work was better known across Scandinavia because his wife, Mette, was Danish and sold his paintings there when he left for the Pacific

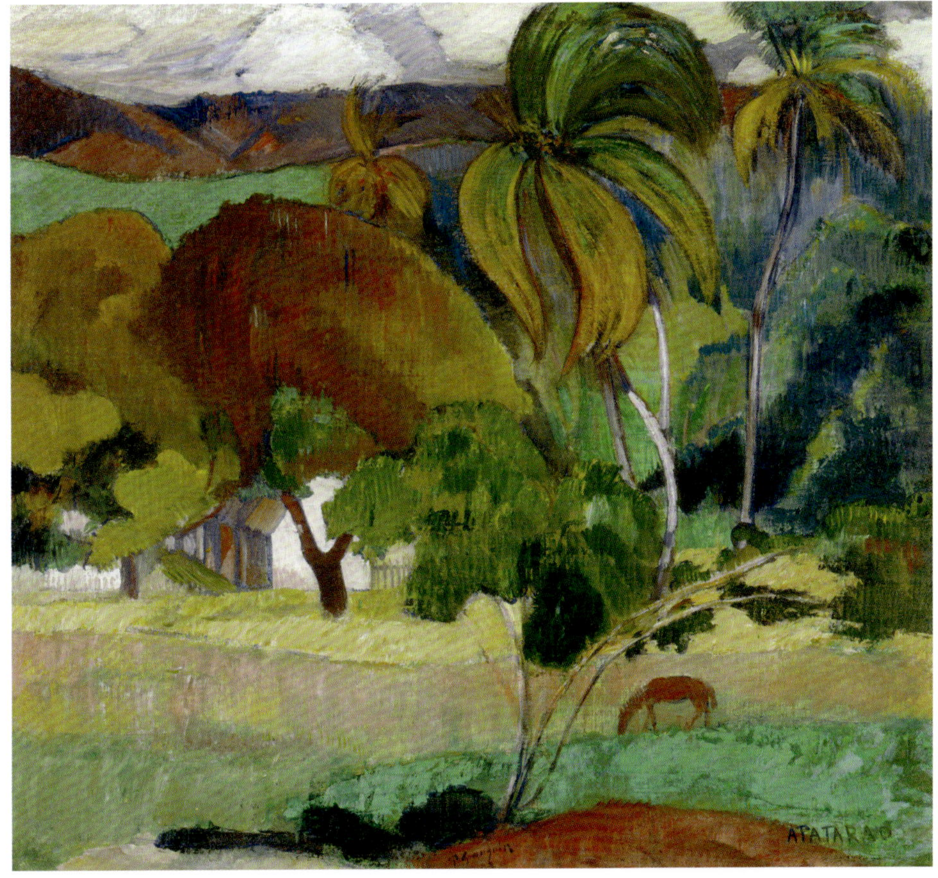

Fig. 14
Paul Gauguin (1848–1903),
Landscape from Tahiti, 1891.
Oil on canvas, 49 x 54 cm.
Ny Carlsberg Glyptotek,
Copenhagen

(Hansen later bought Gauguin's *The Little One Is Dreaming, Étude* [cat. 50] from Mette in 1916).[9] In 1914, however, the Statens Museum for Kunst (the Danish National Gallery) organised an important exhibition of French nineteenth-century art that turned into a great opportunity for Danish collectors. The show spanned Neoclassicism, Romanticism, Realism, Impressionism and Post-Impressionism, and included important loans from Parisian dealers such as the Galeries Durand-Ruel and Bernheim-Jeune, and Ambroise Vollard. The exhibition closed in June but when war broke out in the summer, many of the paintings were stranded in Copenhagen, offering collectors there the chance to acquire works that had been little seen in Scandinavia.[10] Equally importantly, its extensive range provided the blueprint for a collection narrative, one that Hansen was to follow at Ordrupgaard.[11]

The successful engineer and socialist politician Johannes Rump (1861–1932) seized this opportunity to expand his collection and bought several works that had been exhibited in 1914, including Matisse's *Place des Lices, Saint-Tropez* (1904, now in the Statens Museum for Kunst). Much like Hansen, Rump was not new to collecting, having assembled the largest

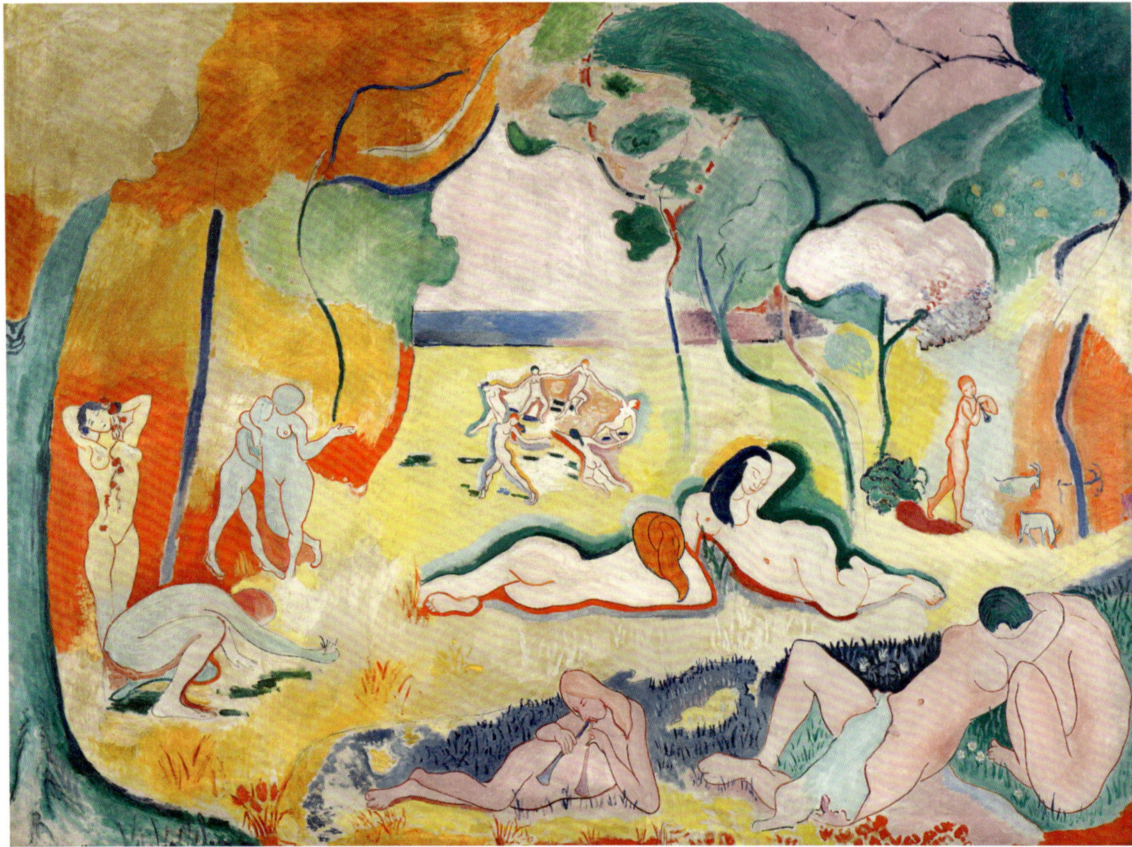

private collection of old-master drawings in Denmark between 1898 and 1907.[12] He credited his interest in art to an earlier meeting with Carl Jacobsen, acknowledging the older collector's influential role. Rump's passion for French art was sparked when he spent six months in Paris in 1912 and started collecting works by André Derain, Matisse and Maurice Utrillo, also acquiring a few works by Impressionists and Neo-Impressionists.[13] During the First World War, when Denmark remained neutral, Rump established an art centre (the Danish Art Trade) to support young Danish artists and, after the war, continued to collect, focusing his collection on Matisse. Although it was on a more

modest scale than the Jacobsens' holdings, Rump also gave his collection to Denmark, presenting it to the Statens Museum for Kunst in 1928.

Helge Jacobsen (1882–1946), Carl's son, was the third generation of his family to become a patron of the arts. Unlike his father, Helge embraced Impressionism and Post-Impressionism, and shifted the focus of the Glyptotek's collection after he became chairman of the Ny Carlsberg Foundation following his father's death in 1914. Like Rump, Jacobsen made important additions to his collection after the 1914 Statens Museum for Kunst exhibition, acquiring five out of the nine Gauguins exhibited,

28

including *Landscape from Tahiti* (fig. 14), and works by Manet, Monet, Sisley and Courbet.[14] When Hansen started collecting, he became Jacobsen's greatest rival in Copenhagen. Indeed, several paintings from his collection were eventually to join Jacobsen's collection following the failure of the Danish Landmandsbank in 1922, as a result of which Hansen was forced to sell part of his French collection.[15]

Perhaps the Danish collector with the closest trajectory to Hansen was Christian Tetzen-Lund (1852–1936), a wealthy wholesaler of animal feed and grain, who also initially focused his collection on Danish and Scandinavian art. He too started collecting French painting in 1916 (buying Renoir's *Le Moulin de la Galette, Sketch* [cat. 44], later acquired by Hansen) and opened his home to the public in 1917, but he preferred avant-garde works including those by Picasso. Within just a few years he acquired a vast collection, and by 1920 he owned almost 500 paintings, including works by Renoir, Cézanne and Van Gogh, more than 20 by Picasso and 12 by Matisse, among them *The Joy of Life* (fig. 15), which he sold to Albert C. Barnes in 1922.[16]

Copenhagen in the 1910s, therefore, was a vibrant centre for art collecting in which the newly wealthy bourgeoisie, who had witnessed the success of Carl Jacobsen's Glyptotek, spurred each other on to broaden their collections from national art to include French painting. Rump, Helge Jacobsen and eventually the Hansens all followed Carl Jacobsen's example, giving their collections to Denmark, perhaps also competing to endow their country with significant examples of international art.[17]

'A wartime price'

As we have seen, Hansen was one of several collectors who, having already built significant collections of Danish or Scandinavian art, radically changed their focus to French art during the First World War. In 1916, the year both Hansen and Tetzen-Lund started collecting French modern art, France was embroiled in the First World War, with the devastating battles of Verdun and the Somme being fought on its territory. During the first years of the war, and until early 1917, few paintings were sold at the Hôtel Drouot, then the most important auction house in Paris.[18] The art market gradually revived between 1916 and 1917 but prices were lower relative to the pre-war years.[19] The prices that fell most were those of recent works, and more expensive works became harder to sell.[20]

Letters from Hansen's advisor, the critic and champion of Impressionism Théodore Duret (1838–1927), repeatedly refer to the fall in prices. In one, written in October 1916, Duret discussed Manet's *Le Petit Lange* (1862), a portrait of a young boy, and suggested that although the owner had been asking 80,000 francs before the war, it might now be possible to acquire for between 30,000 and 50,000 francs.[21] Duret again emphasised how low prices were when he offered Hansen a Courbet still-life in July 1917, and once more later that year when proposing that Hansen should buy Delacroix's *Ugolino and His Sons* (cat. 3), adding that the proposed price of 35,000 francs was 'a low price, a wartime price'.[22] Even if this was Duret's ploy to persuade him to buy, Hansen no doubt realised the wartime market offered a unique opportunity to create an outstanding collection of

French art. With his eye for quality and buying works with prestigious provenances from leading Parisian dealers, Hansen made the most of this opportunity.[23]

As a neutral country during the war, Denmark offered art collectors favourable circumstances in which to buy. Denmark's policy of neutrality stemmed from its traumatic defeat by the German States in the Second Schleswig War of 1864, when it lost three duchies, Schleswig, Holstein and Lauenburg, which accounted for nearly half its population and substantial territory. When war broke out across Europe in 1914, neutrality seemed the only strategy for the country to survive.[24] Thus Denmark was able to continue trading with both Britain and Germany, and although communication and shipping were necessarily complicated, Hansen was still able to correspond with his advisors.[25] During these years, Copenhagen temporarily became a European centre for modern art with a vibrant avant-garde that may have fostered collectors' interests.[26]

Denmark witnessed uneven economic growth during the war. Inflation was high and the cost of living almost doubled. A Danish report published in 1921 suggests that the wartime economy most benefited those who were already wealthy, especially bankers and industrialists, who saw their incomes rise.[27] Although it is not known to what extent this affected the Hansens' fortunes, the context explains why Hansen, and several of his contemporaries, began collecting French nineteenth-century art in earnest during the war and were able to amass spectacular collections of works that had previously been highly sought after by international collectors.

Danish collectors saw a brief opportunity to build their collections while international rivals, especially Americans and Russians, were no longer driving prices up during the war, and before they resumed collecting aggressively after the armistice.[28]

Hansen's collection as French propaganda
Collected in the midst of war, Hansen's new collection could perhaps be interpreted as a covert expression of support for France. Very few Danes publicly voiced an opinion or took sides, but defeat by the German States in 1864 had fostered strong anti-German feeling among the Danish population, extending to intellectuals, politicians and the royal family.[29] As a prominent figure in Copenhagen, Hansen would have been bound to remain neutral.

Even before the war, Danish art critics had tended to express pro-French and anti-German views, pitting French and German art against one another.[30] An art critic in the French press in April 1918 wrote about Hansen's growing collection in political terms, arguing that it was propaganda promoting French culture.[31] In Copenhagen, too, art could be used to serve political ends. In late 1918 Herwarth Walden, a Berlin magazine editor and gallery owner who worked for the German Central Office for Foreign Services, organised an exhibition entitled 'International Art: Expressionists and Cubists', which sought to demonstrate Germany's artistic superiority.[32] In such a context, a public appreciation of French painting may have been viewed as a silent expression of support for France. Significantly, in 1920 Hansen donated money to the reconstruction

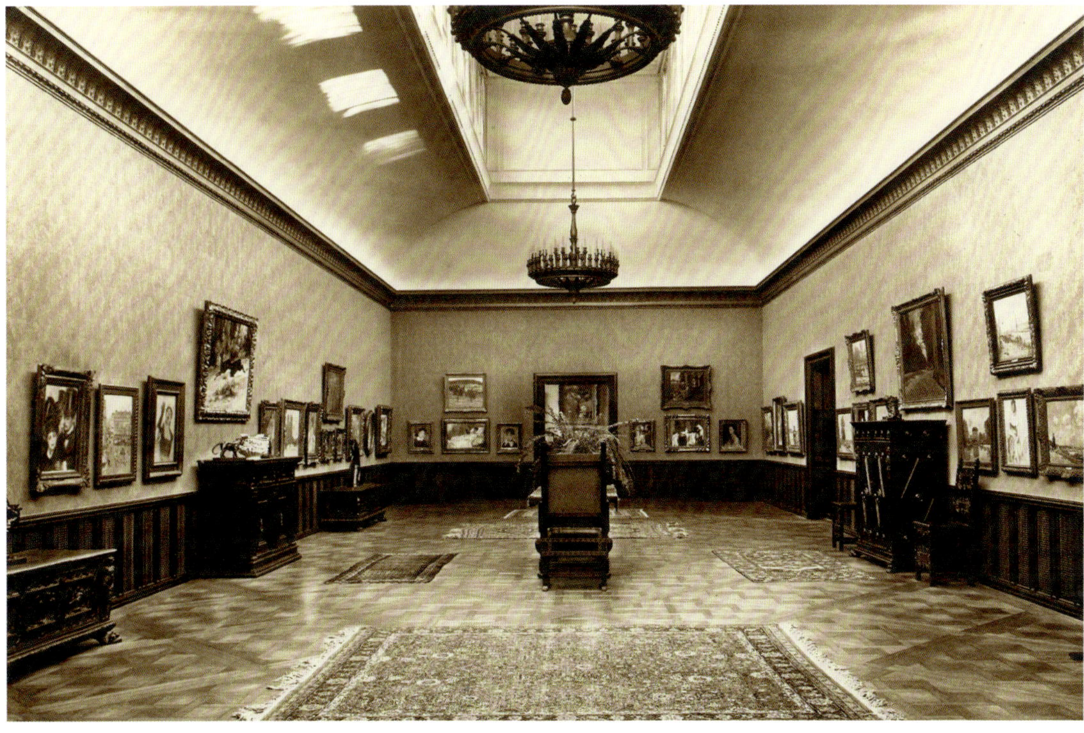

of Reims Cathedral, making a powerful statement in support of the French. A masterpiece of Gothic architecture only a few kilometres from the front line, the cathedral is a site of national and historic importance in which French kings had been crowned since the Middle Ages. Its partial destruction by German shelling in 1914 profoundly shocked France and images of the ruined cathedral served as powerful tools of French anti-German propaganda, demonstrating the enemy's barbarity and disregard for cultural heritage.[33] Ultimately, Hansen was a committed Francophile and, when he inaugurated his collection at Ordrupgaard in 1918, he also established the French Art Society in Copenhagen, which promoted French culture in Scandinavia, through which he organised exhibitions of French art until he died in 1936.[34]

It was no coincidence then that Hansen began collecting what was to become an outstanding collection of Impressionist art in 1916. Although he sheepishly confessed to Henny in September 1916 that he had 'been reckless and [had] made considerable purchases' when he bought paintings by Sisley, Pissarro, Monet and Renoir, this was no irrational spree. Instead, Hansen was competing with his peers, who all seized the opportunity created by Denmark's neutrality to acquire prestigious works of Impressionist art, emulating the wealthiest international patrons of the pre-war years.

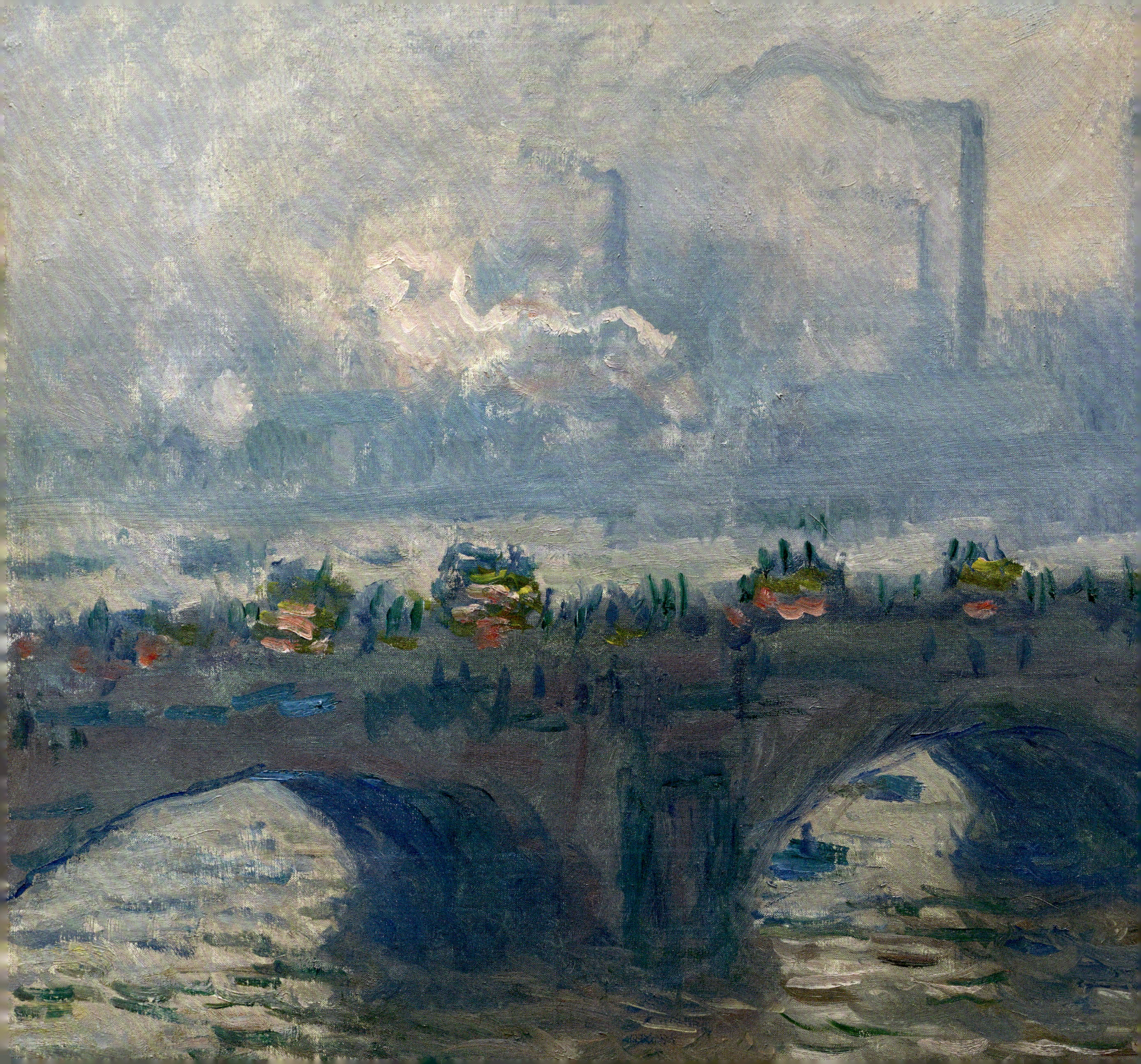

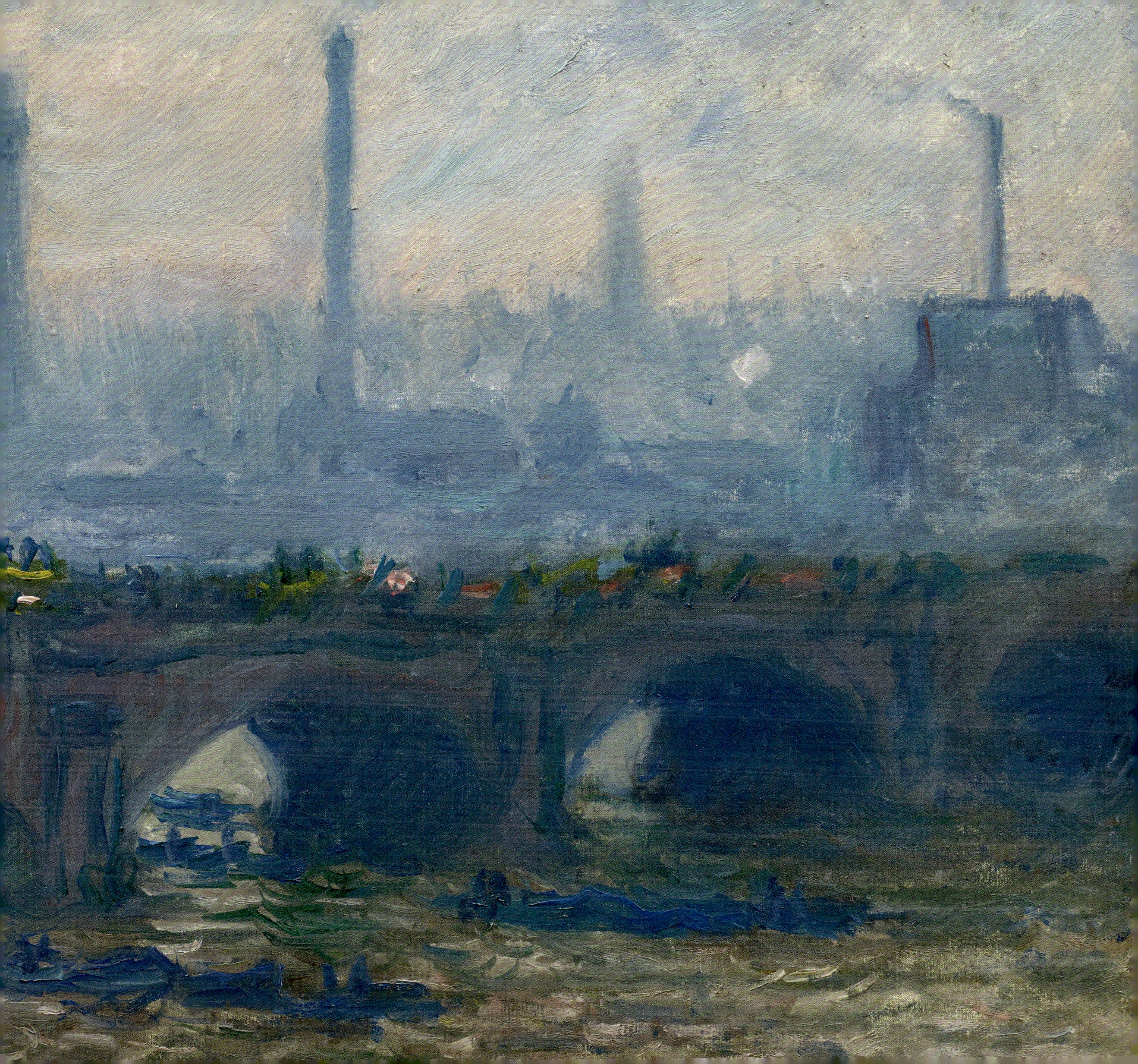

1
Jean-Auguste-Dominique Ingres (1780–1867)
Dante Offering the Divine Comedy to Homer,
c. **1827 and** *c.* **1864–65**
Oil on three pieces of canvas mounted on wood,
38 × 35.5 cm
Inv. no. 248 WH

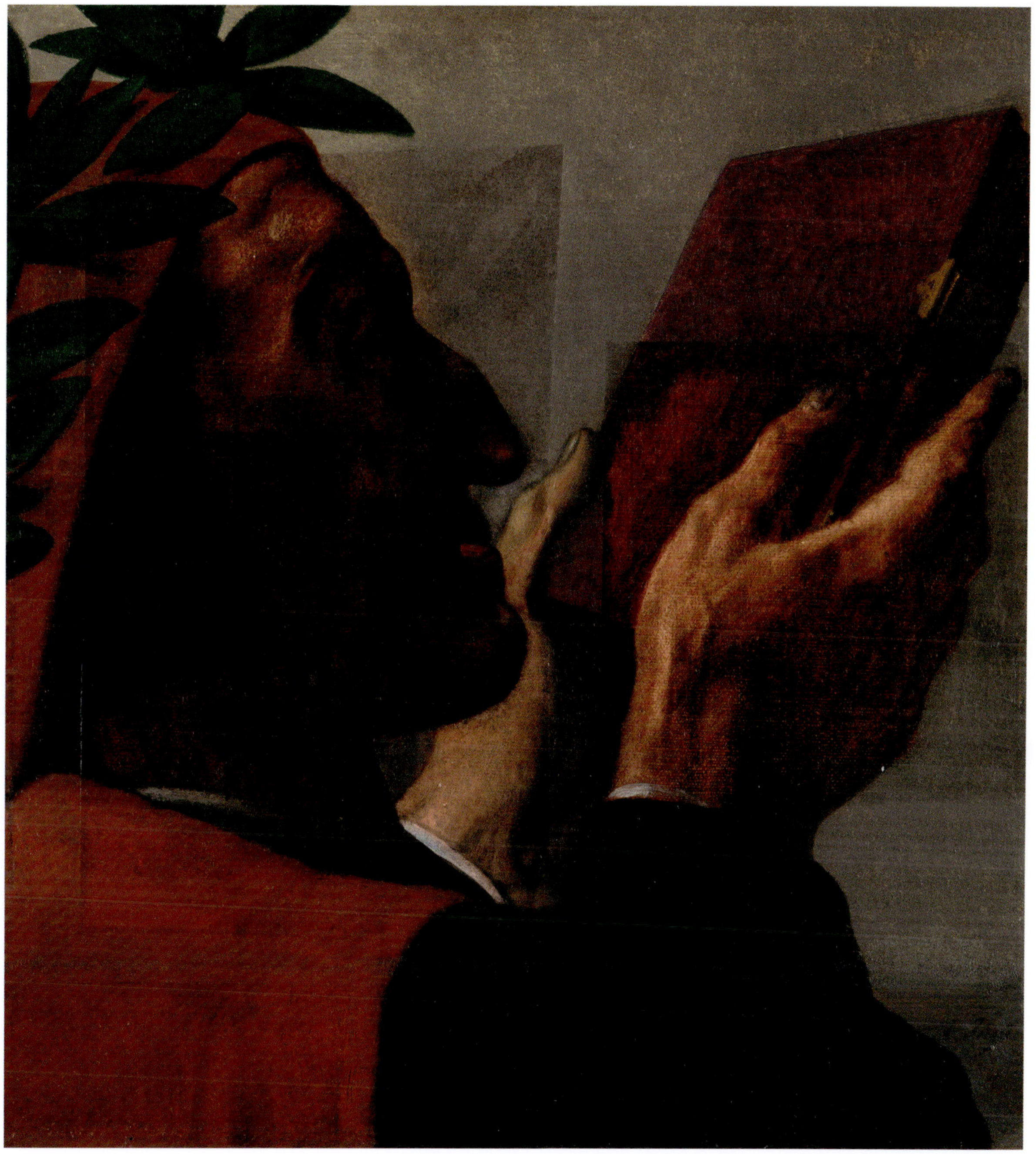

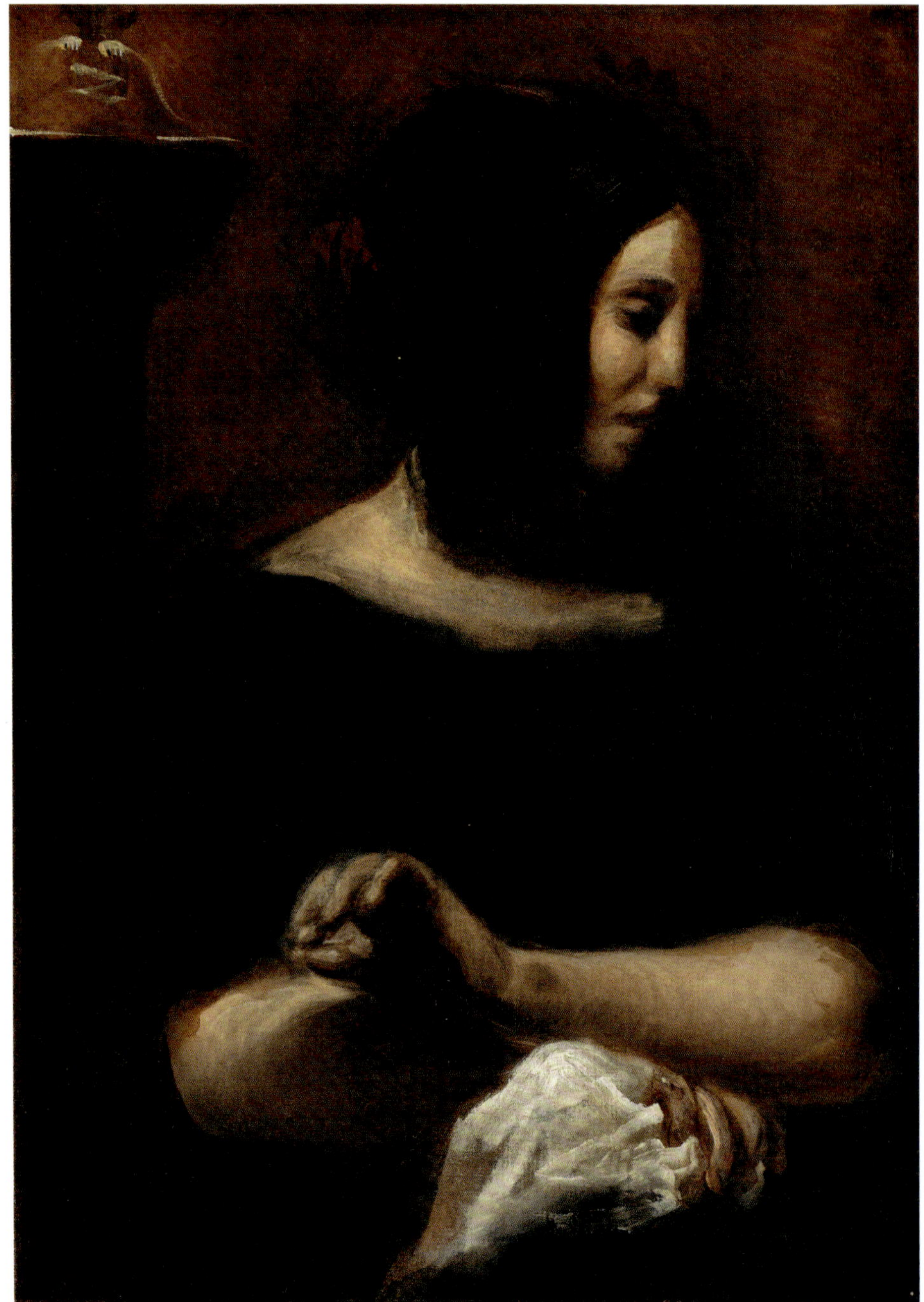

2
Eugène Delacroix (1798–1863)
George Sand, 1838
Oil on canvas, 78 × 56.5 cm
Inv. no. 280 WH

3
Eugène Delacroix (1798–1863)
Ugolino and His Sons, 1860
Oil on canvas, 50 × 61 cm
Inv. no. 212 WH

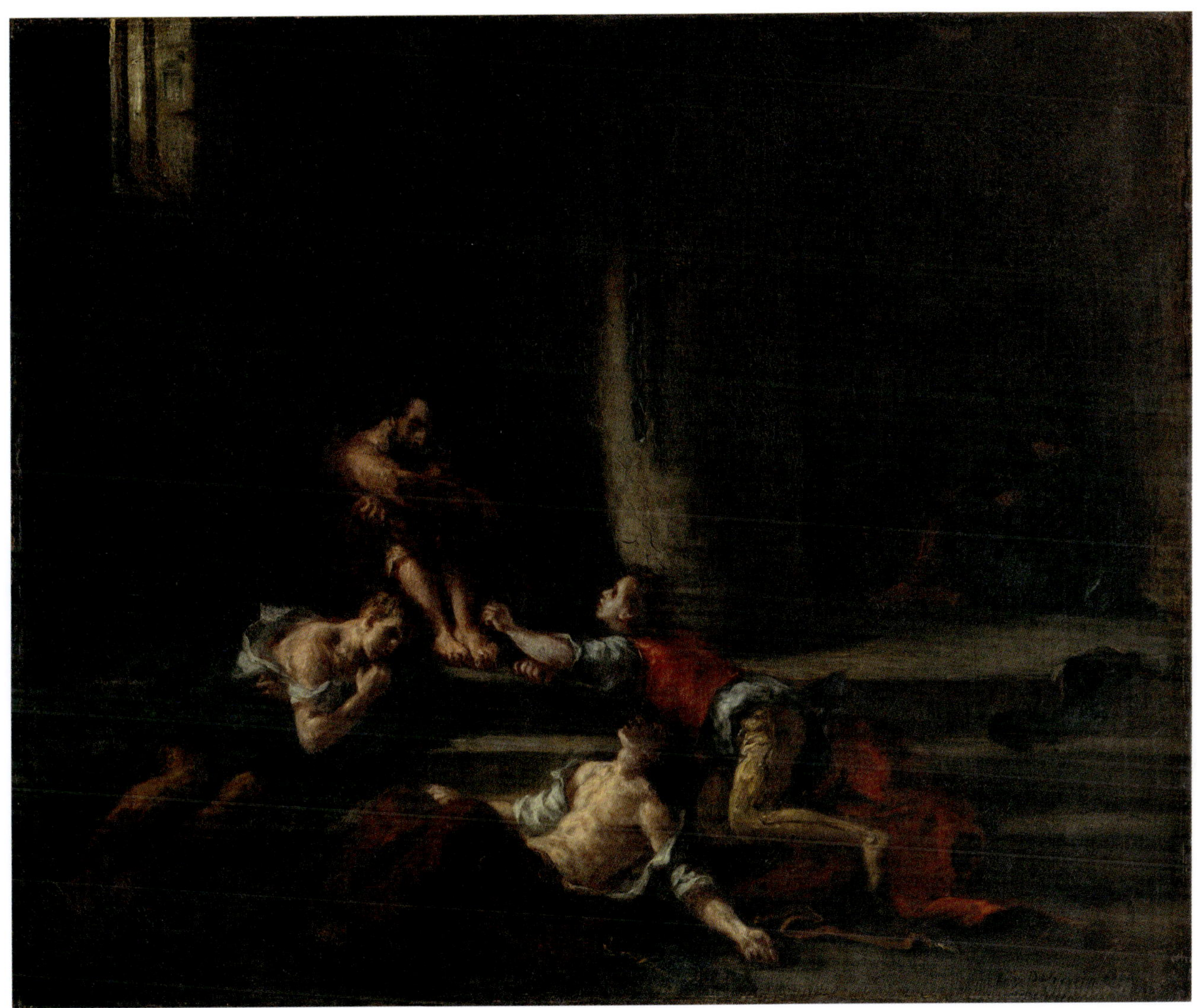

4
Thomas Couture (1815–1879)
The Death of Seneca, Sketch, date unknown
Oil on canvas, 32 × 40.5 cm
Inv. no. 188 WH

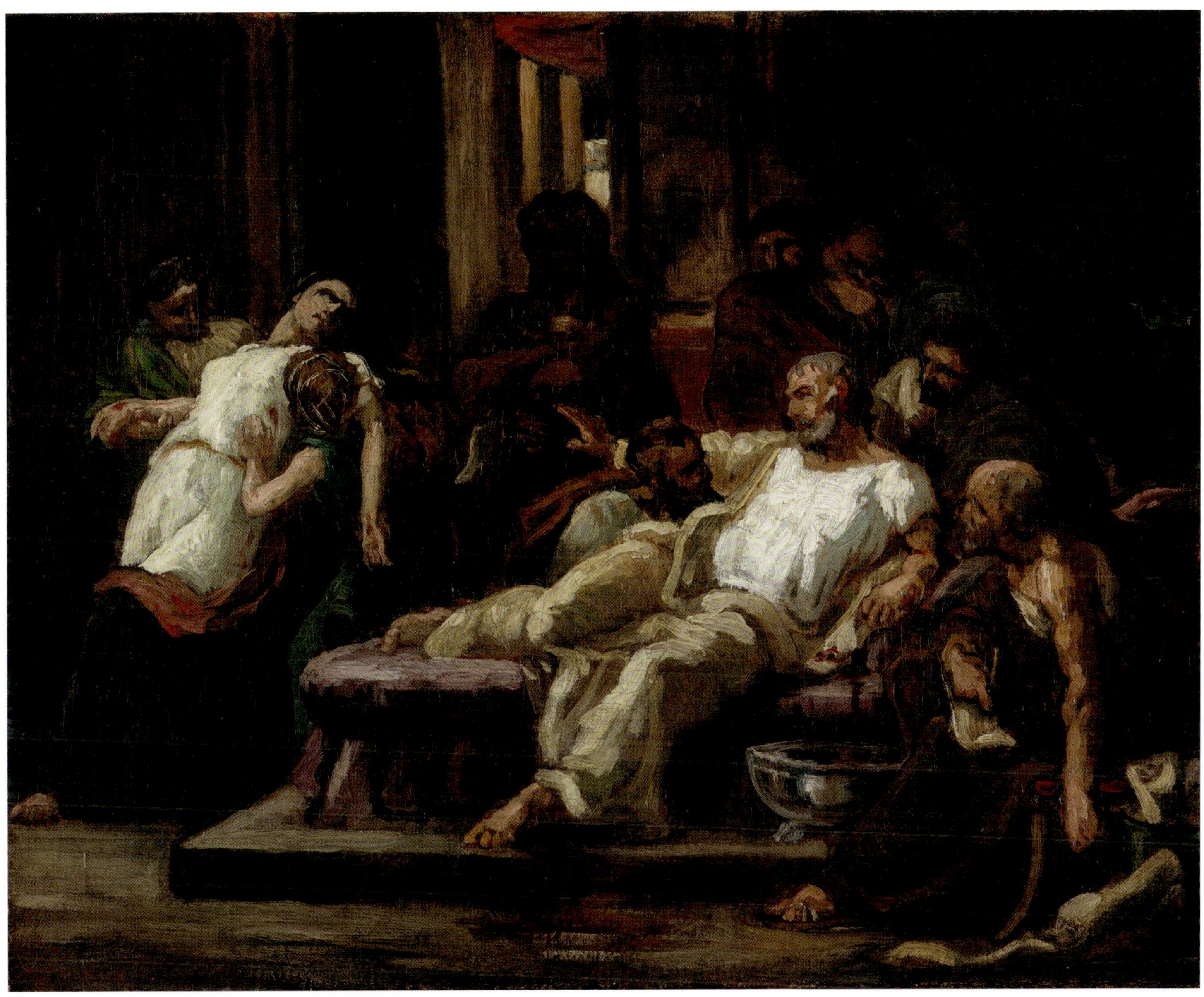

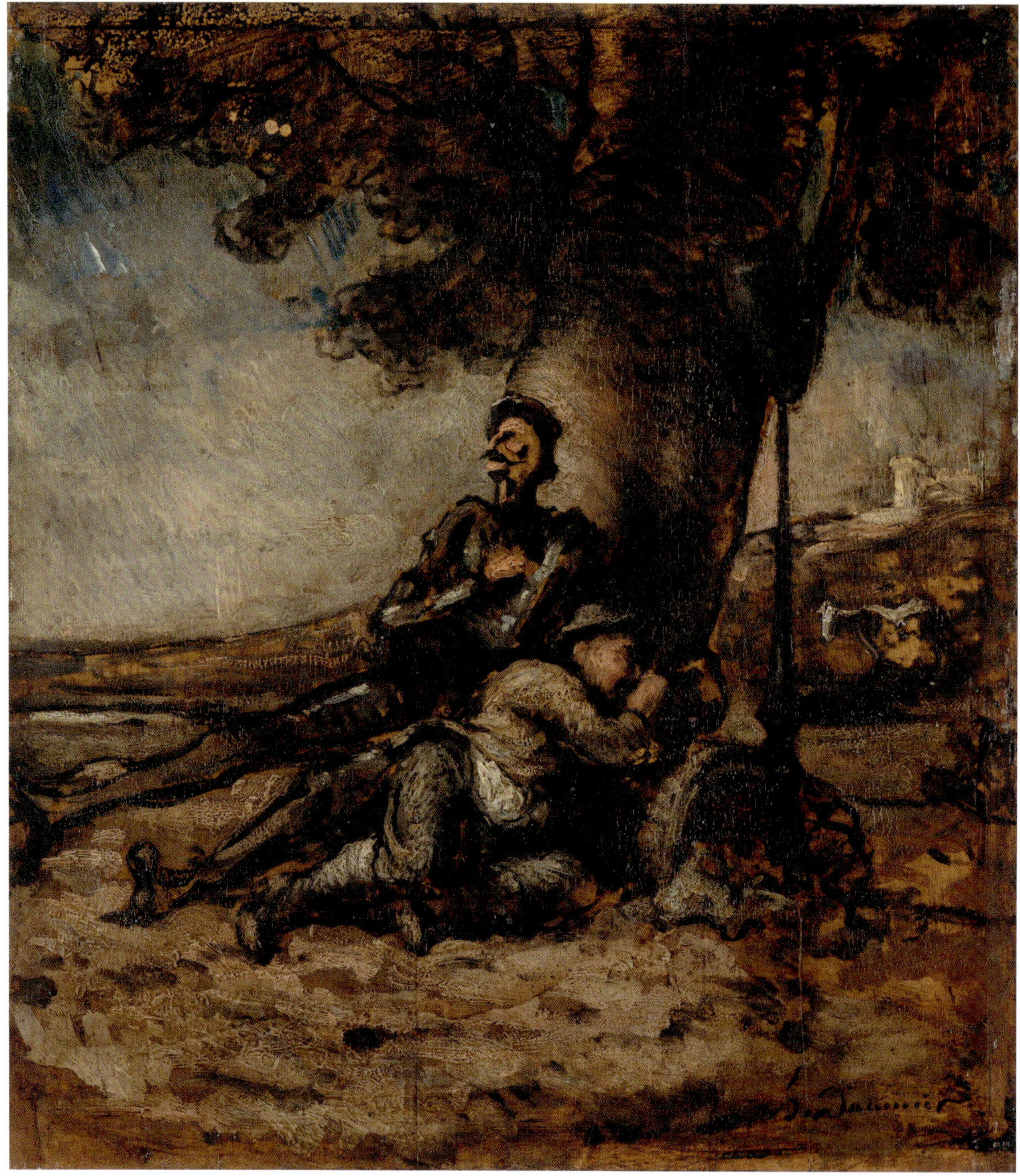

5
Honoré Daumier (1808–1879)
*Don Quixote and Sancho Panza
Resting under a Tree*, c. 1864–66
Oil on wood, 42.5 × 38.5 cm
Inv. no. 211 WH

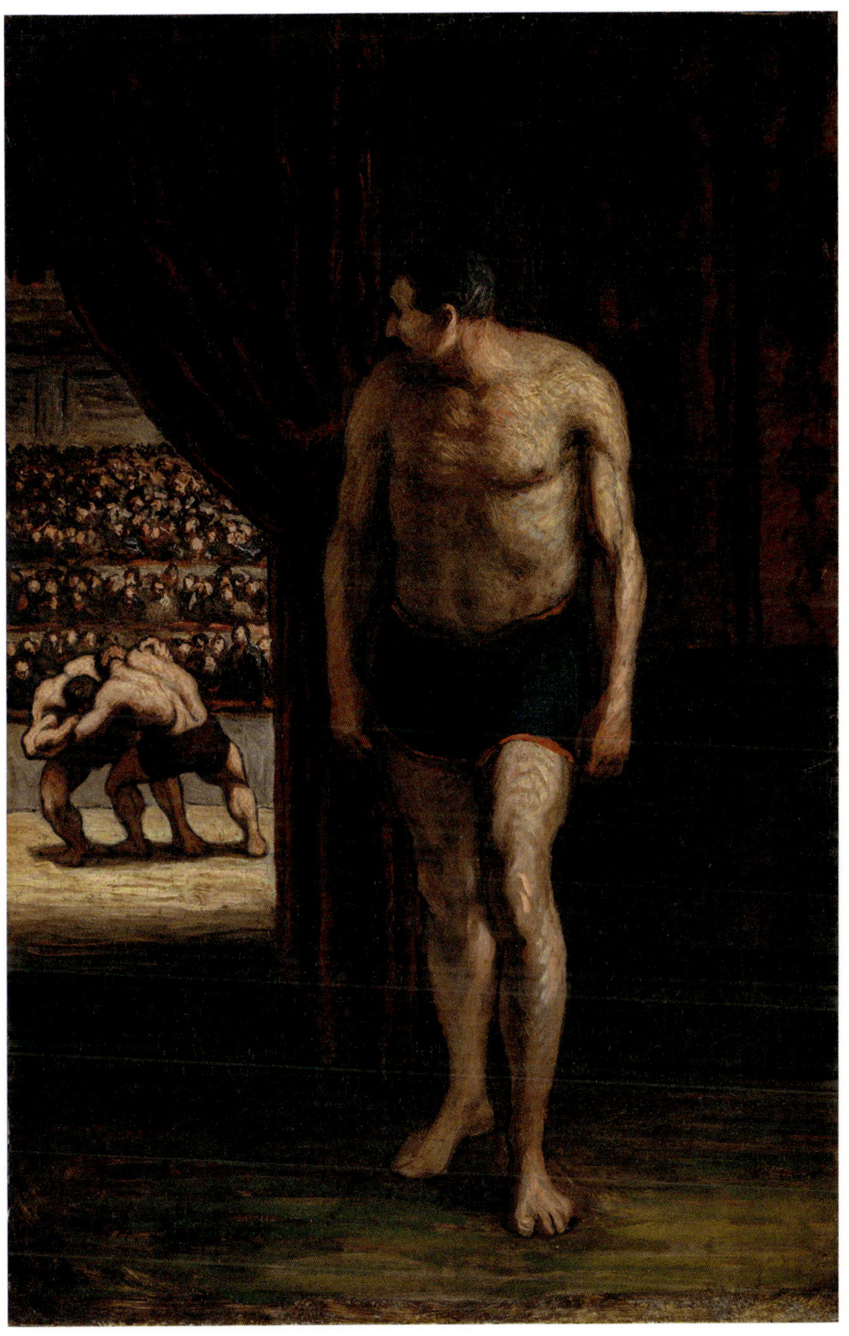

7
Gustave Courbet (1819–1877)
The Ruse, Roe Deer Hunting Episode
(Franche-Comté, 1866), 1866
Oil on canvas, 97 × 130 cm
Inv. no. 277 WH

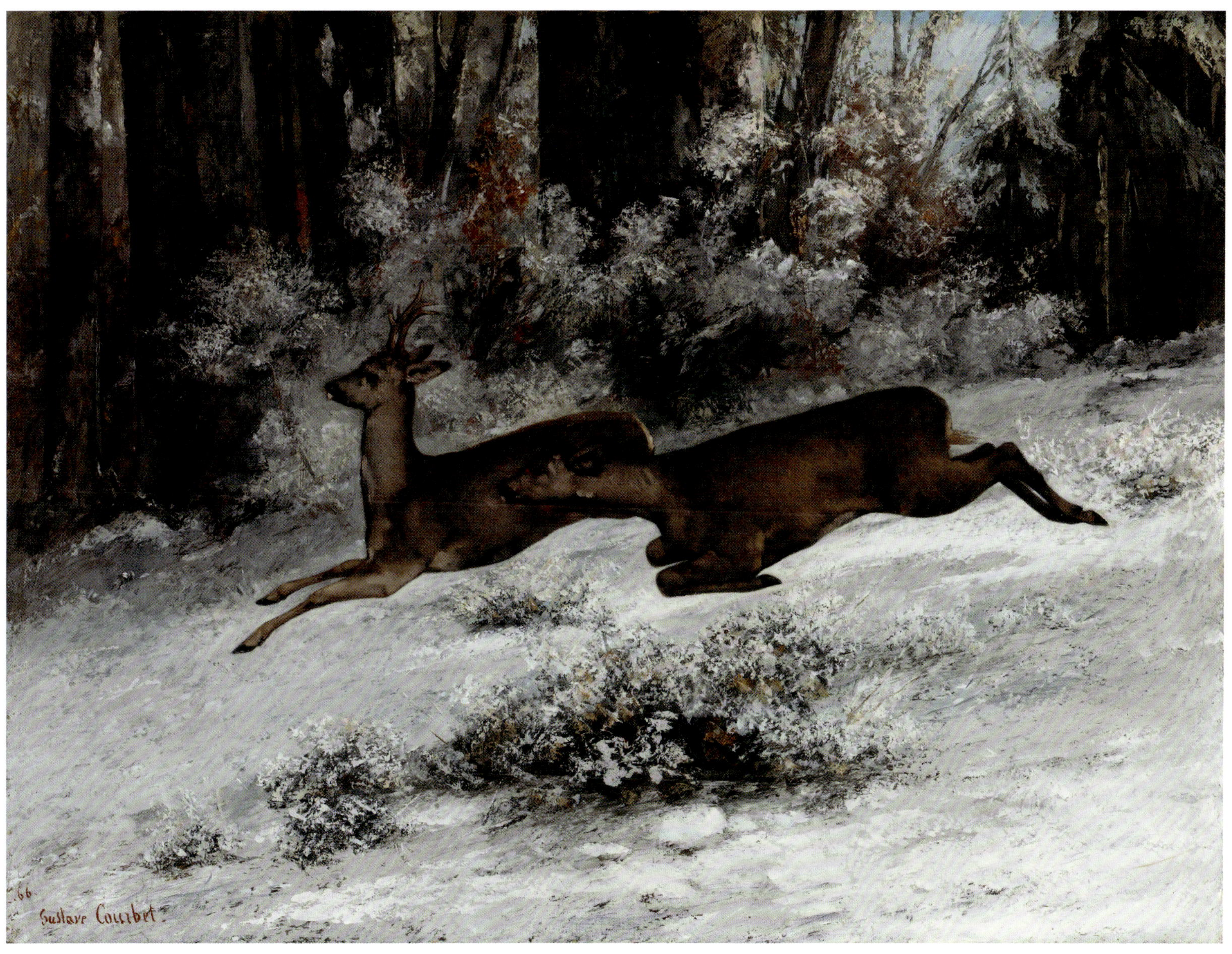

66.
Gustave Courbet

8

Gustave Courbet (1819–1877)
The Cliffs near Étretat, 1869
Oil on canvas, 62 × 88 cm
Inv. no. 236 WH

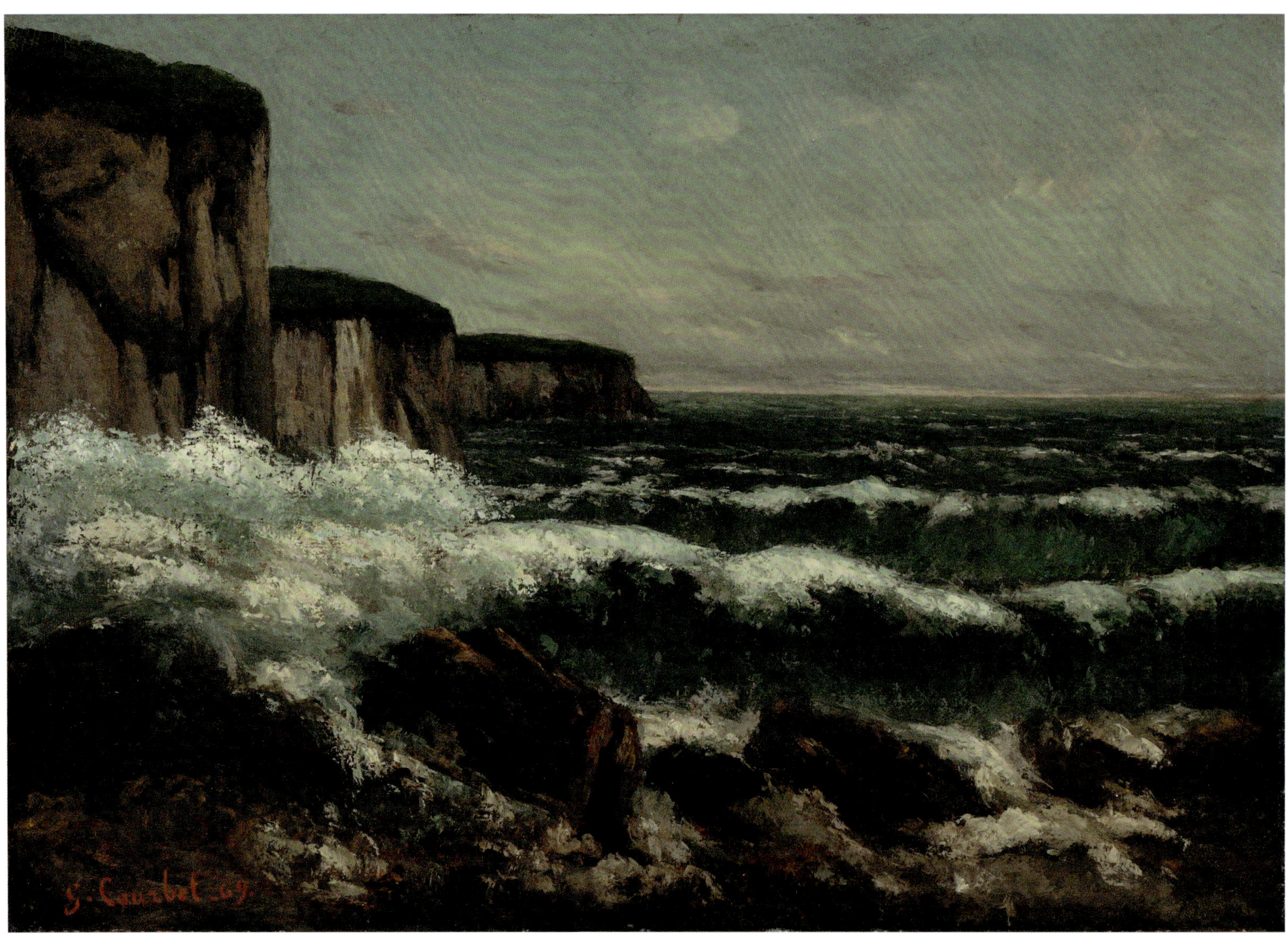

Gustave Courbet (1819–1877)
The Wiremakers' Workshops on the River Loue, near Ornans, 1861
Oil on canvas, 55 × 66 cm
Inv. no. 186 WH

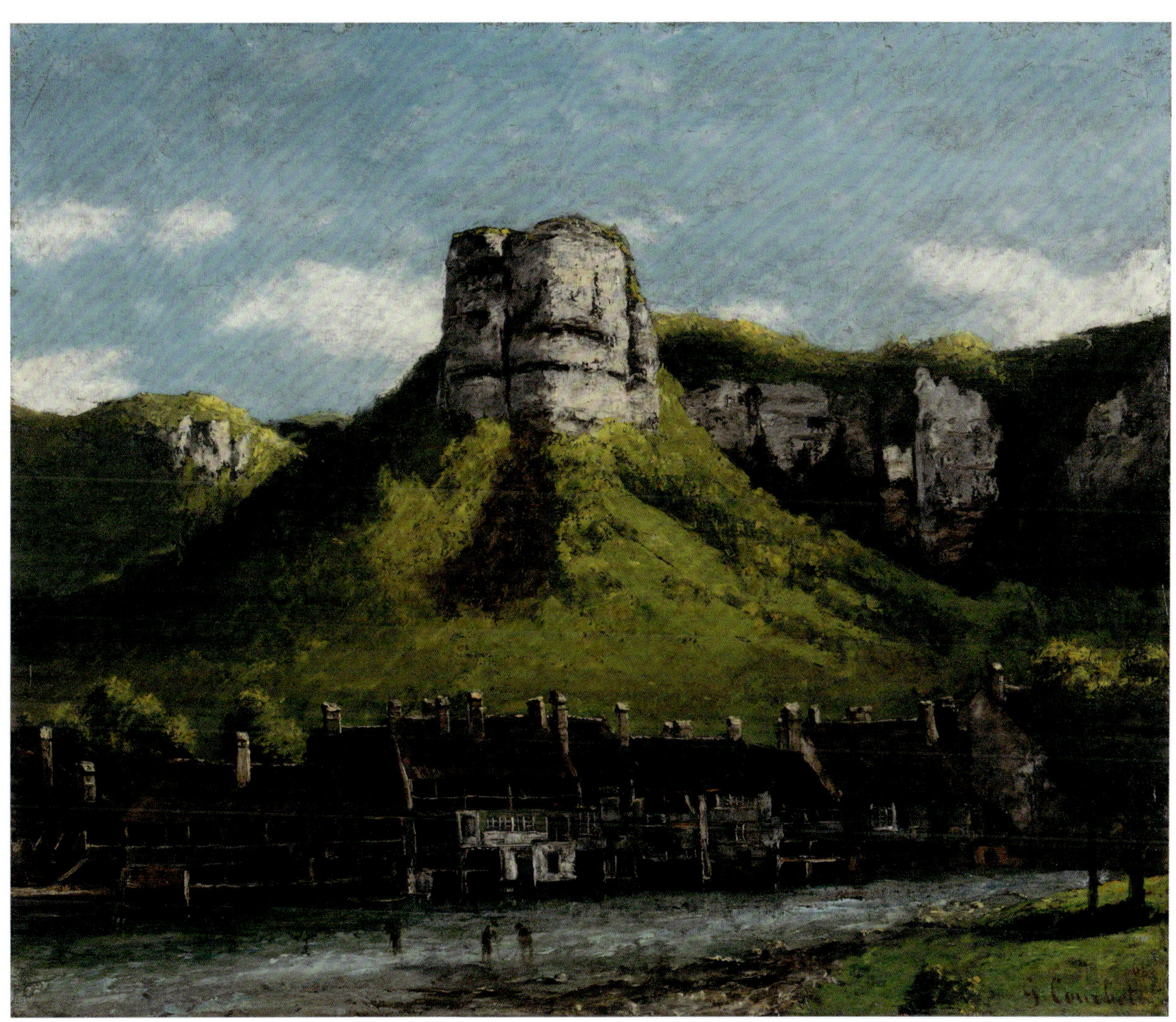

**10
Jean-Baptiste-Camille Corot (1796–1875)**
The Windmill, c. 1835–40
Oil on canvas, 25 × 39.5 cm
Inv. no. 286 WH

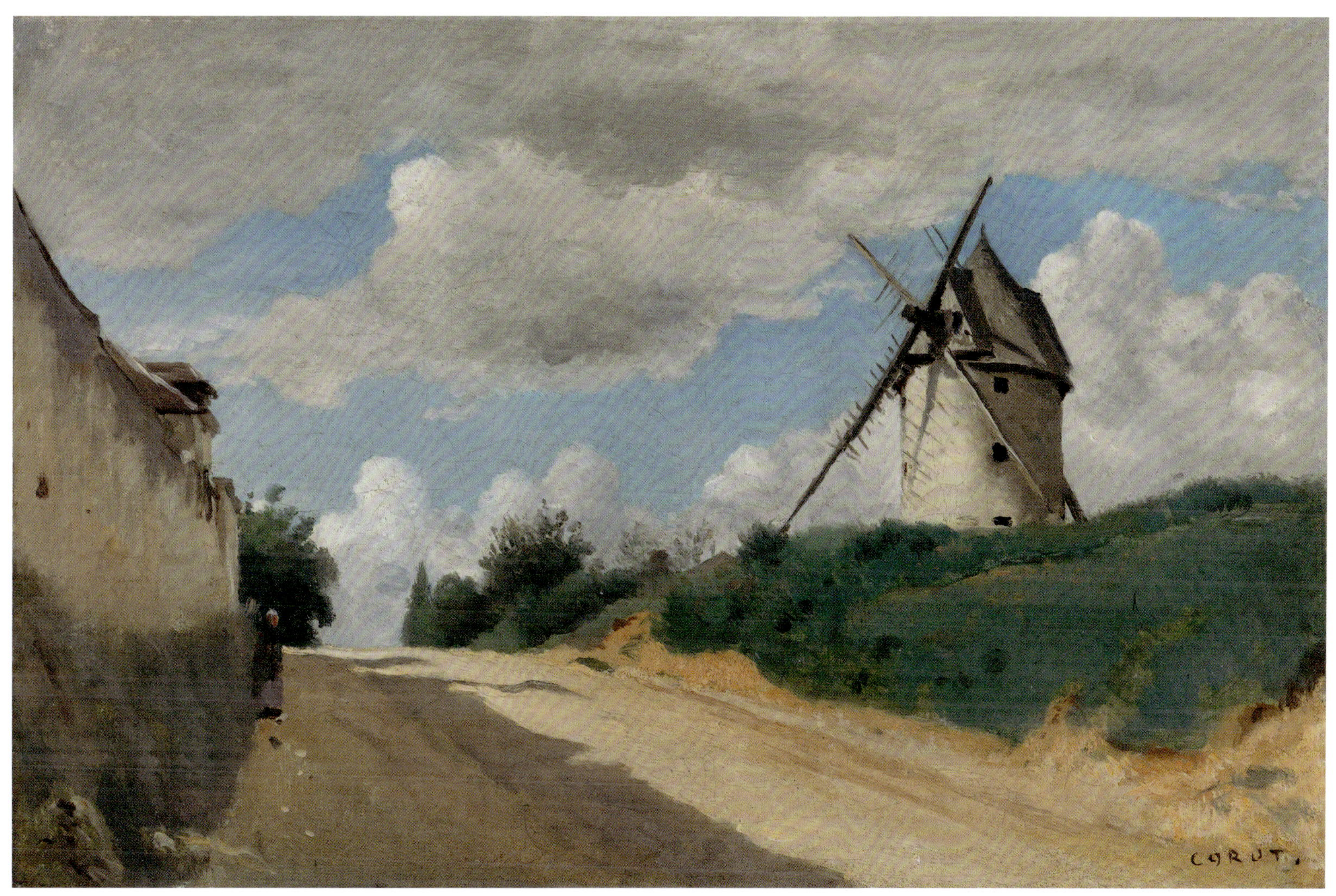

11
Jean-Baptiste-Camille Corot (1796–1875)
Young Italian Woman Seated near a Lake,
c. 1850–55
Oil on canvas, 40.5 × 32 cm
Inv. no. 275 WH

12
Jean-Baptiste-Camille Corot (1796–1875)
*Dancing Nymphs, c.*1850
Oil on canvas, 27 × 34 cm
Inv. no. 294 WH

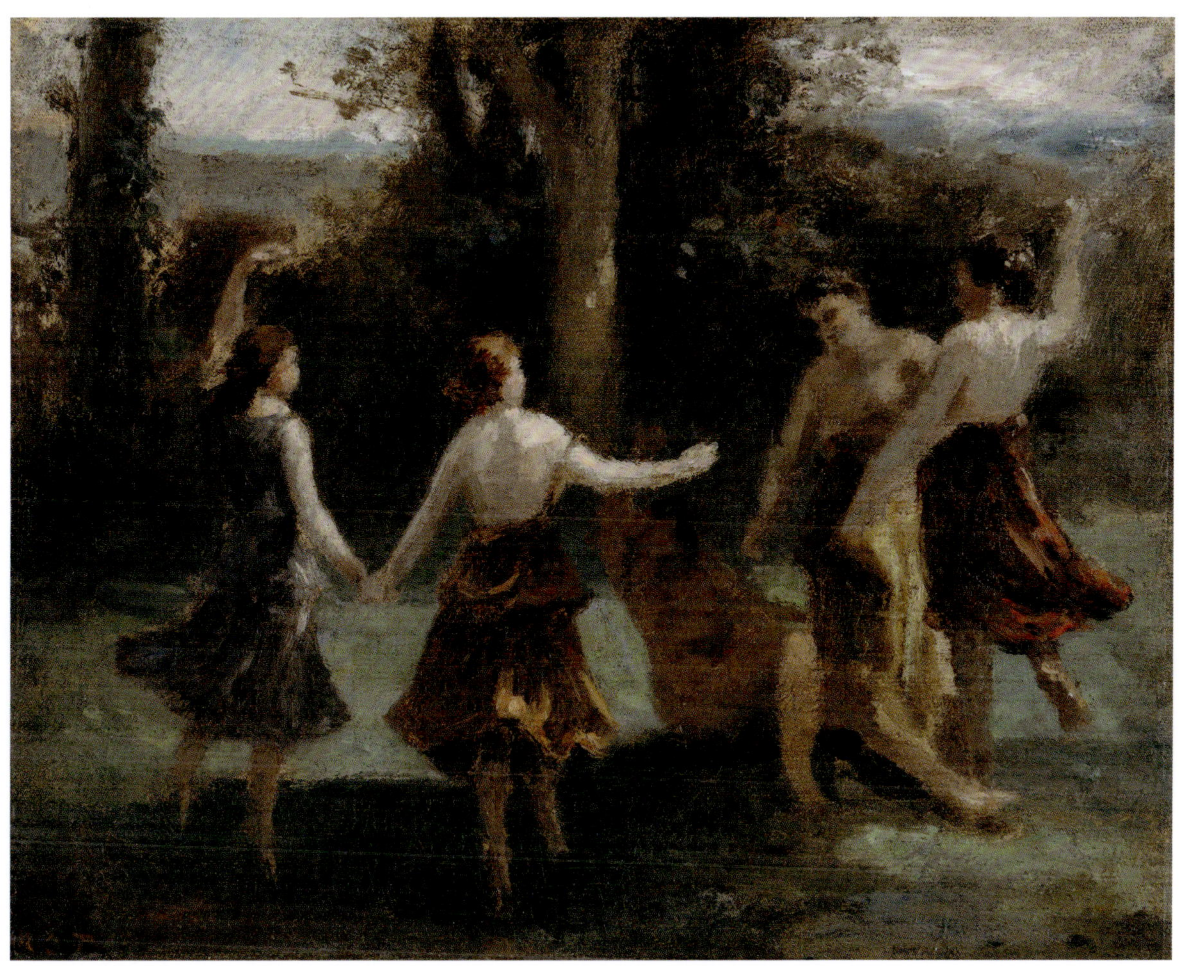

13
Jean-Baptiste-Camille Corot (1796–1875)
Country Road, Côte-d'Or, c. 1840–60
Oil on canvas, 22.5 × 35 cm
Inv. no. 299 WH

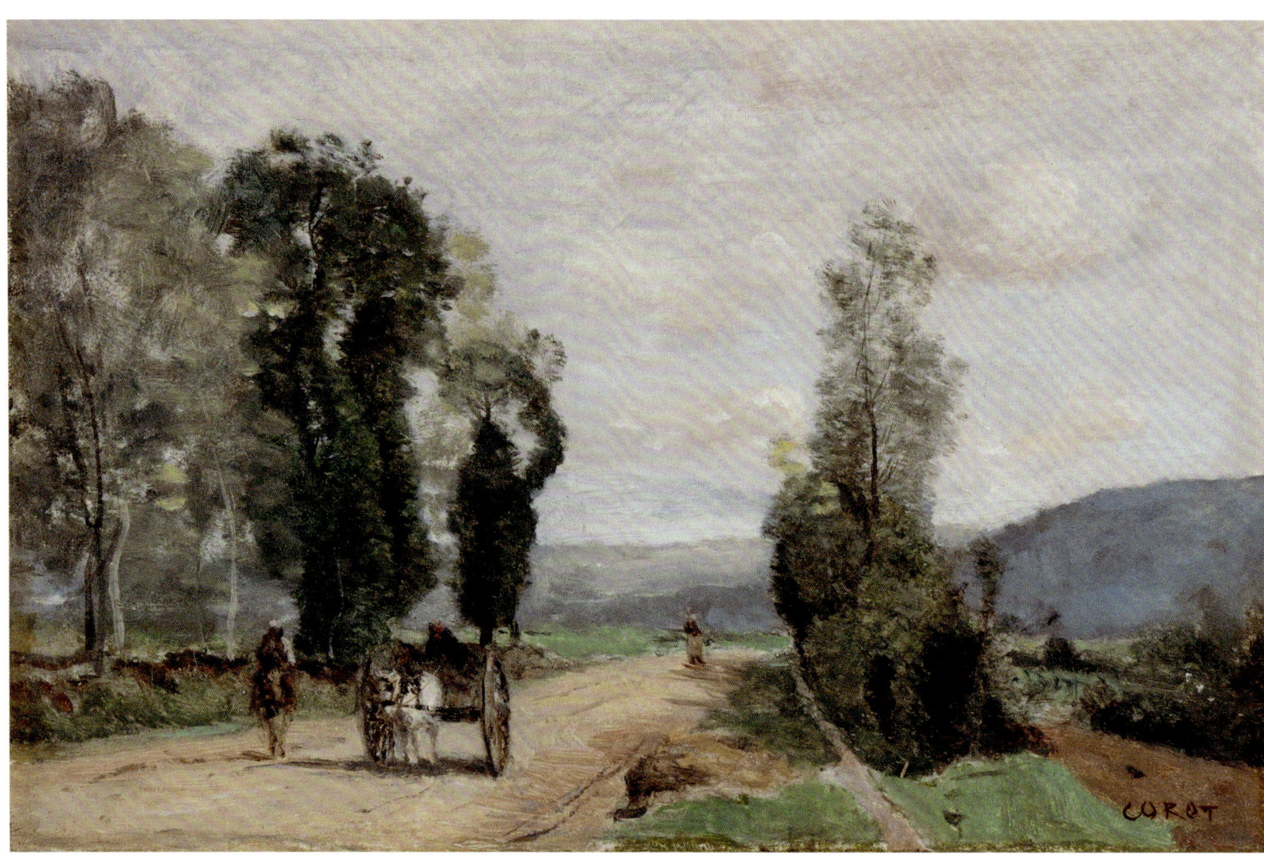

14
Jean-Baptiste-Camille Corot (1796–1875)
The Bridge at Mantes, c. 1850–54
Oil on canvas, 38 × 46 cm
Inv. no. 214 WH

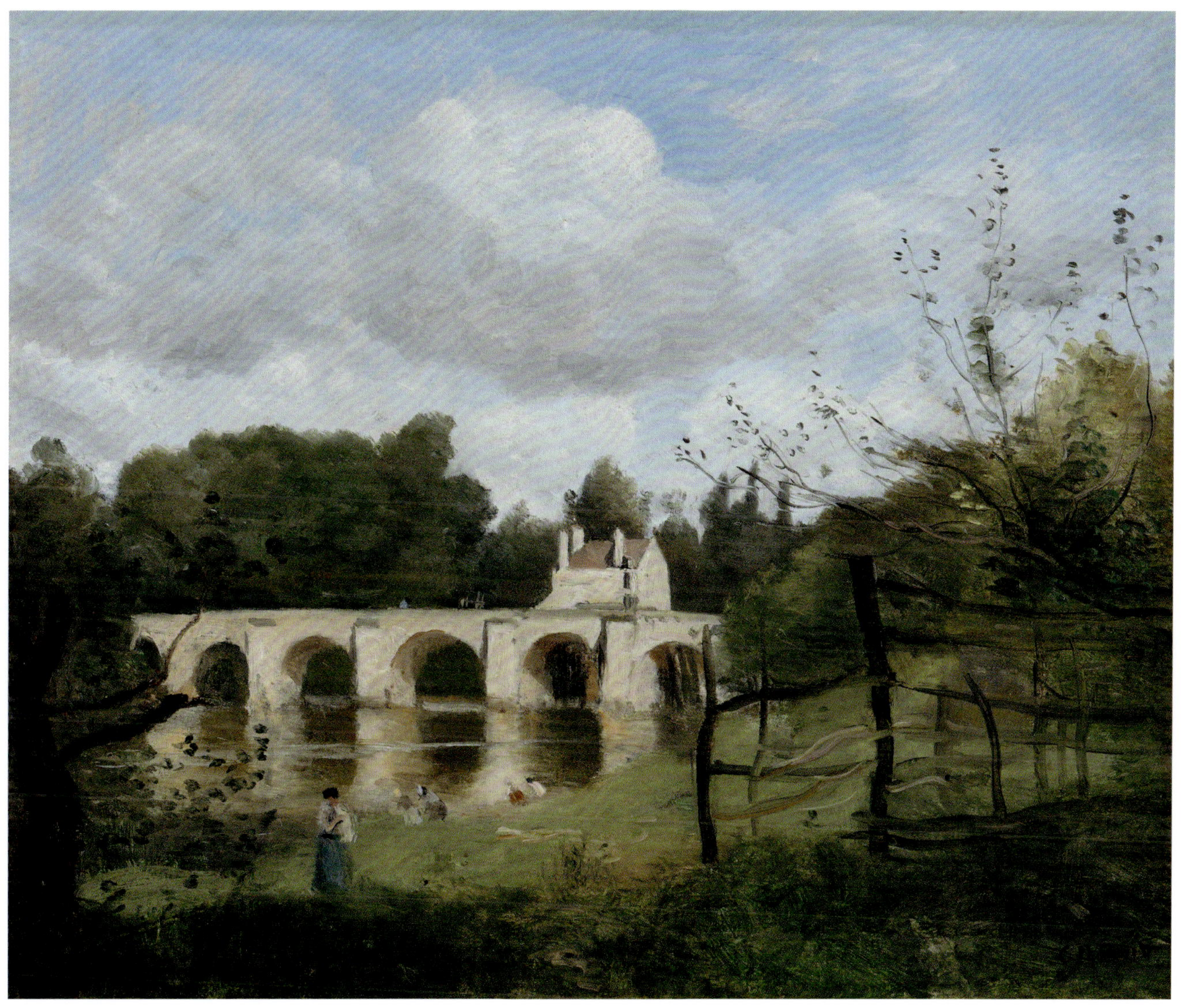

15
Jean-Baptiste-Camille Corot (1796–1875)
The Town of Isigny, Les Hagues, Manche, c. 1855
Oil on canvas, 34 × 32 cm
Inv. no. 235 WH

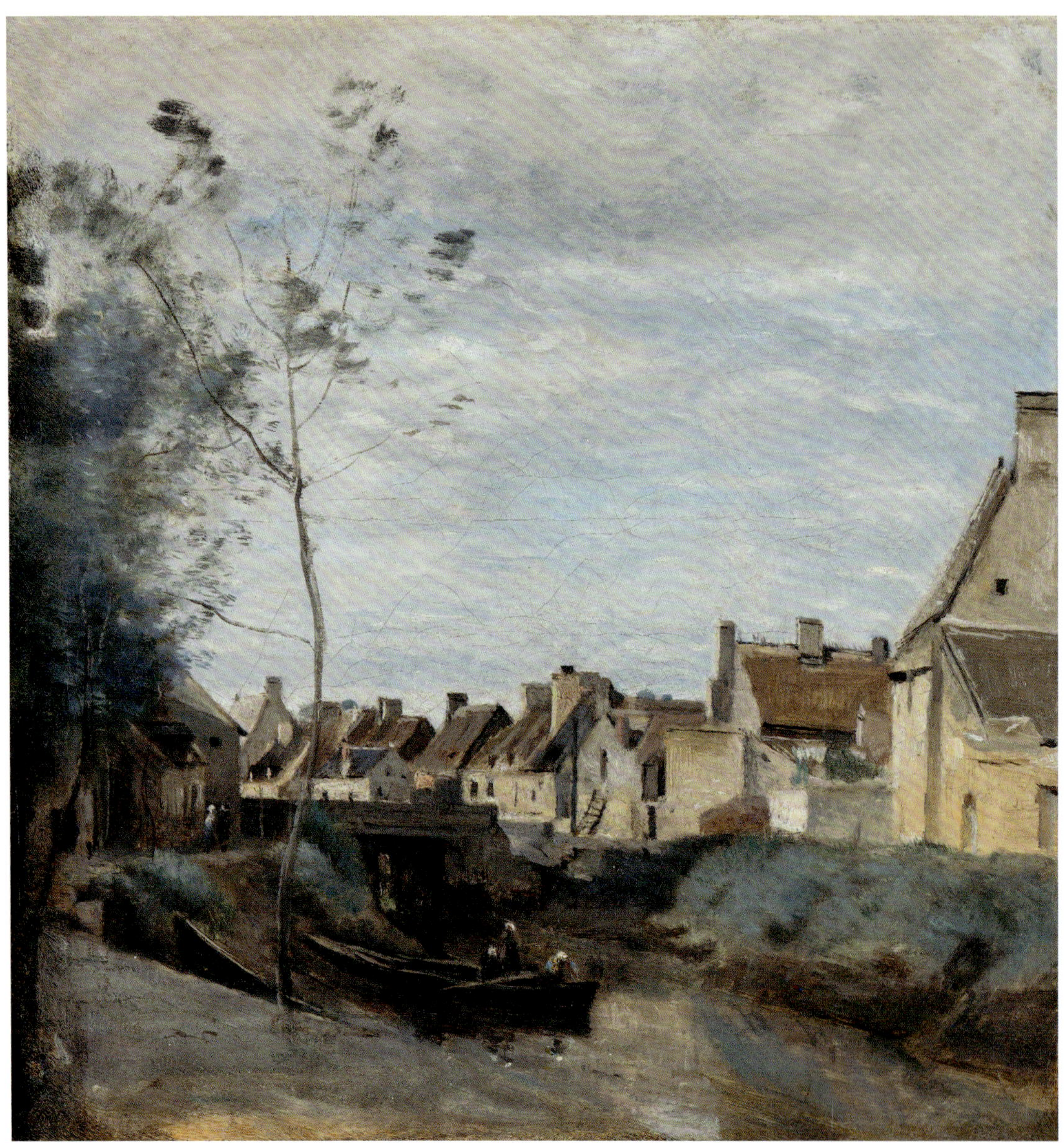

16
Jean-Baptiste-Camille Corot (1796–1875)
Souvenir of a Pond in the Limoges Area, 1855–60
Oil on canvas, 31.5 × 48 cm
Inv. no. 276 WH

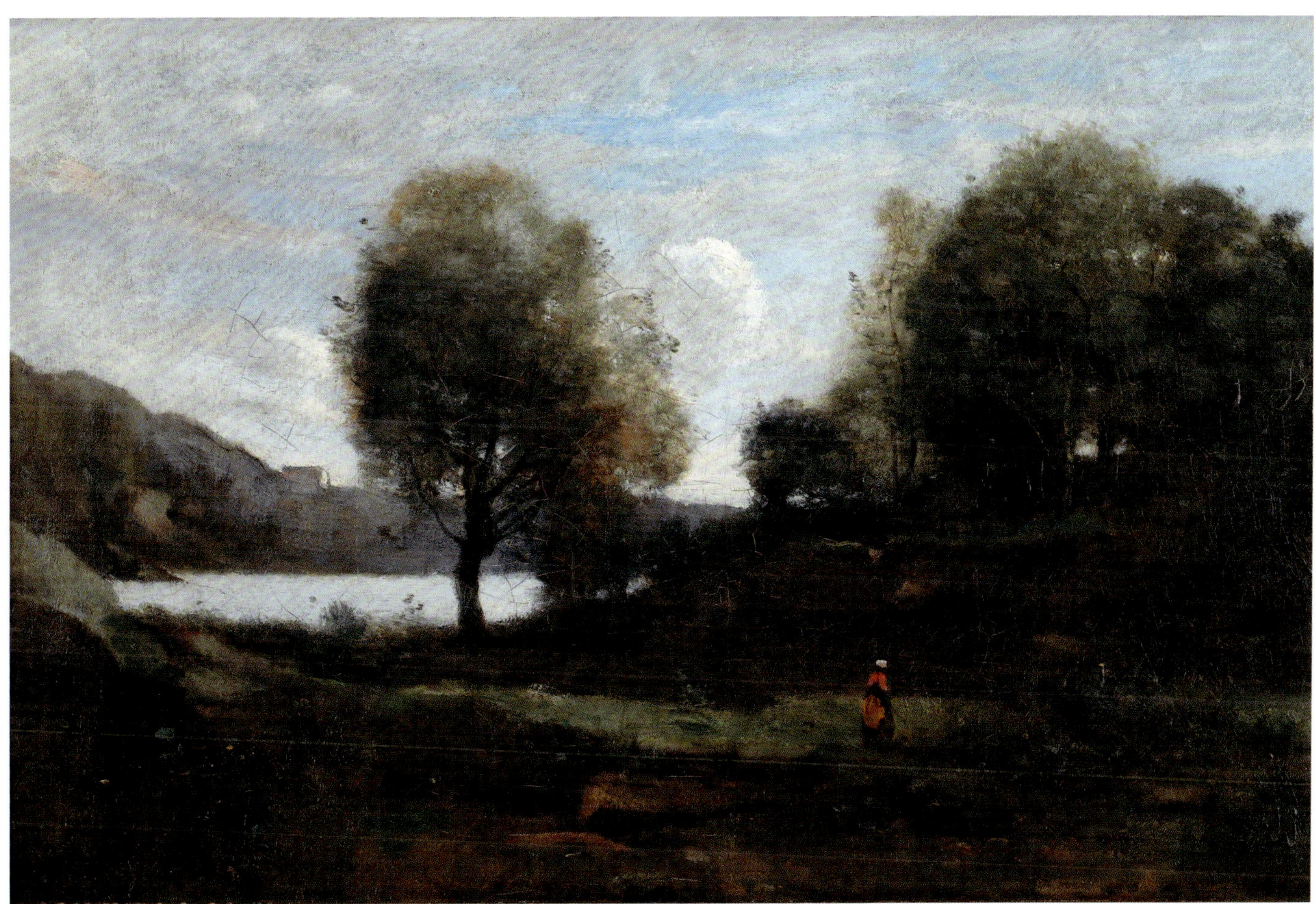

Jean-Baptiste-Camille Corot (1796–1875)
Hamlet and the Gravedigger, c. 1870–75
Oil on canvas, 50 × 80.5 cm
Inv. no. 293 WH

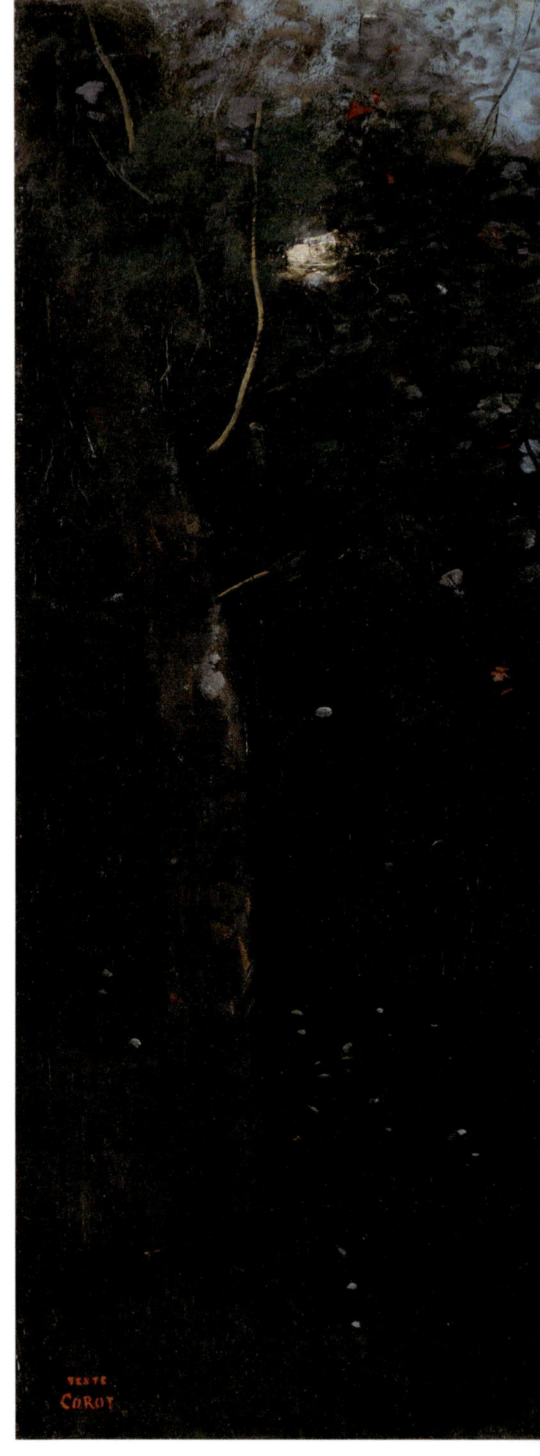

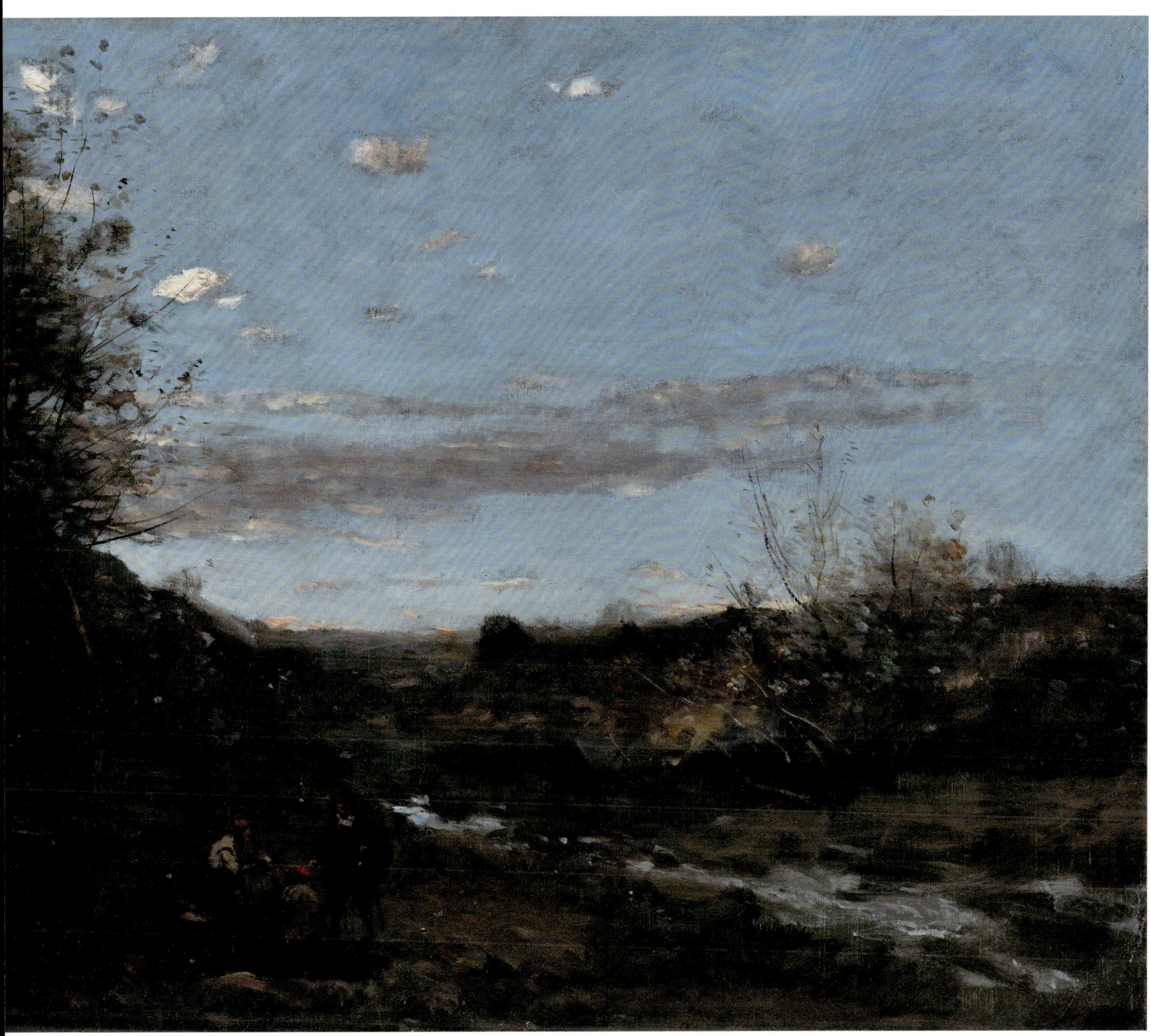

Jules Dupré (1811–1889)
The Sea, after 1875
Oil on canvas, 59.5 × 73.5 cm
Inv. no. 222 WH

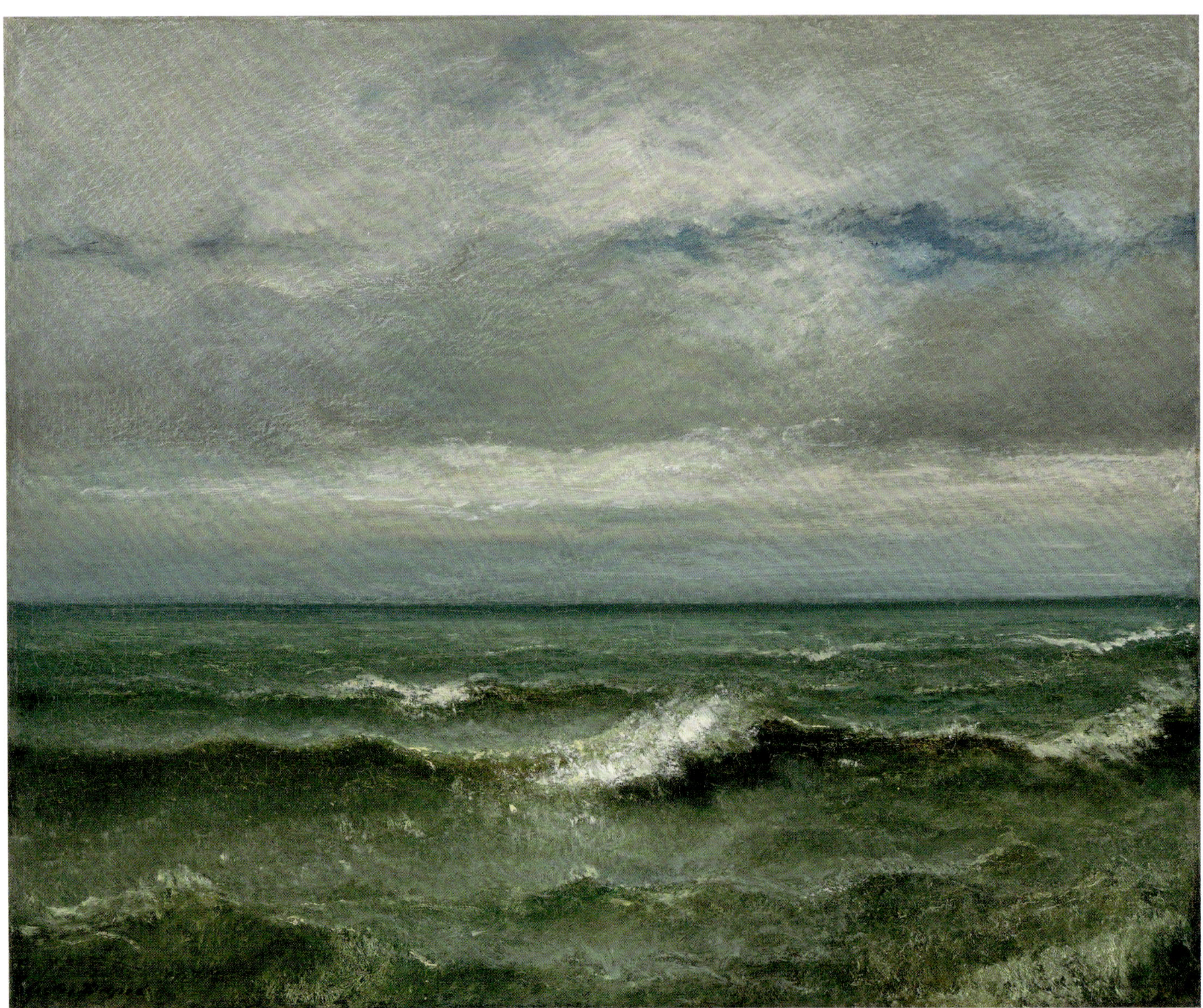

19
Jules Dupré (1811–1889)
A Clearing in the Forest, after 1875
Oil on canvas, 56.5 × 43.5 cm
Inv. no. 241 WH

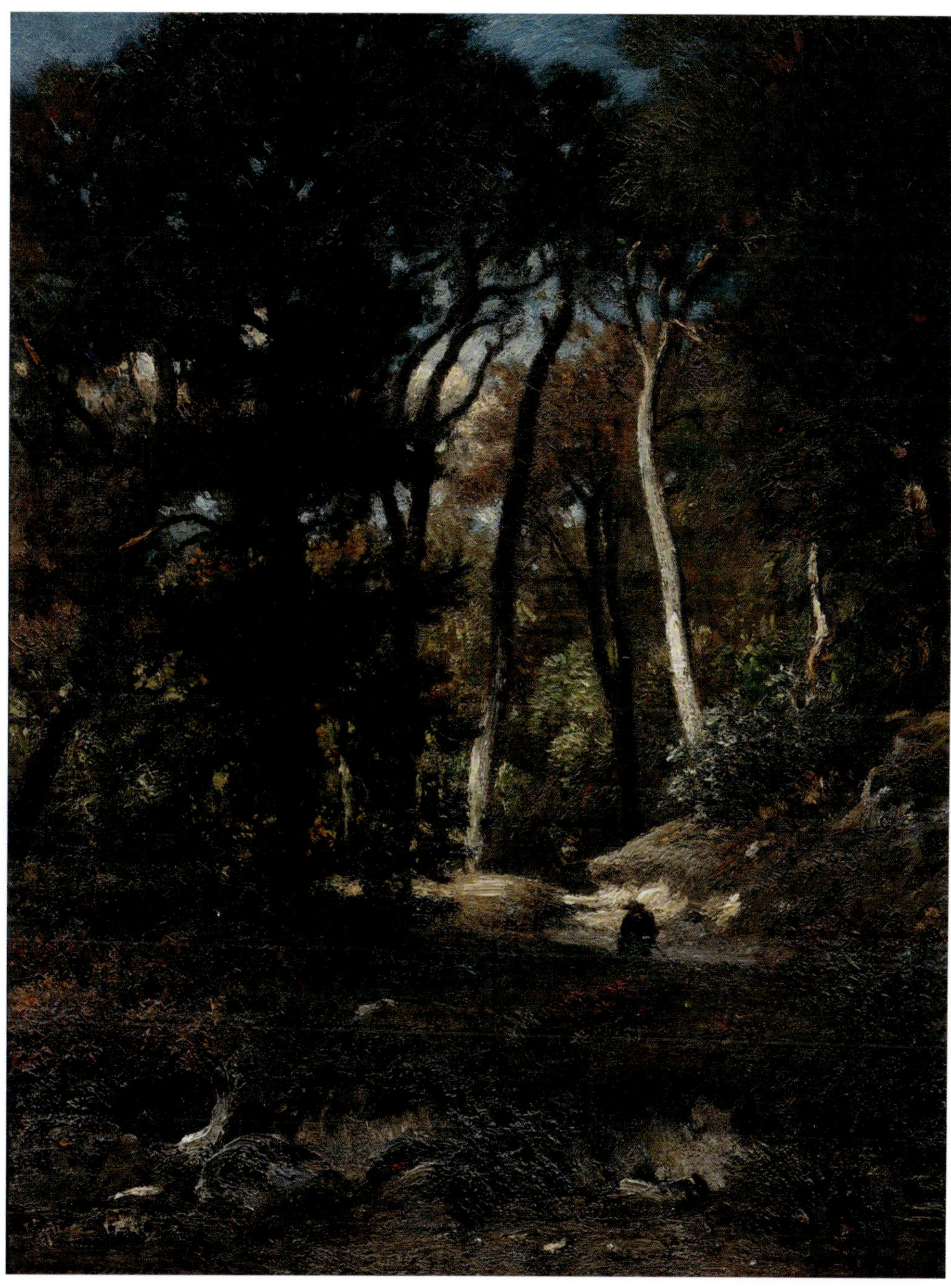

20
Charles-François Daubigny (1817–1878)
Seascape, Overcast, 1874
Oil on canvas, 83.5 × 147 cm
Inv. no. 189 WH

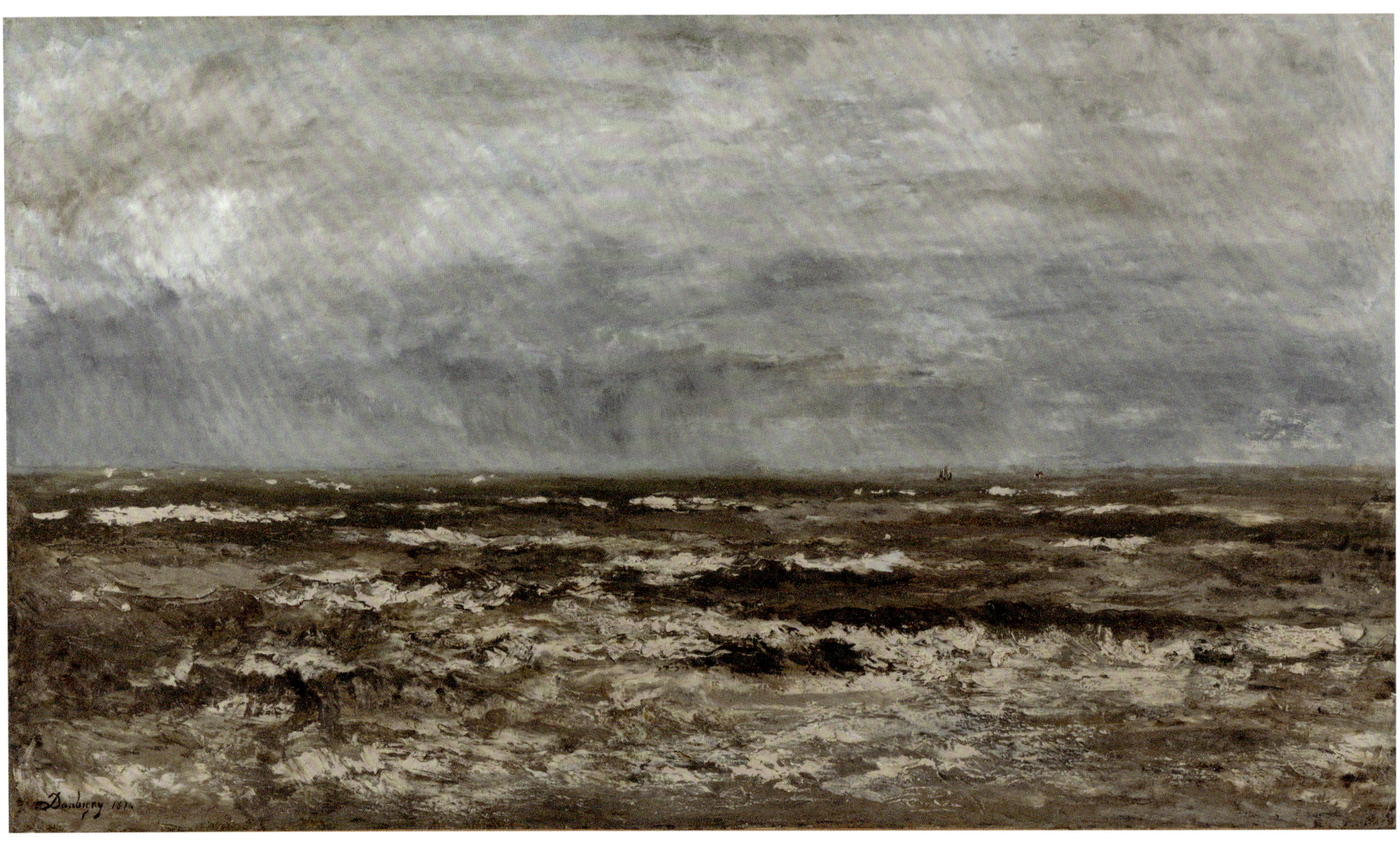

21
Karl Daubigny (1846–1886)
Boat on the River Oise, 1868
Oil on wood, 30 × 55 cm
Inv. no. 237 WH

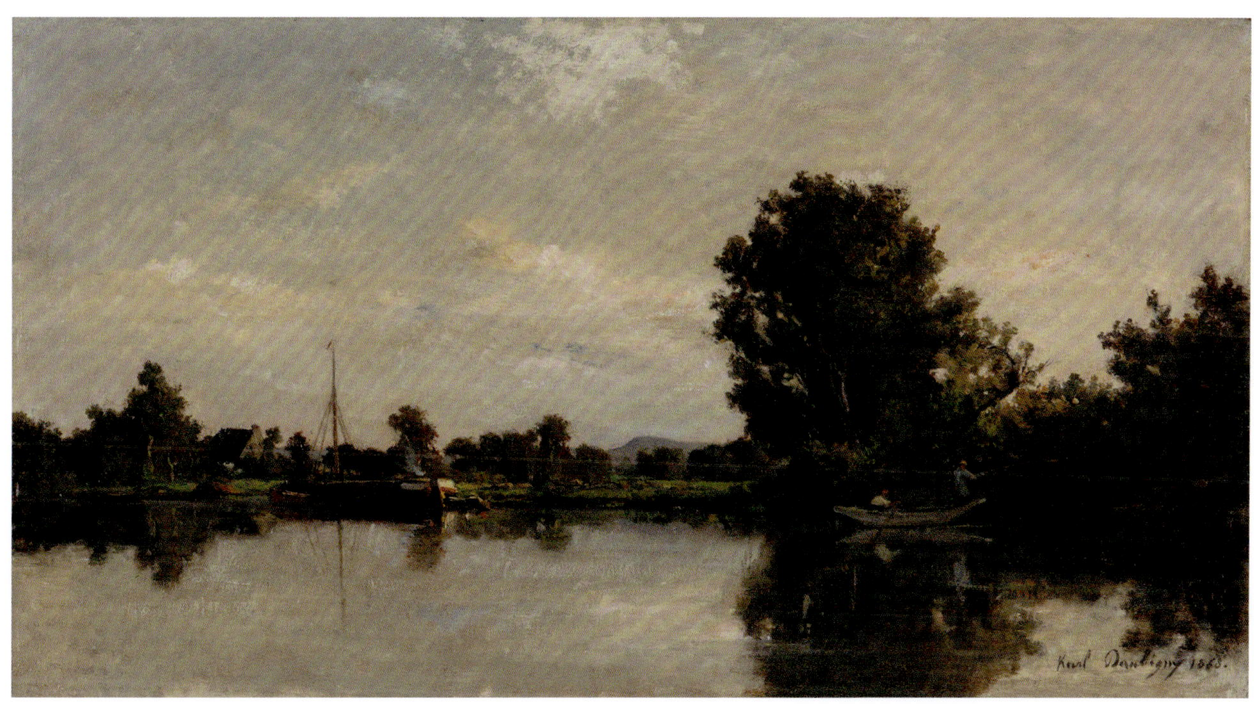

22
Eugène Boudin (1824–1898)
The Pier at Trouville, 1867
Oil on canvas, 47 × 64 cm
Inv. no. 185 WH

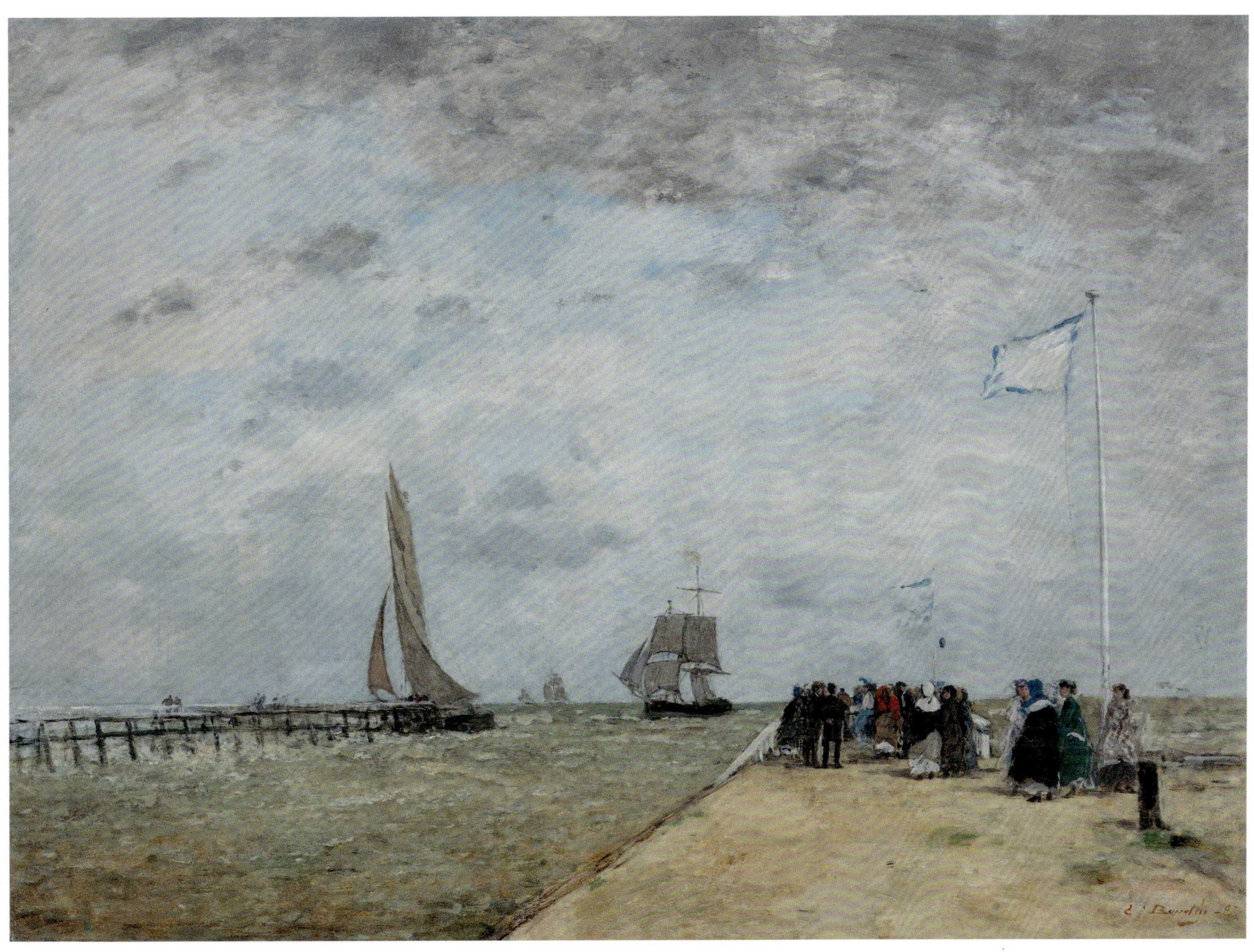

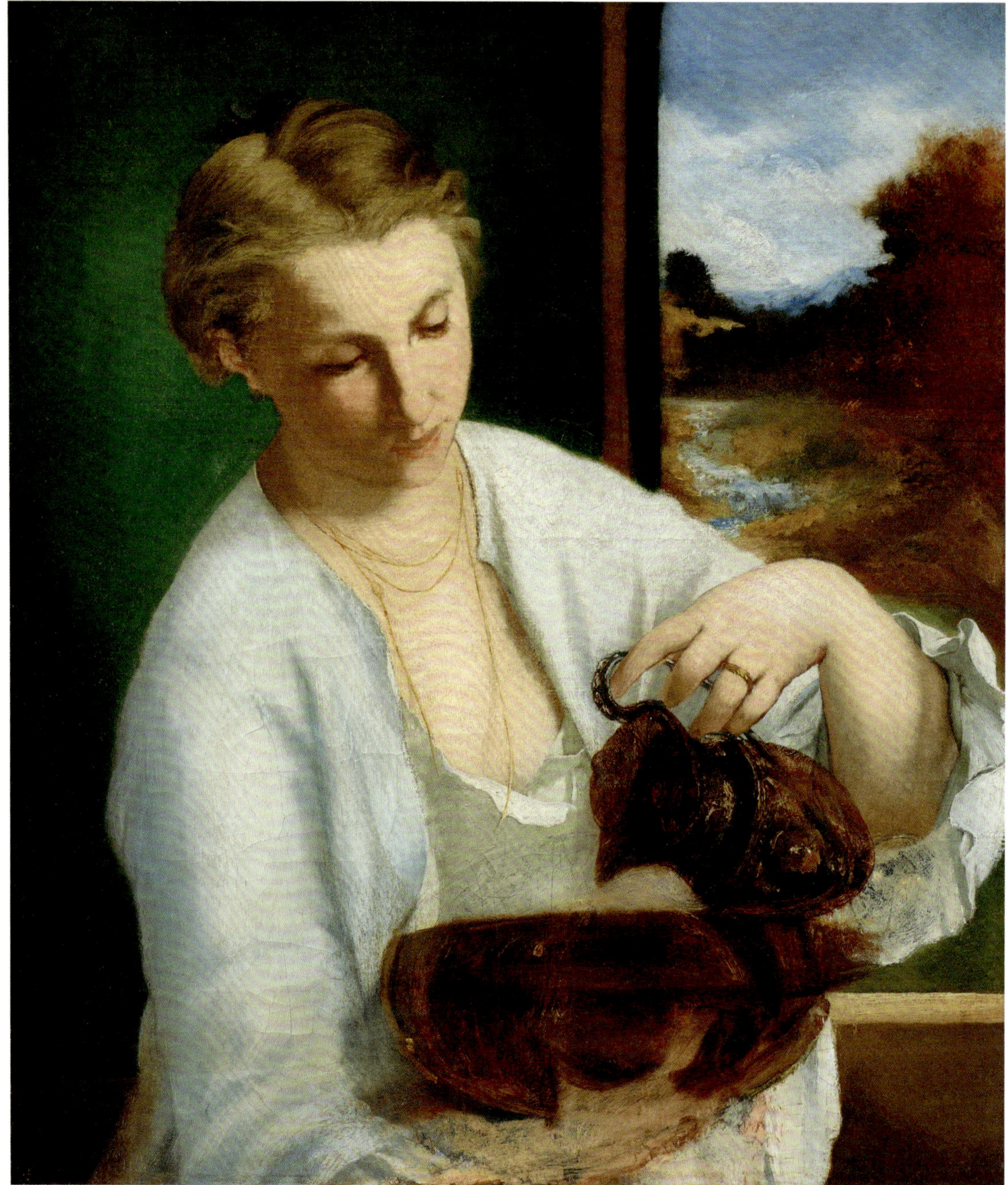

23
Édouard Manet (1832–1883)
Woman with a Jug (Suzanne Leenhoff, later Manet), c. 1858–60
Oil on canvas, 61 × 54.5 cm
Inv. no. 282 WH

24
Édouard Manet (1832–1883)
Basket of Pears, 1882
Oil on canvas, 35 × 41 cm
Inv. no. 197 WH

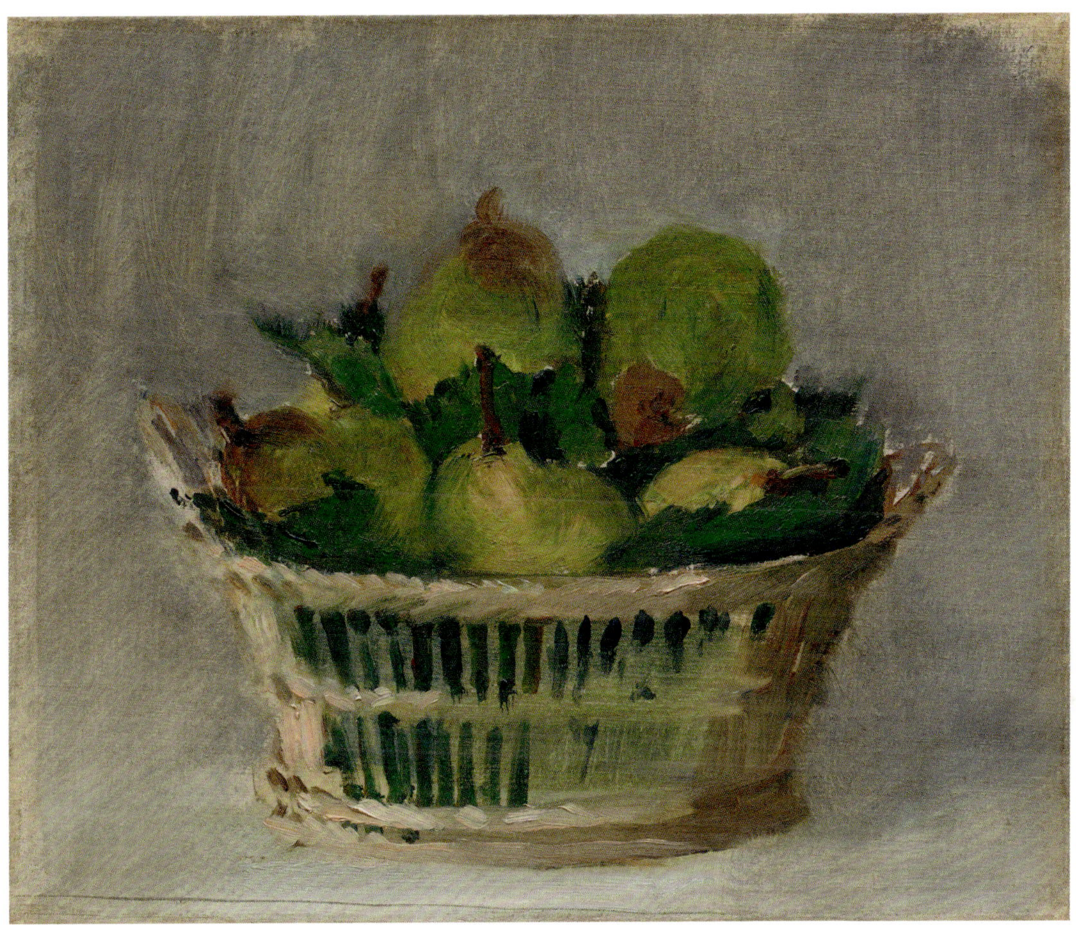

25
Claude Monet (1840–1926)
The Chailly Road through the Forest of Fontainebleau, 1865
Oil on canvas, 97 × 130.5 cm
Inv. no. 250 WH

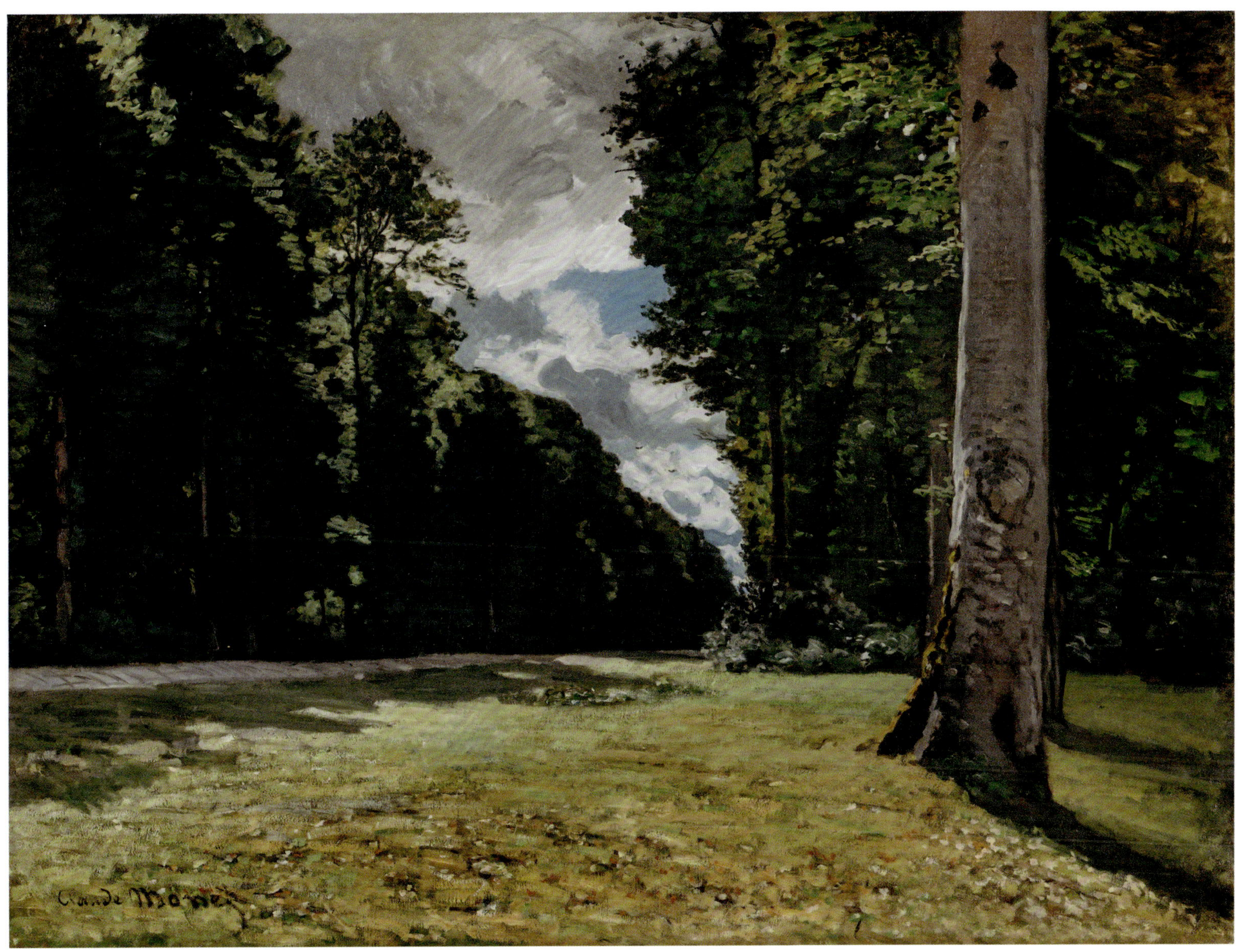

26
Claude Monet (1840–1926)
Seascape, Le Havre, c. 1866
Oil on canvas, 43 × 59.5 cm
Inv. no. 264 WH

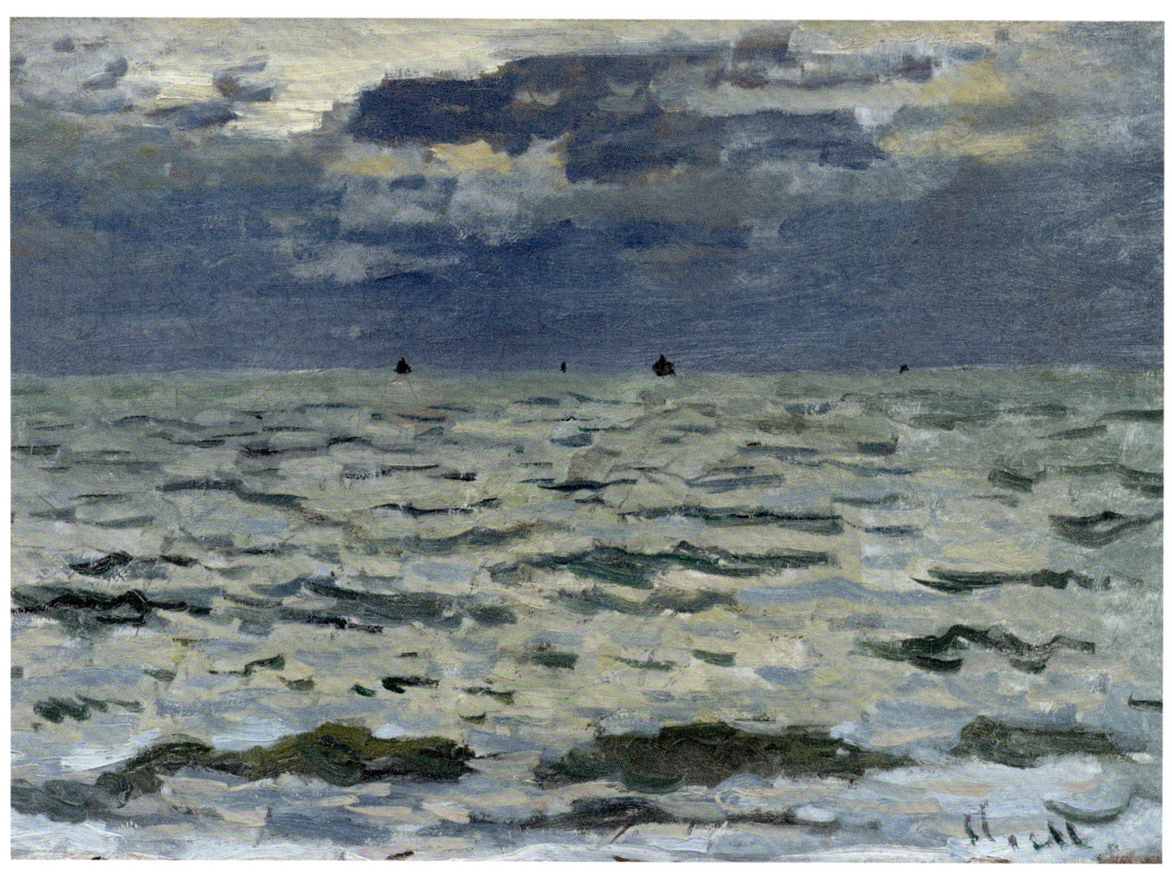

27
Claude Monet (1840–1926)
The Cliff near Sainte-Adresse, Overcast, c. 1881
Oil on canvas, 60 × 73 cm
Inv. no. 283 WH

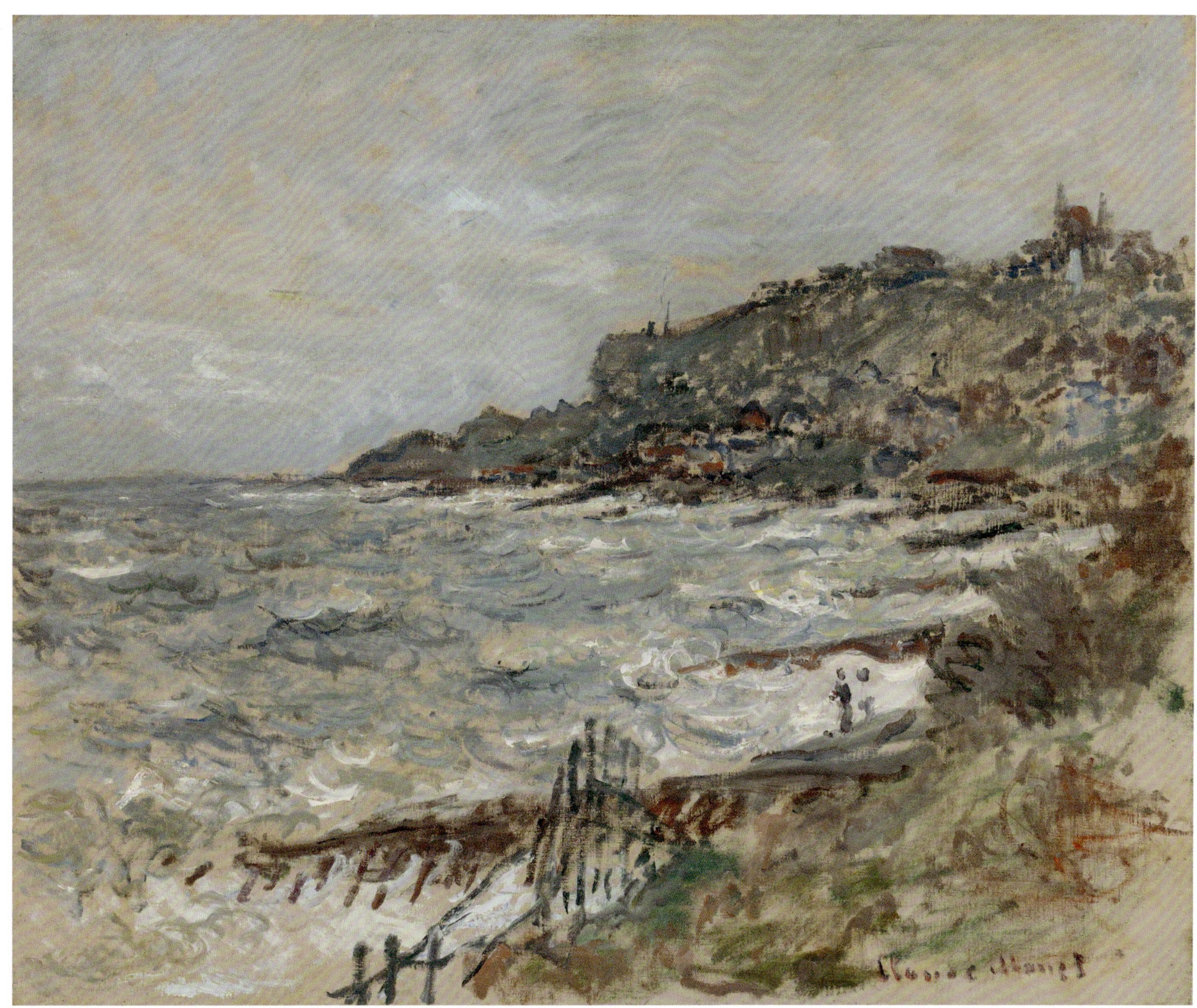

28
Claude Monet (1840–1926)
Waterloo Bridge, Overcast, 1903
Oil on canvas, 65.5 × 100.5 cm
Inv. no. 198 WH

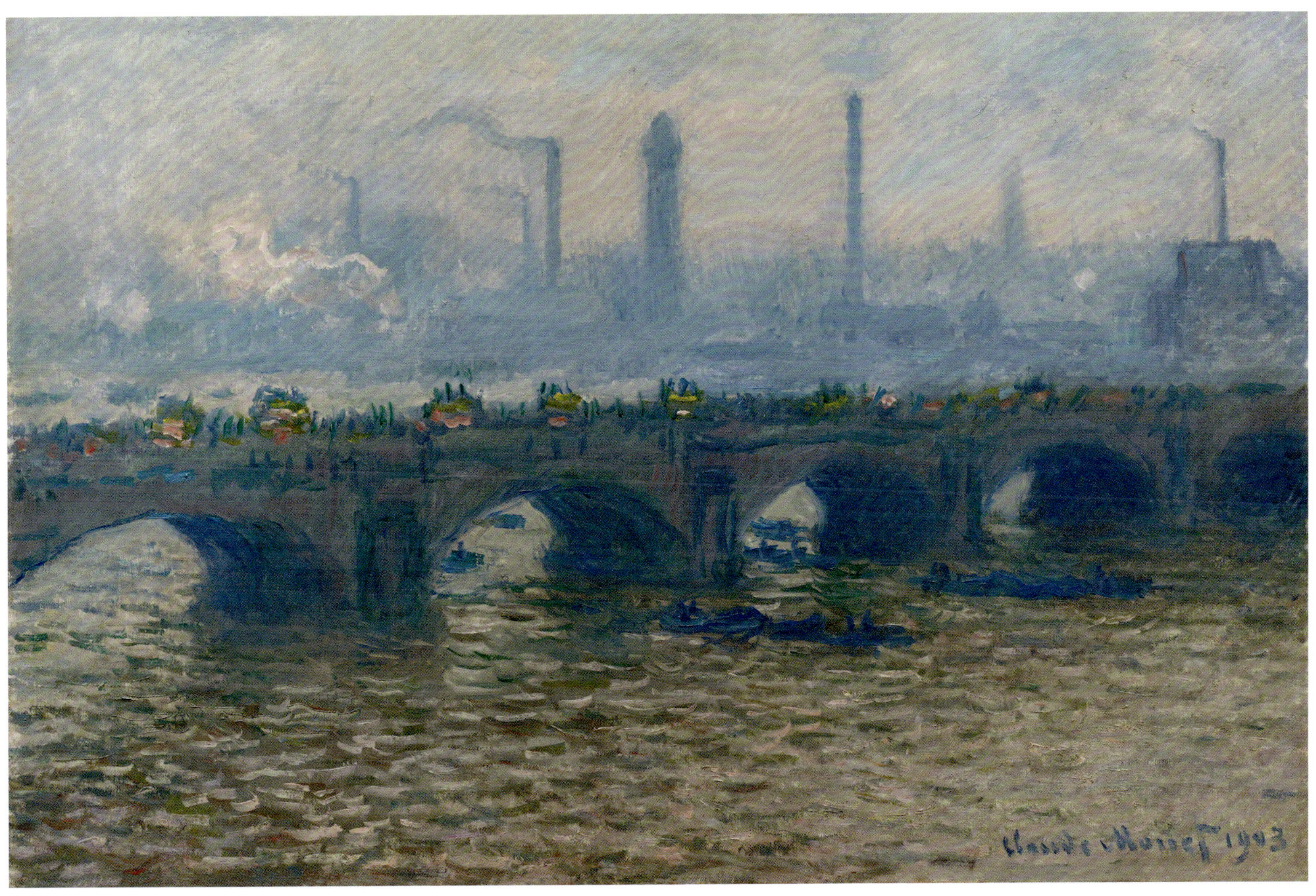

29
Camille Pissarro (1830–1903)
By St Anthony's Brook, The Hermitage, Pontoise, 1876
Oil on canvas, 54 × 65 cm
Inv. no. 260 WH

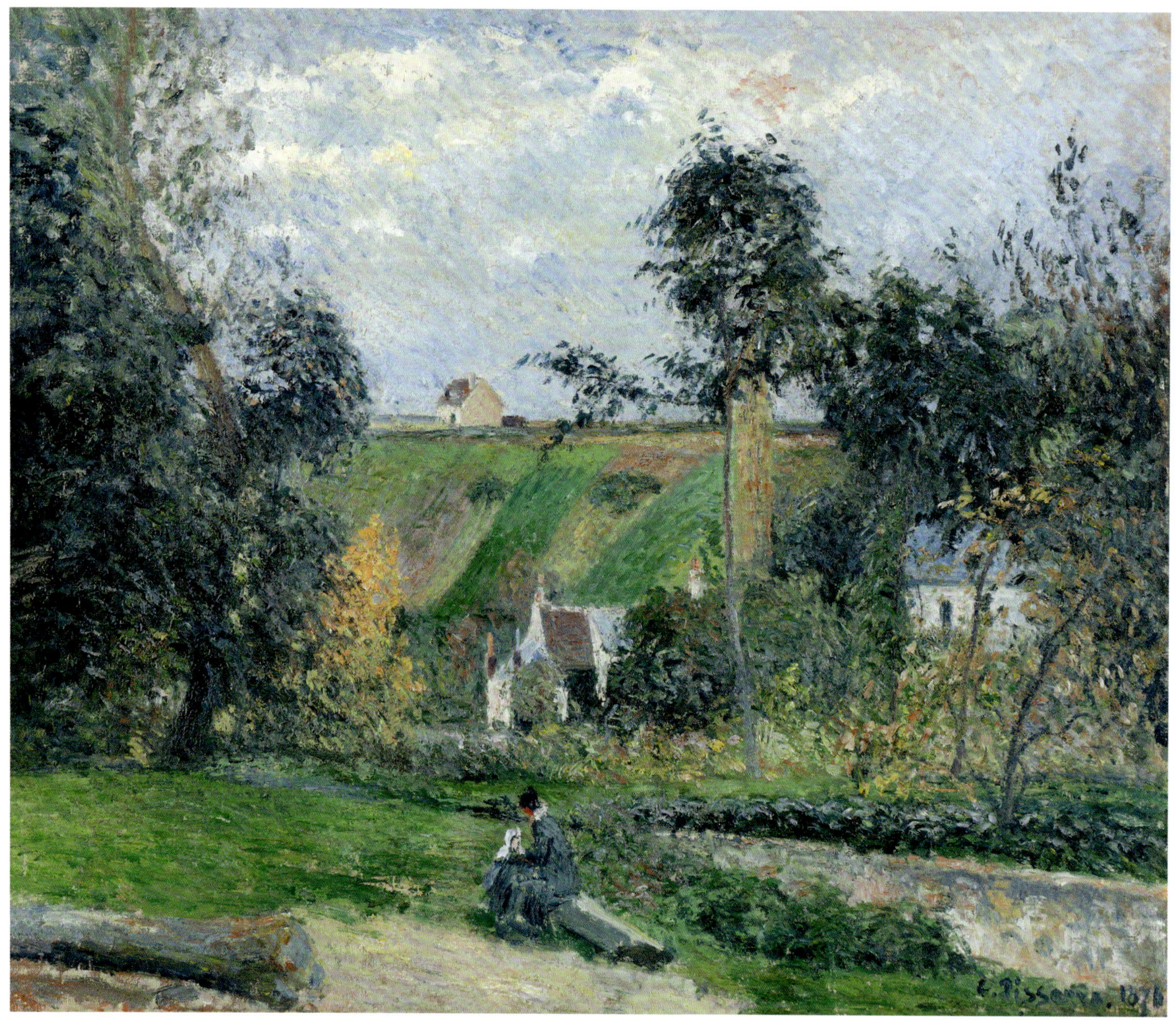

30
Camille Pissarro (1830–1903)
Snowy Landscape, Éragny, Evening, 1894
Oil on canvas, 54.5 × 65 cm
Inv. no. 201 WH

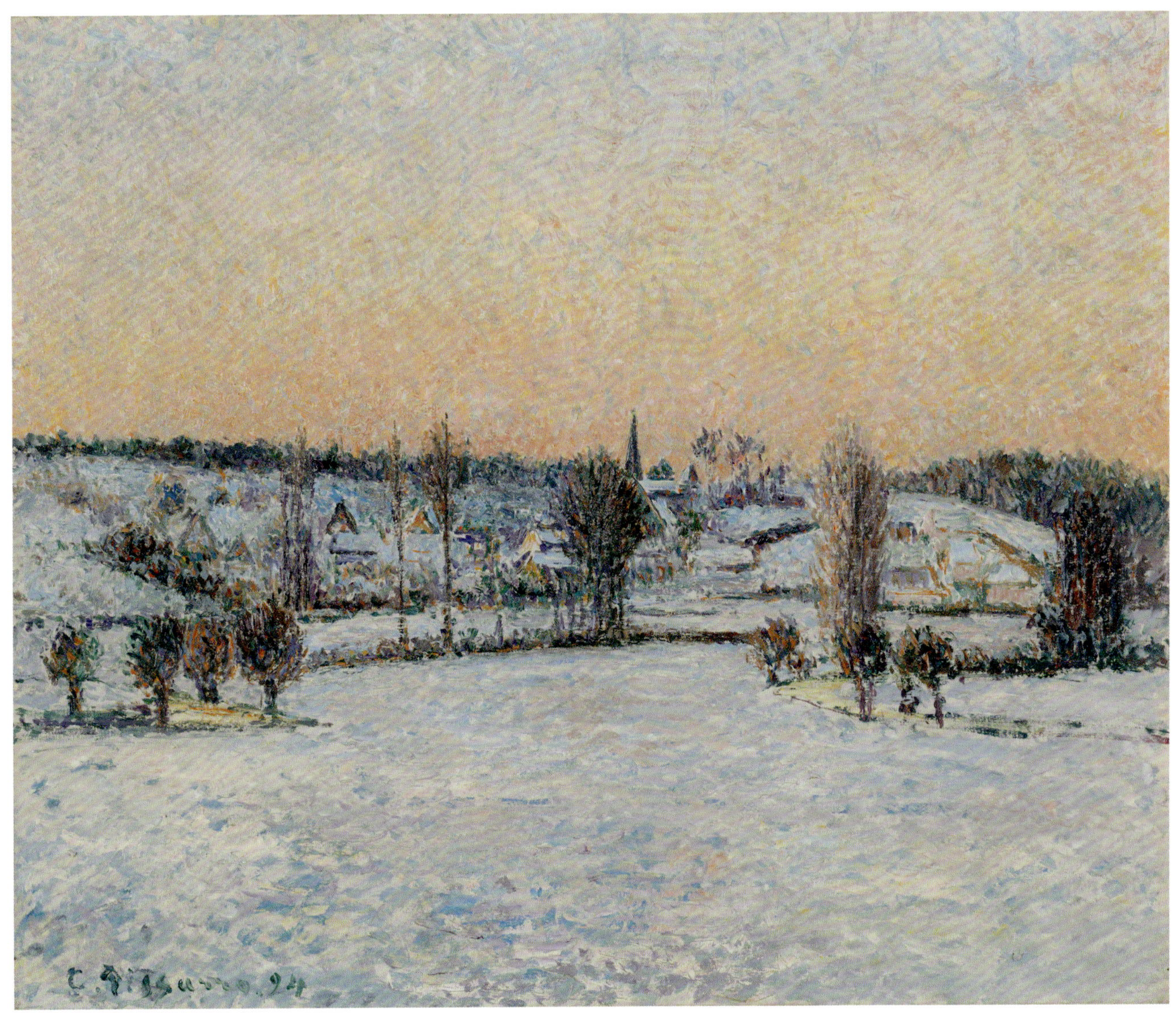

31
Camille Pissarro (1830–1903)
Plum Trees in Blossom, Éragny (The Painter's Home), 1894
Oil on canvas, 60 × 73 cm
Inv. no. 267 WH

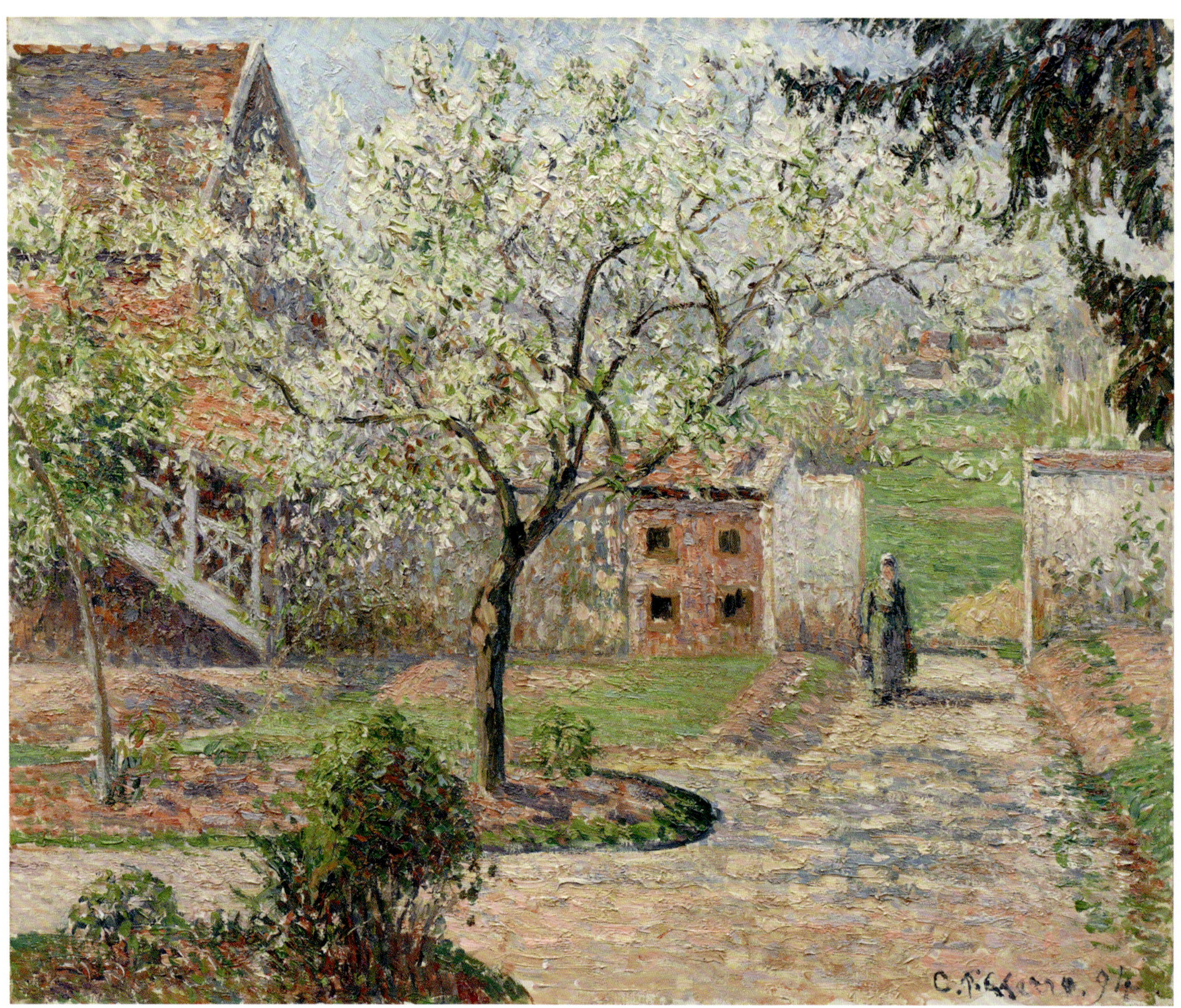

32
Camille Pissarro (1830–1903)
A Corner in the Garden, Éragny, 1897
Oil on canvas, 65.5 × 81 cm
Inv. no. 202 WH

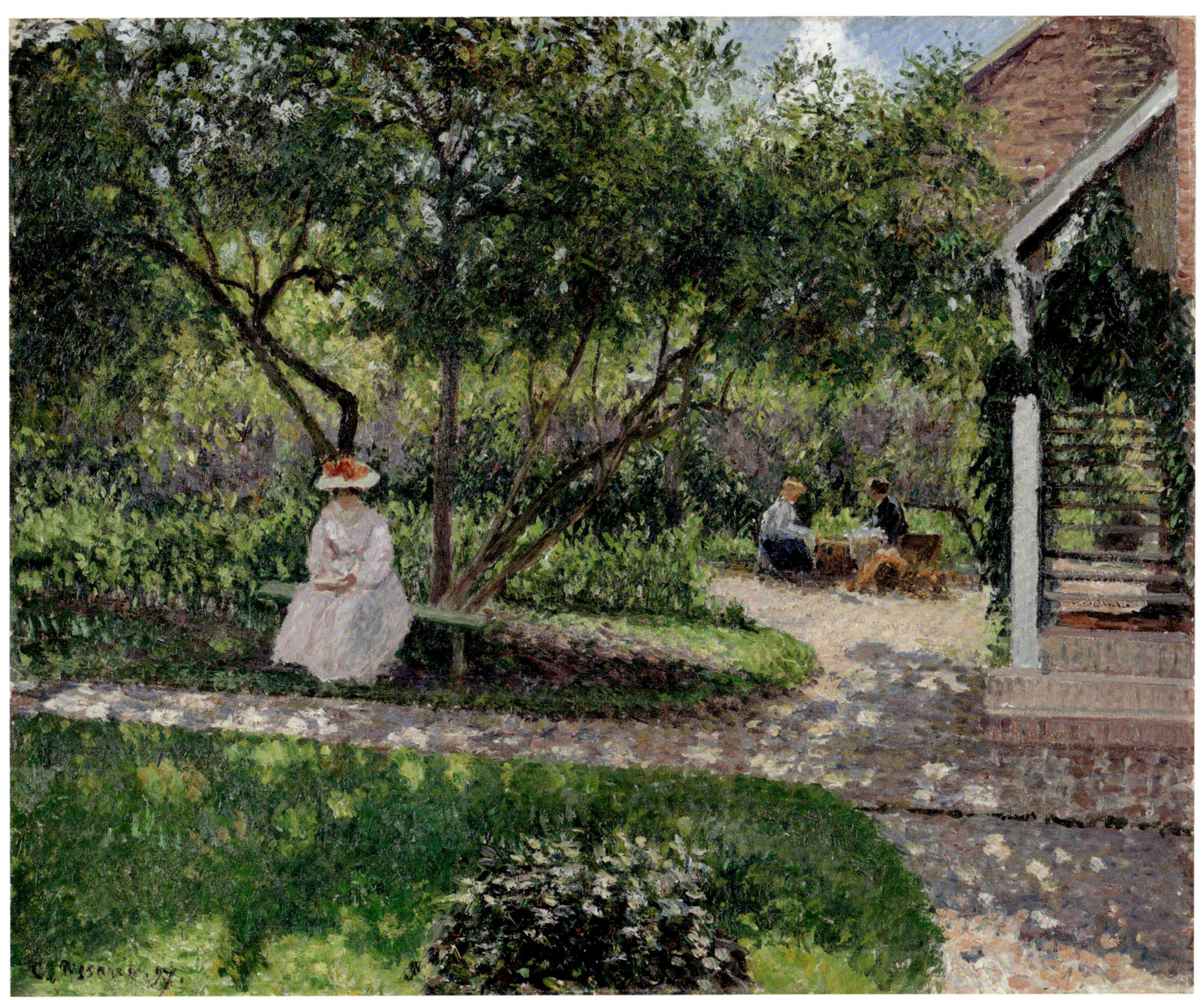

33
Camille Pissarro (1830–1903)
Rue Saint-Lazare, Paris, 1897
Oil on canvas, 35 × 27 cm
Inv. no. 300 WH

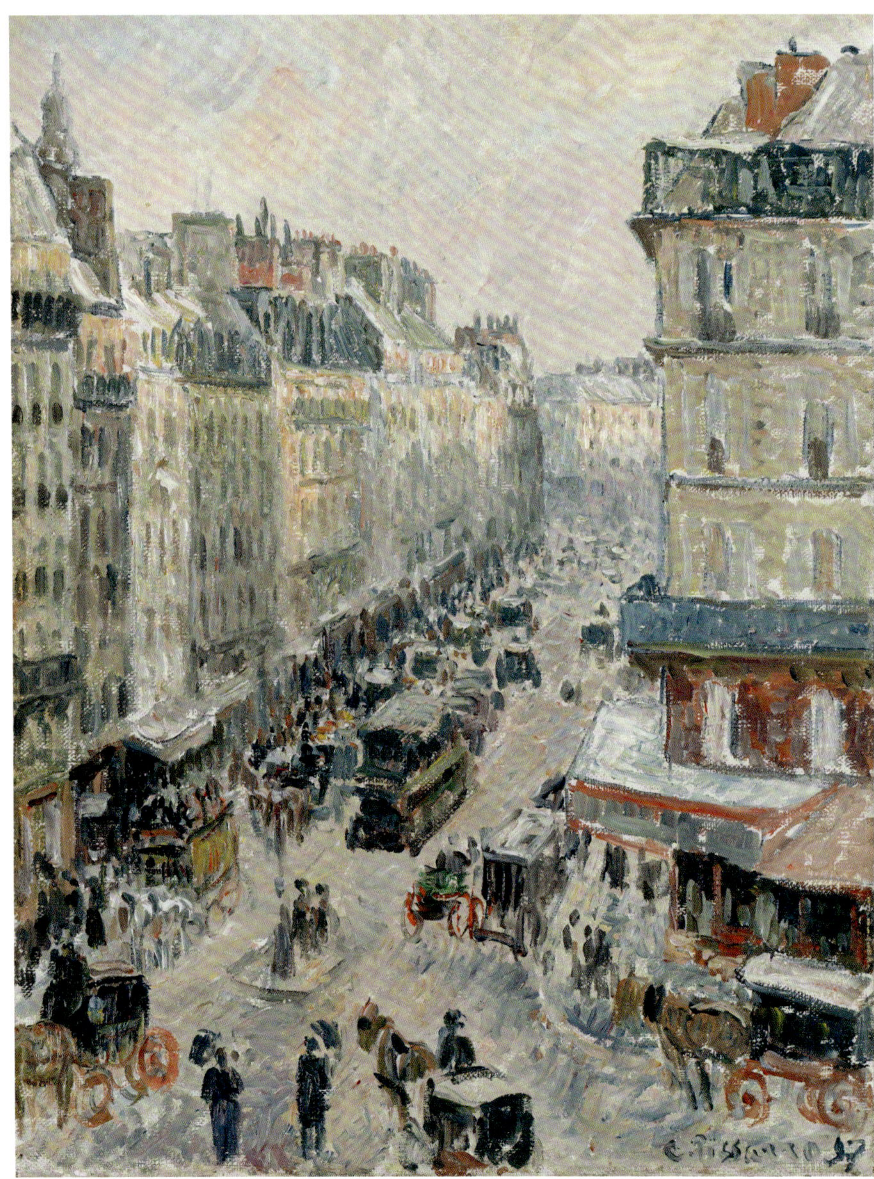

34
Camille Pissarro (1830–1903)
Morning Sun in the Rue Saint-Honoré,
Place du Théâtre Français, 1898
Oil on canvas with underlying
drawing in black crayon, 65.5 × 54 cm
Inv. no. 261 WH

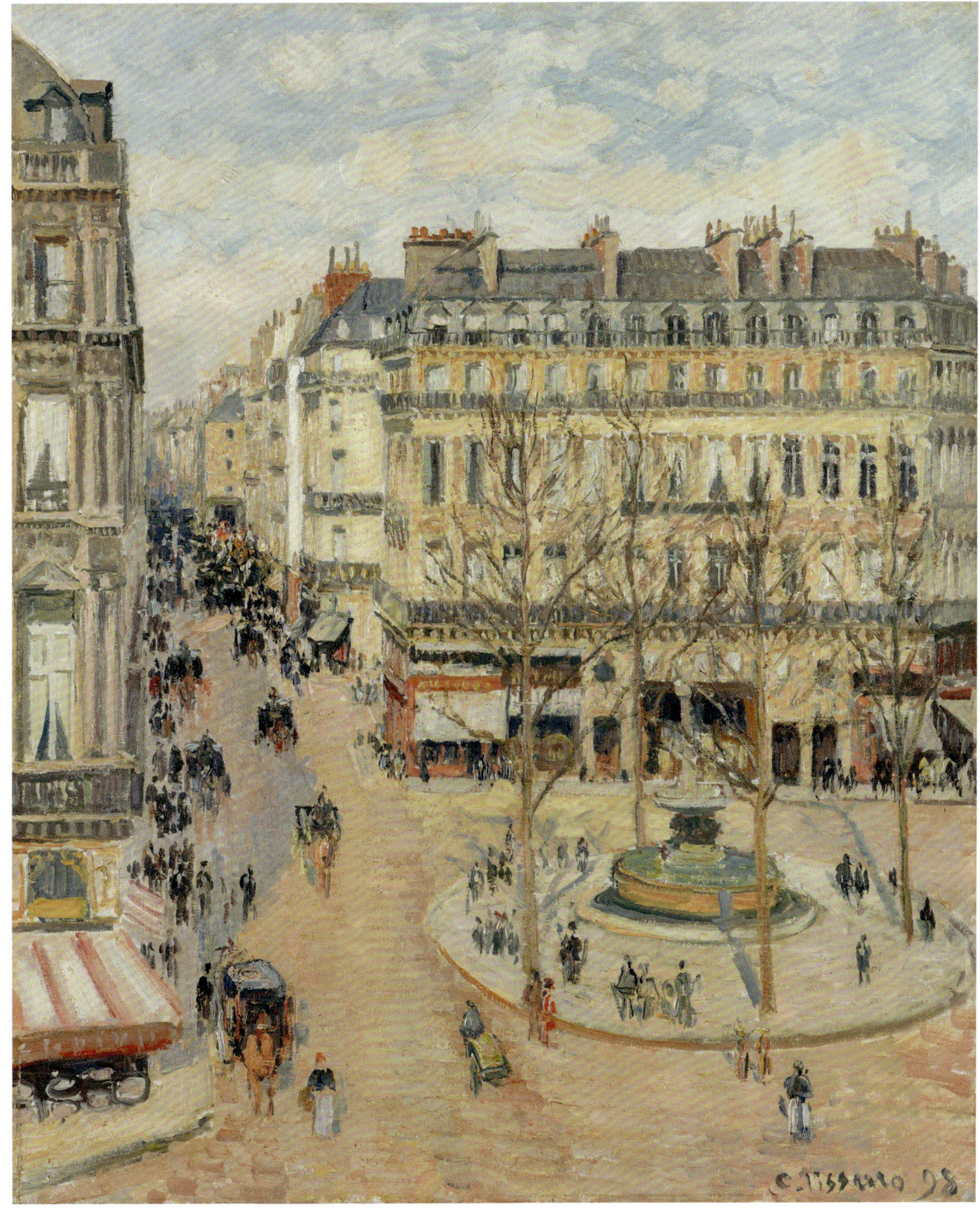

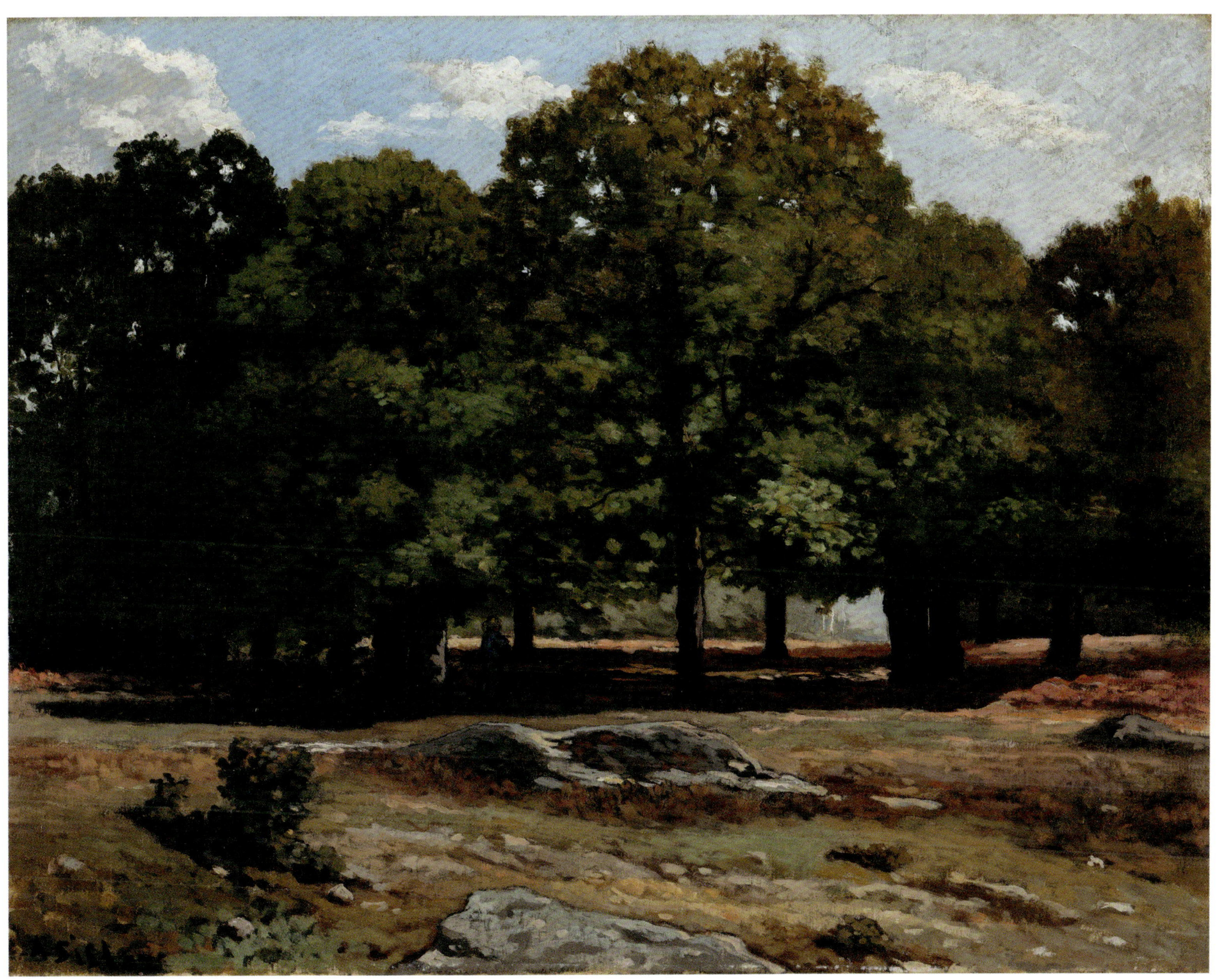

Alfred Sisley (1839–1899)
The Flood, Banks of the Seine, Bougival, 1873
Oil on canvas, 50 × 65.5 cm
Inv. no. 253 WH

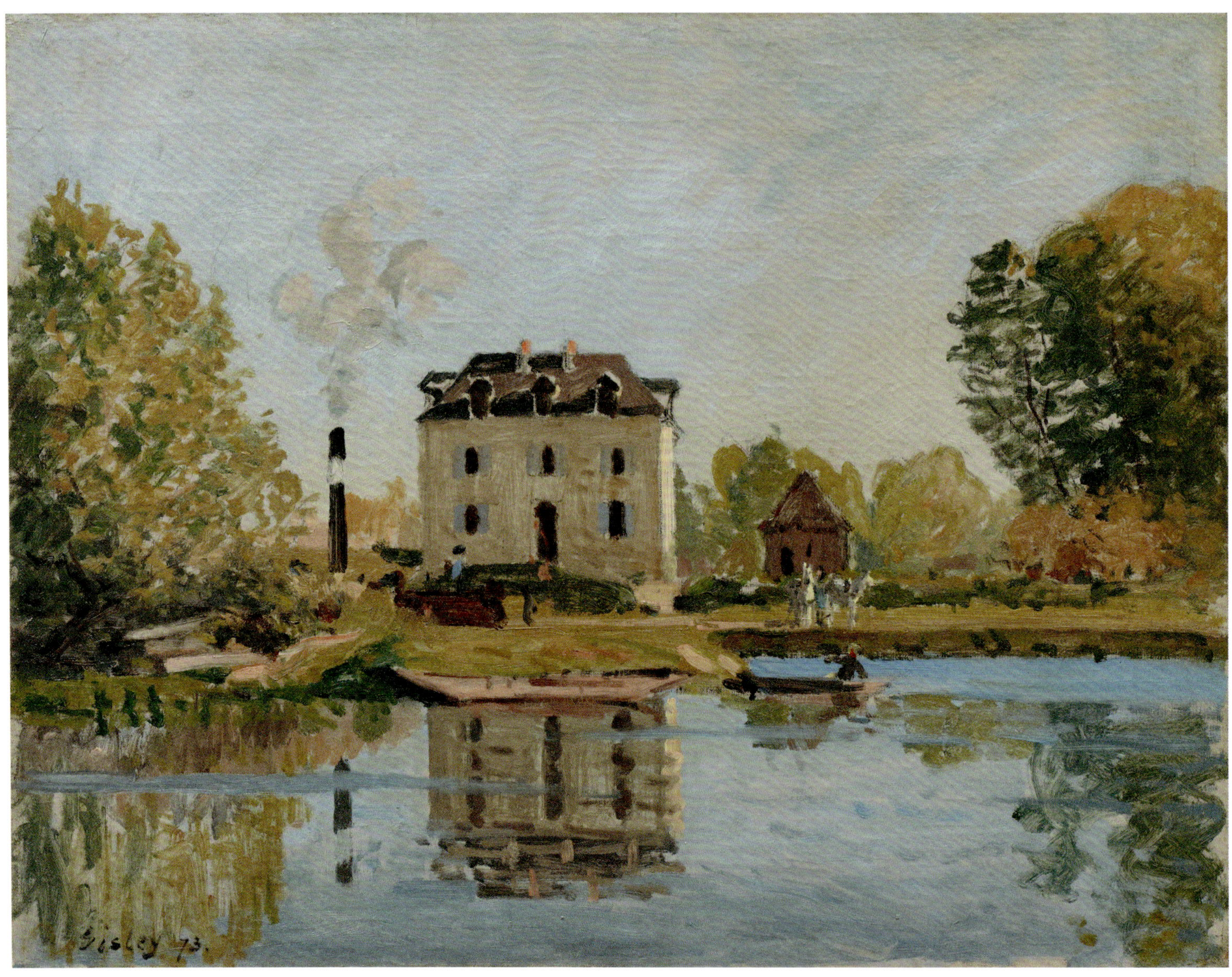

37
Alfred Sisley (1839–1899)
Unloading Barges at Billancourt, 1877
Oil on canvas, 50 × 65 cm
Inv. no. 273 WH

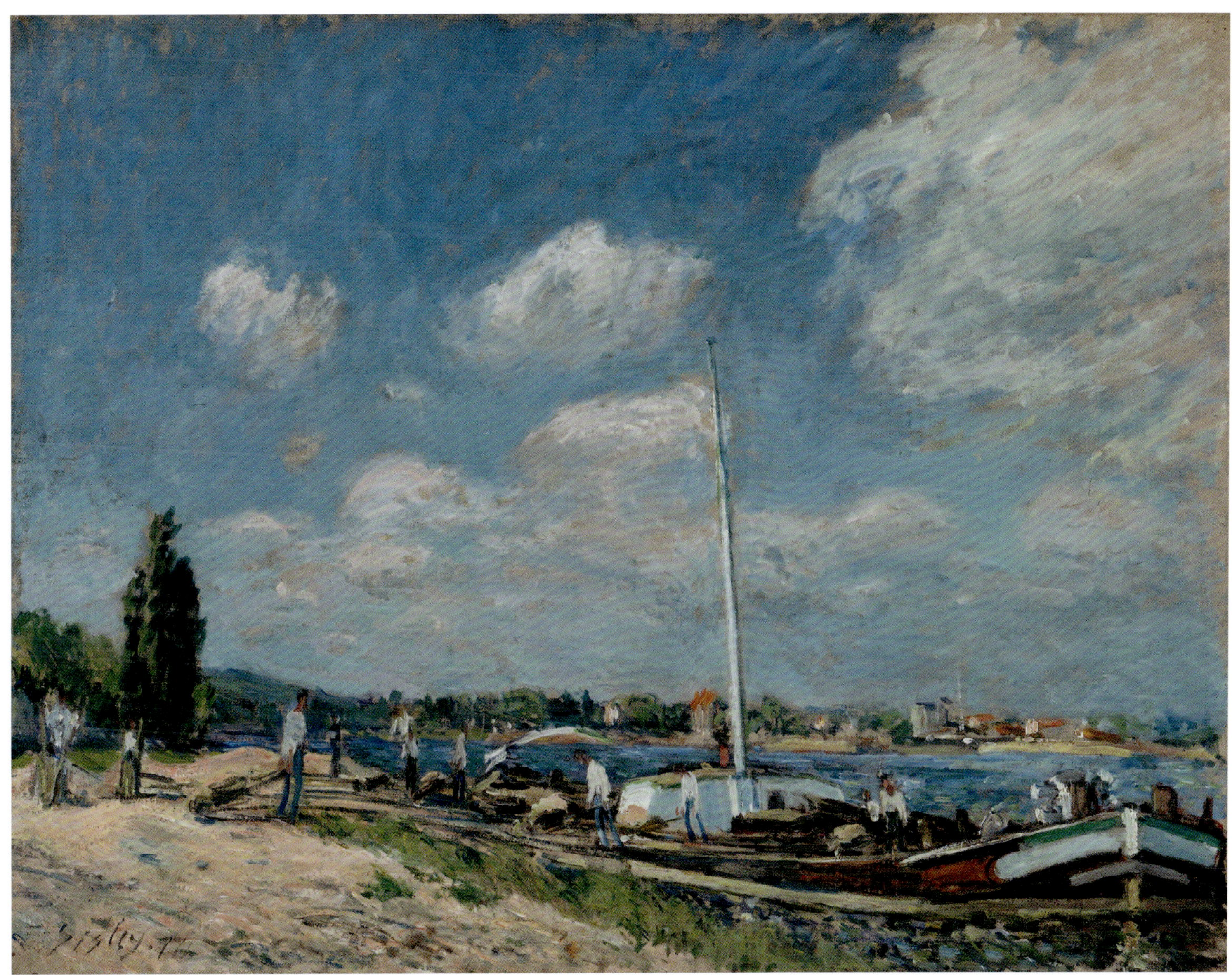

38
Alfred Sisley (1839–1899)
September Morning near Saint-Mammès and the Veneux-Nadon Hills, 1884
Oil on canvas, 54 × 72.5 cm
Inv. no. 269 WH

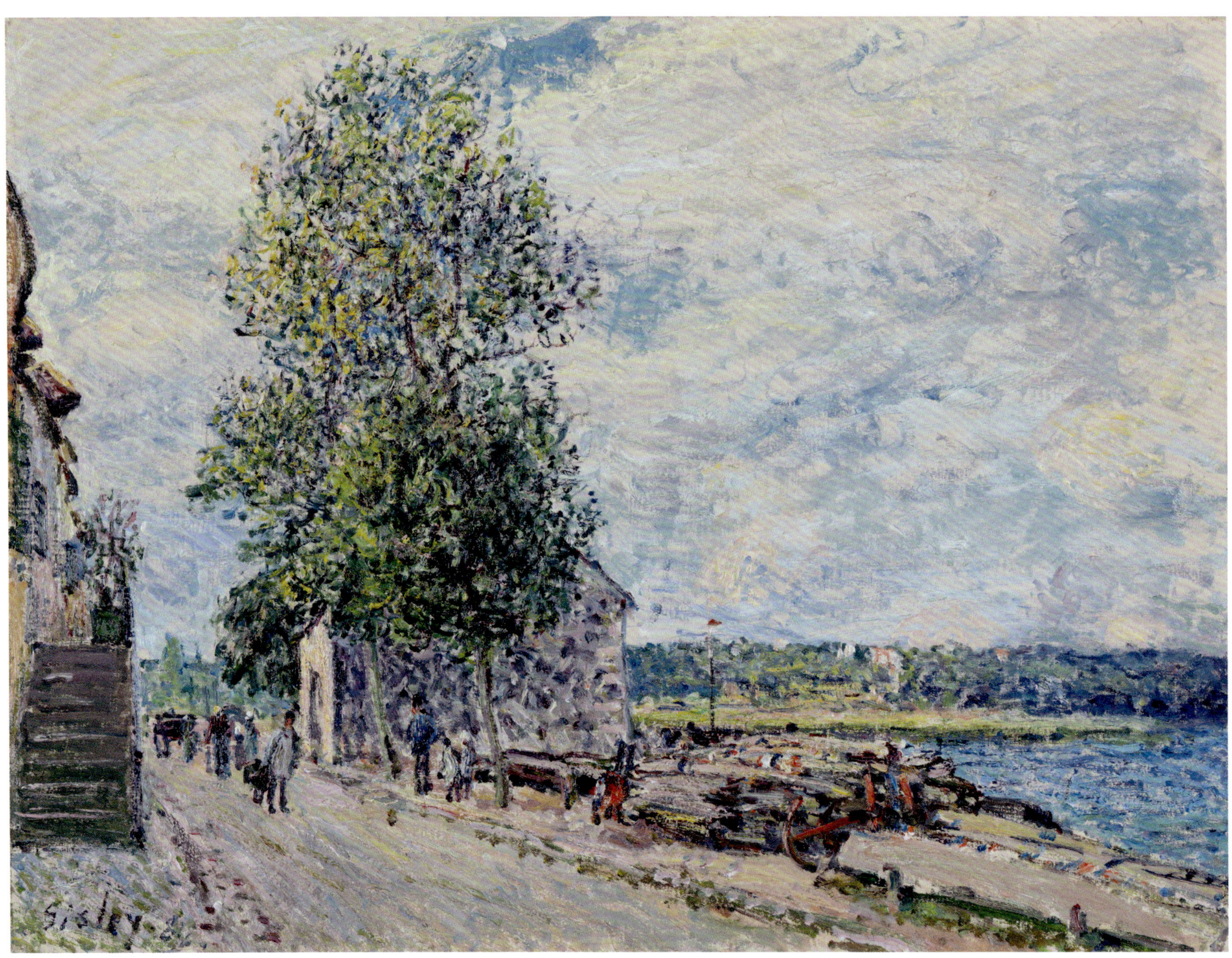

39
Alfred Sisley (1839–1899)
The River Boat Garage, 1885
Oil on canvas, 46 × 56 cm
Inv. no. 230 WH

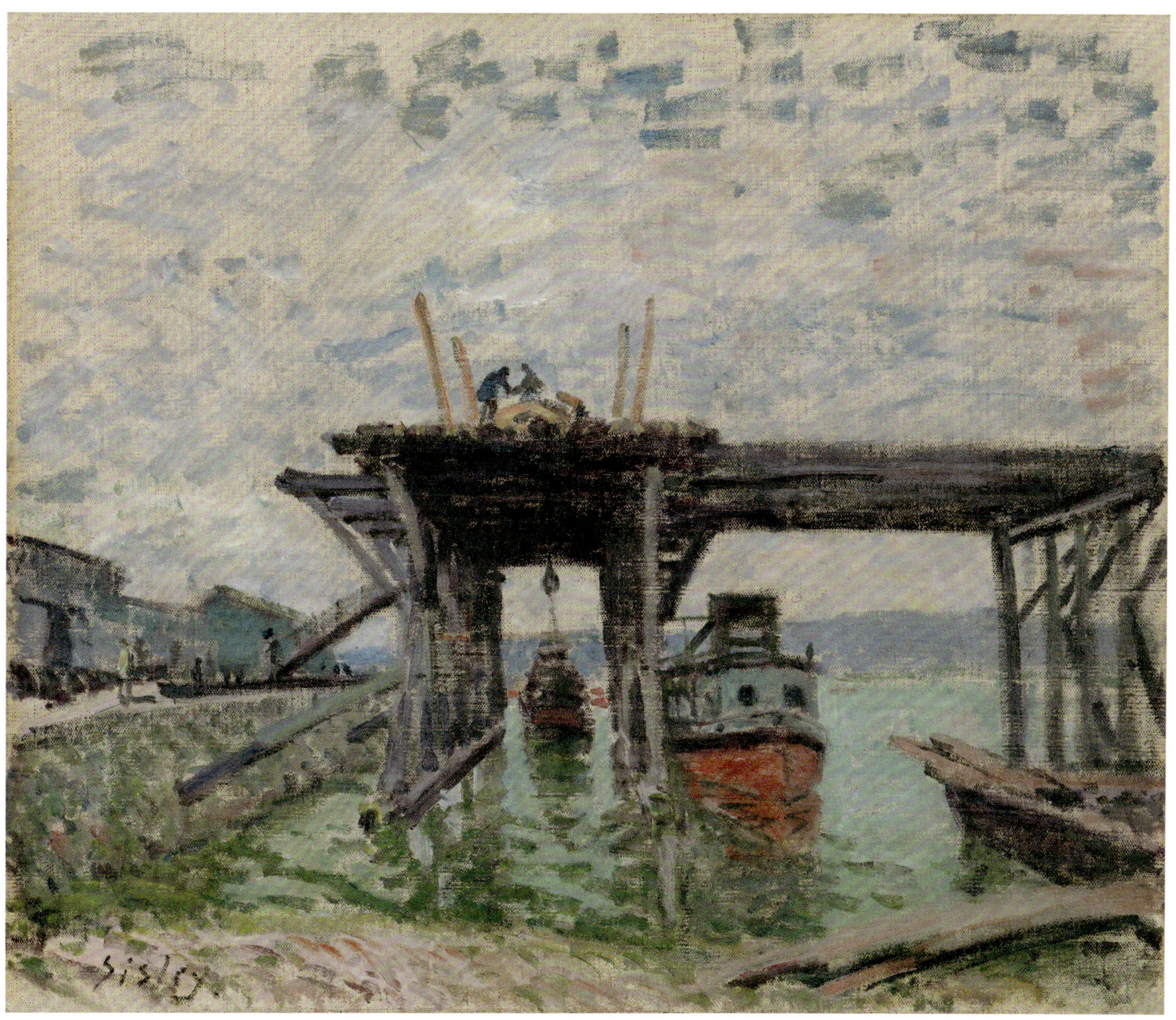

40
Alfred Sisley (1839–1899)
Barges from Berry on the Loing Canal in Spring, 1896
Oil on canvas, 54 × 65 cm
Inv. no. 231 WH

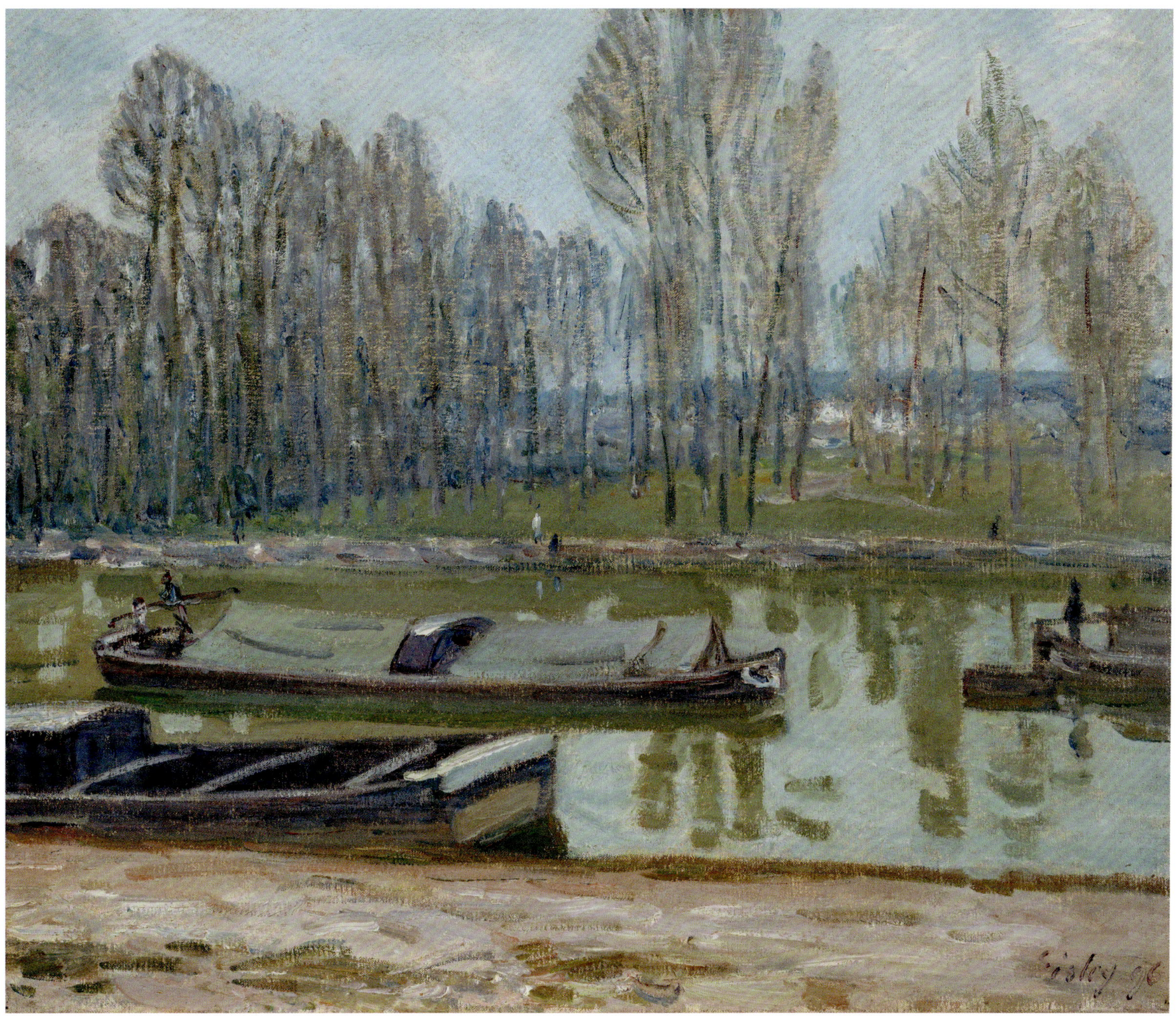

Sisley 96

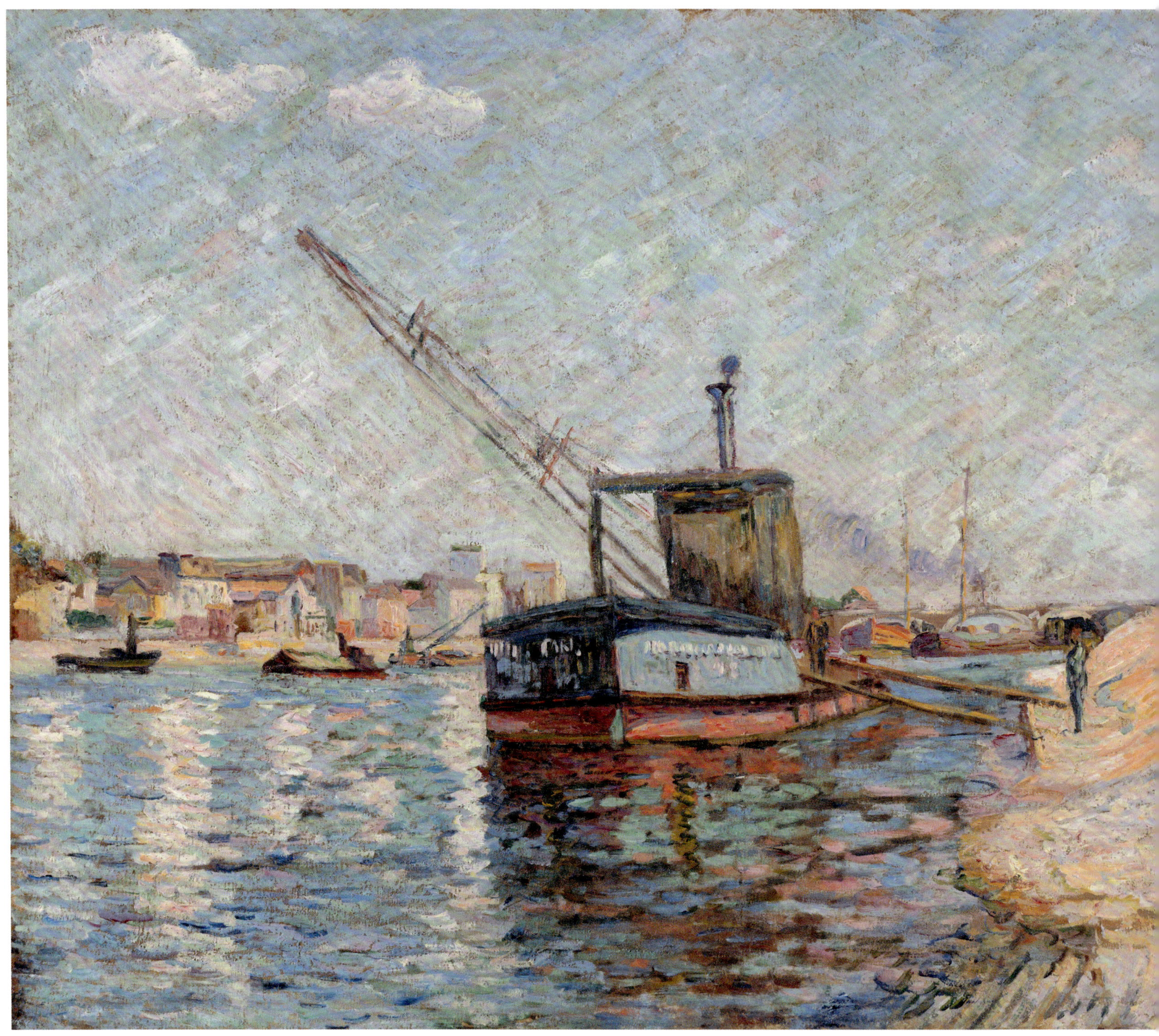

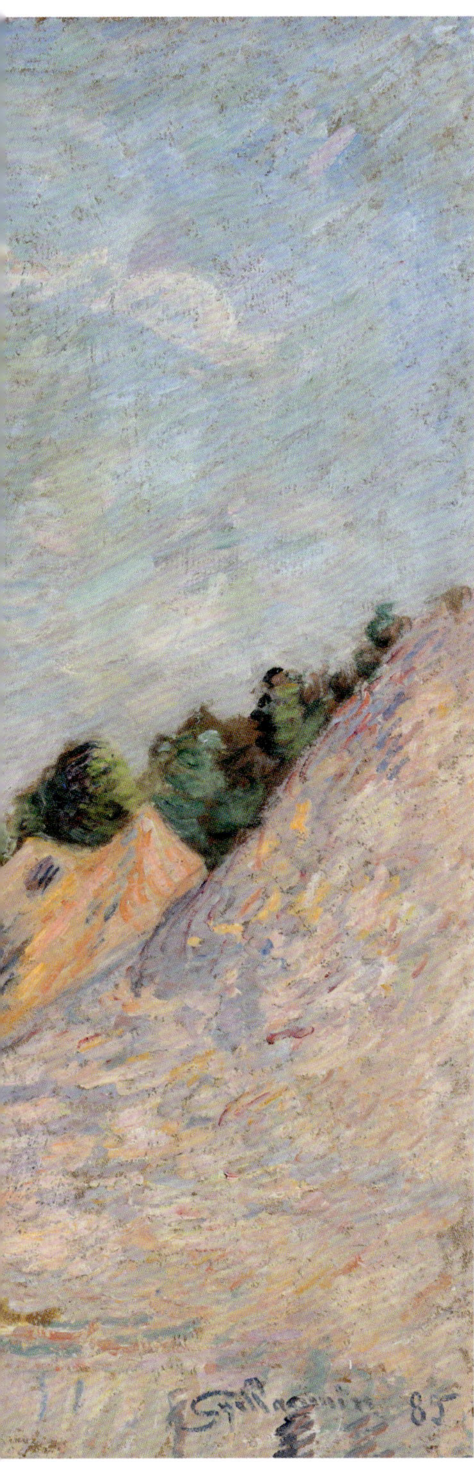

41
Armand Guillaumin (1841–1927)
Quai de Bercy, Paris, 1885
Oil on canvas, 60 × 92 cm
Inv. no. 265 WH

42
Pierre-Auguste Renoir (1841–1919)
Woman in a Meadow (Lise Tréhot), c. 1868
Oil on canvas, 29 × 34.5 cm
Inv. no. 204 WH

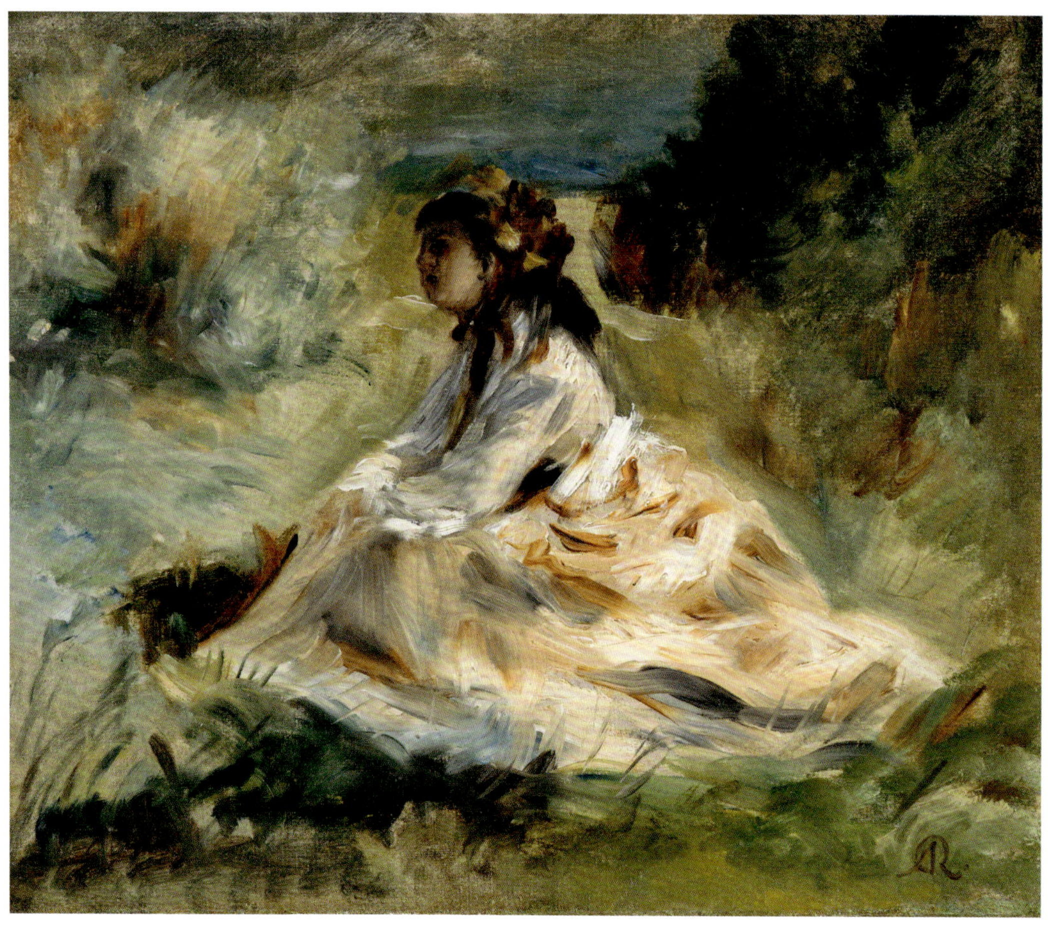

43
Pierre-Auguste Renoir (1841–1919)
Portrait of a Romanian Lady
(Madame Iscovesco), 1877
Oil on canvas, 41 × 33 cm
Inv. no. 205 WH

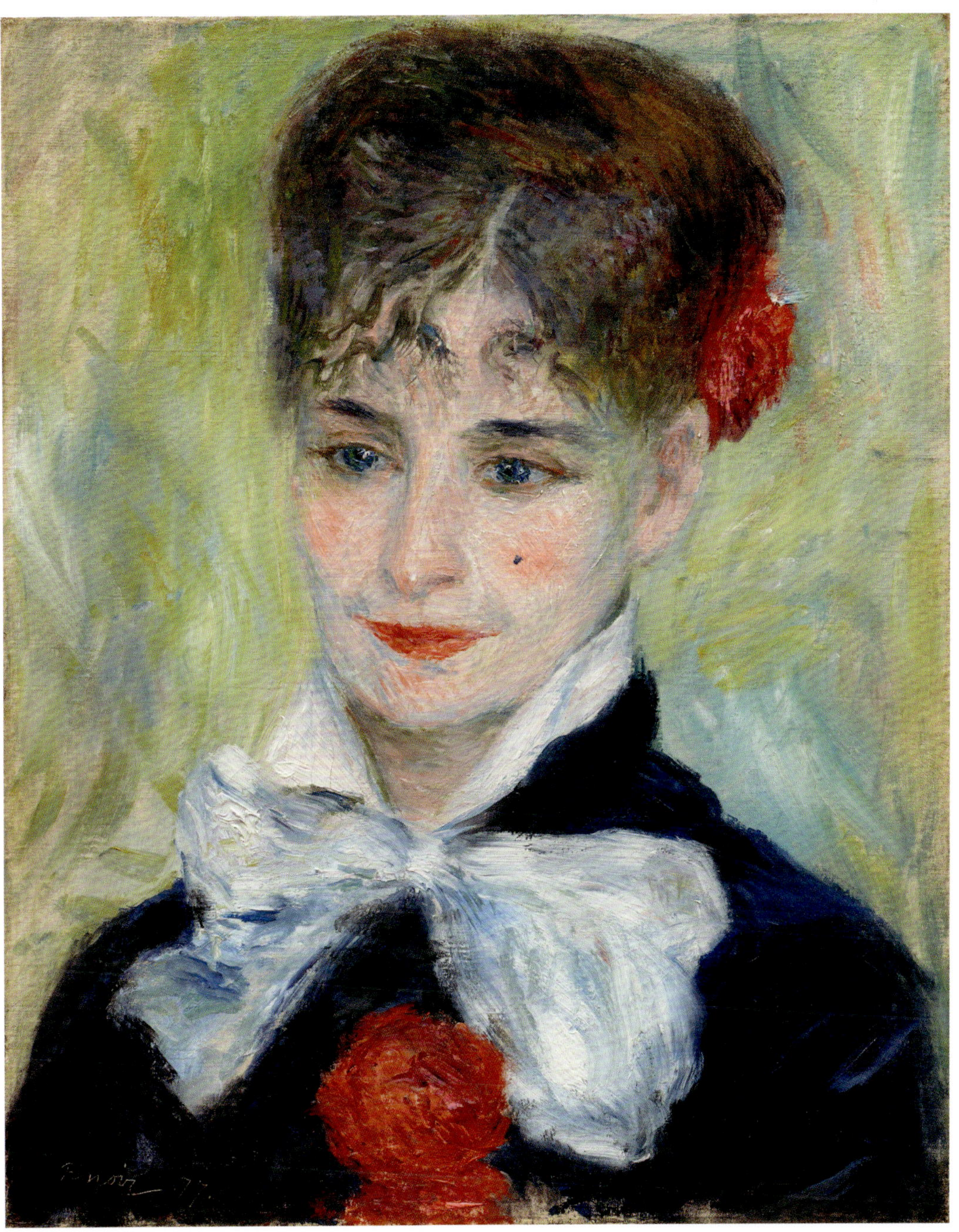

44
Pierre-Auguste Renoir (1841–1919)
Le Moulin de la Galette, Sketch, 1875–76
Oil on canvas, 65 × 85 cm
Inv. no. 271 WH

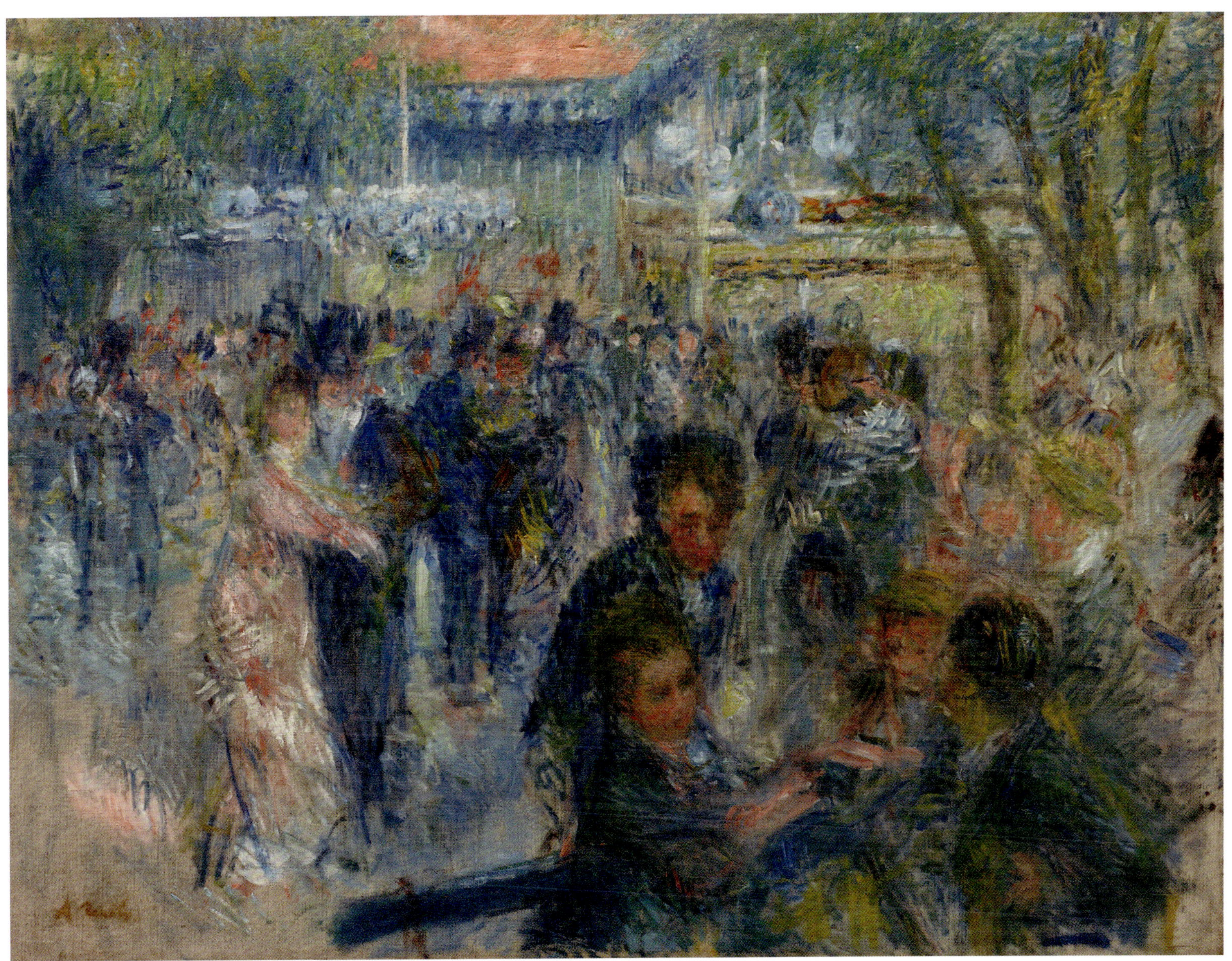

45
Edgar Degas (1834–1917)
Courtyard of a House (New Orleans, Sketch), 1873
Oil on canvas, 60 × 73.5 cm
Inv. no. 238 WH

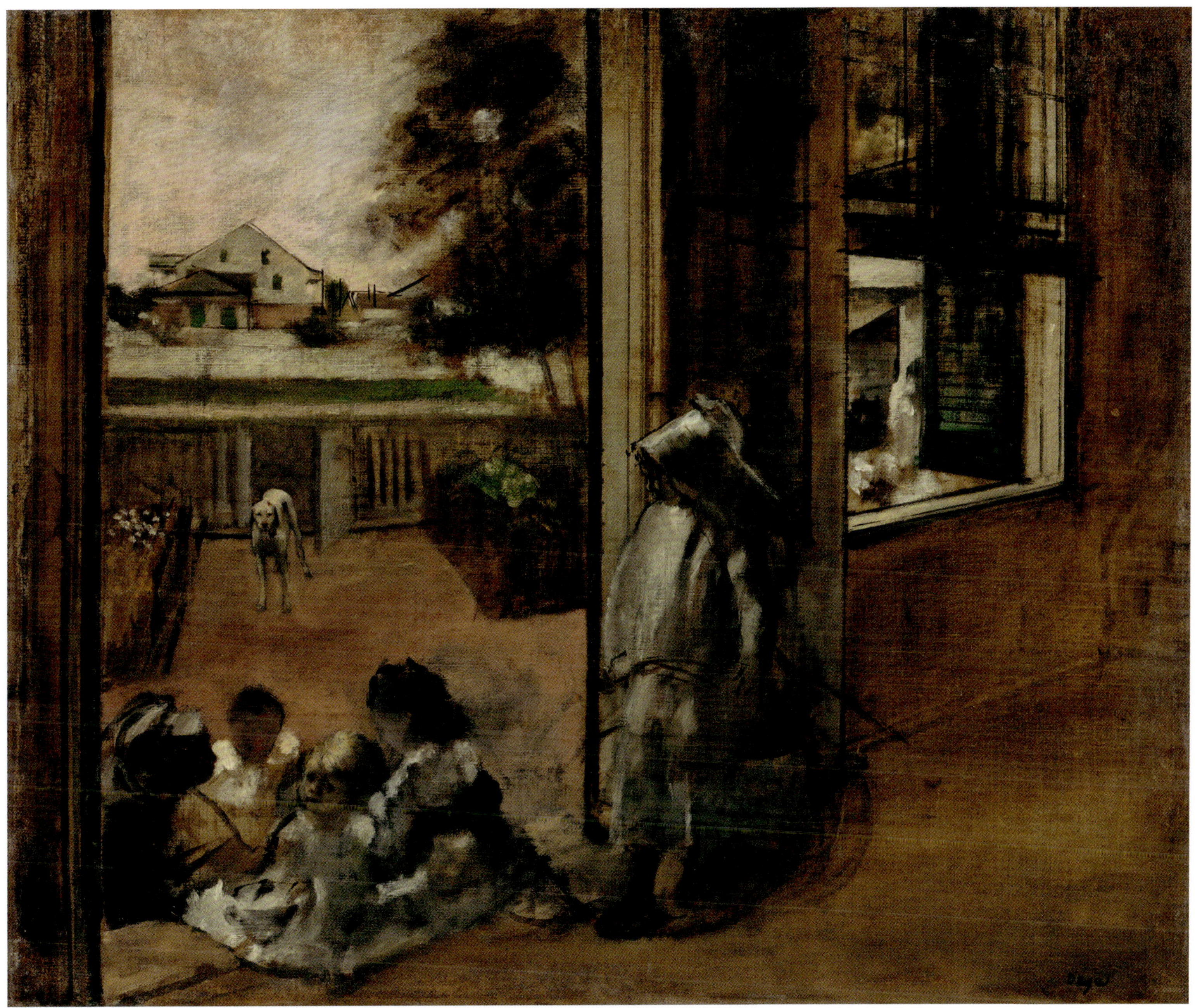

46
Edgar Degas (1834–1917)
Woman Arranging Her Hair, 1894
Oil on canvas, 54 × 40 cm
Inv. no. 290 WH

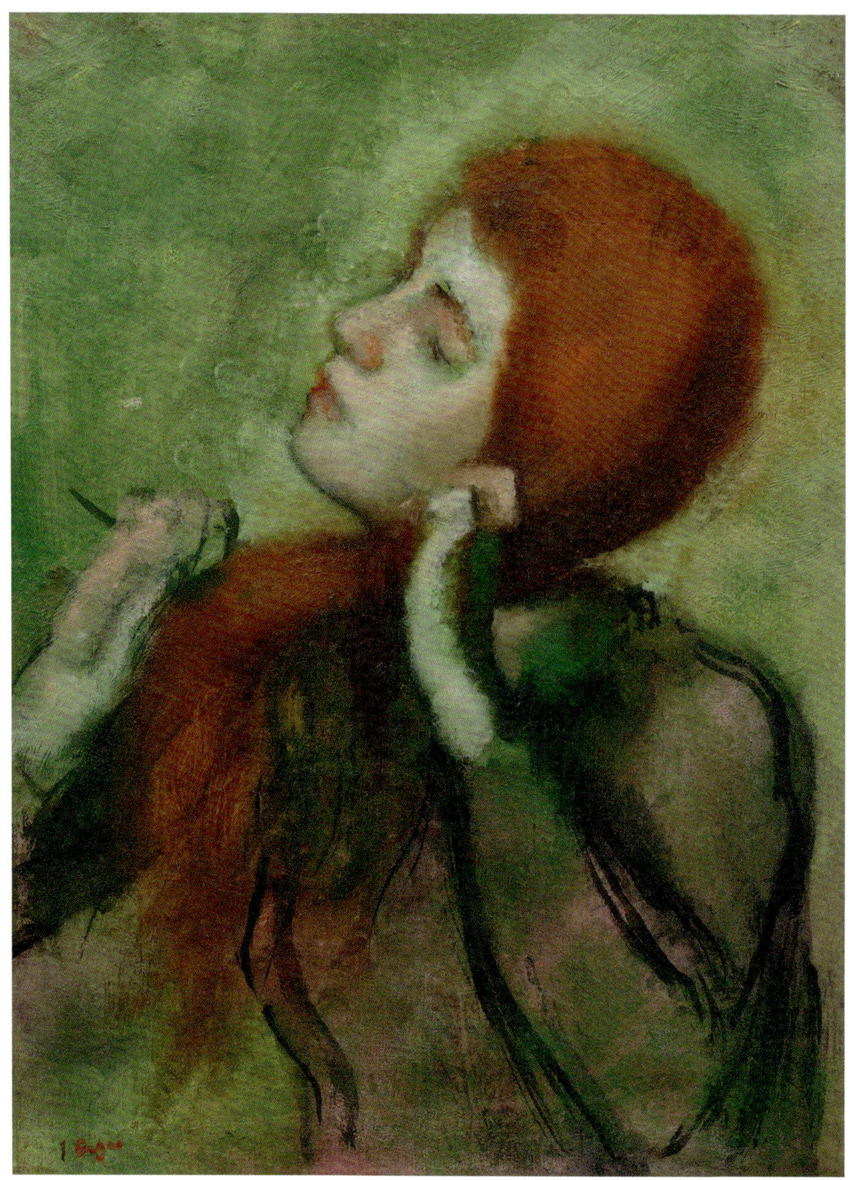

47
Eva Gonzalès (1847–1883)
*The Convalescent (Portrait of
a Woman in White)*, 1877–78
Charcoal and oil on canvas, 86 × 47.5 cm
Inv. no. 245 WH

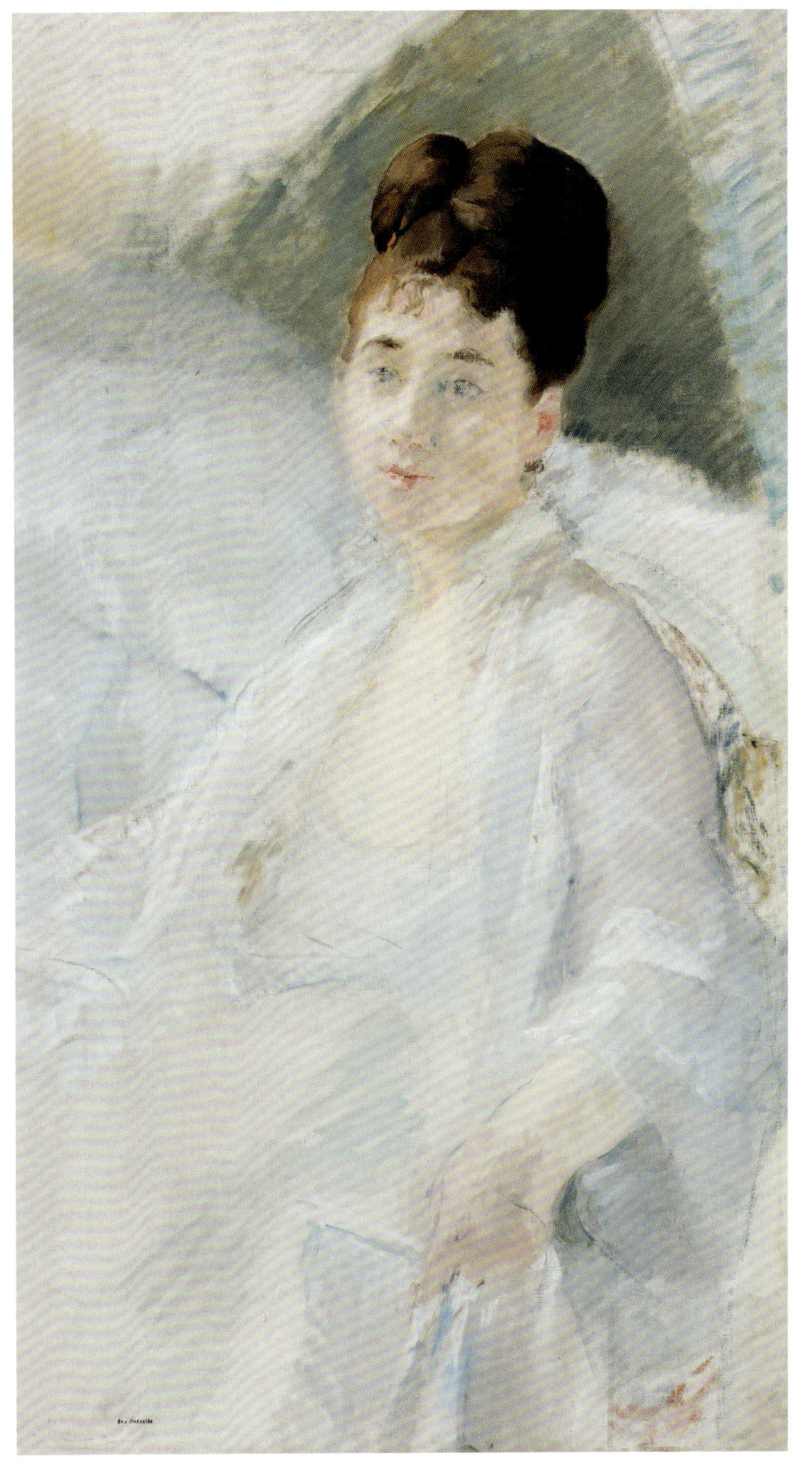

48
Berthe Morisot (1841–1895)
Young Girl on the Grass, the Red Bodice
(Mademoiselle Isabelle Lambert), 1885
Oil on canvas, 74 × 60 cm
Inv. no. 251 WH

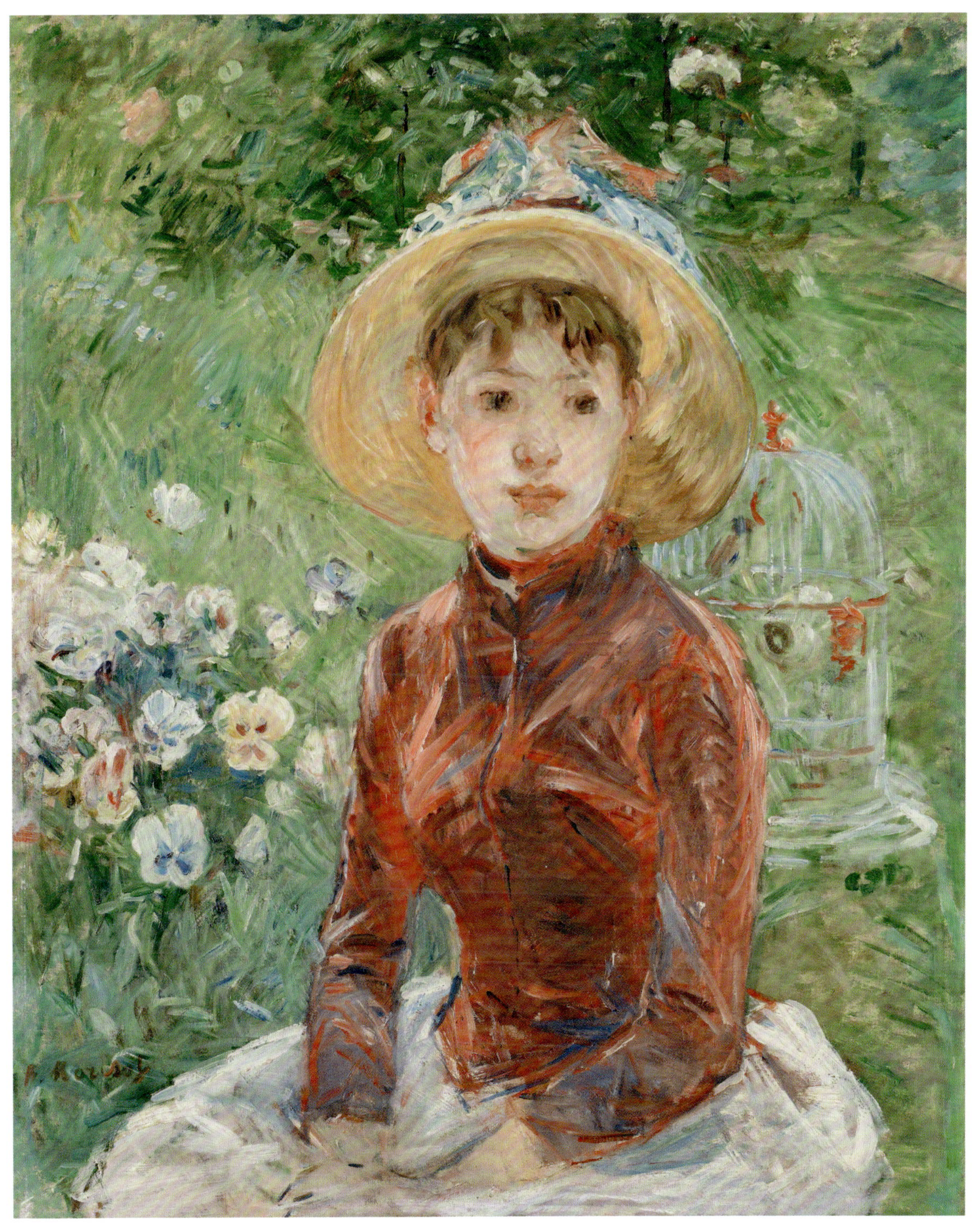

49
Berthe Morisot (1841–1895)
*Woman with a Fan (Portrait of
Madame Marie Hubbard)*, 1874
Oil on canvas, 50.5 × 81 cm
Inv. no. 200 WH

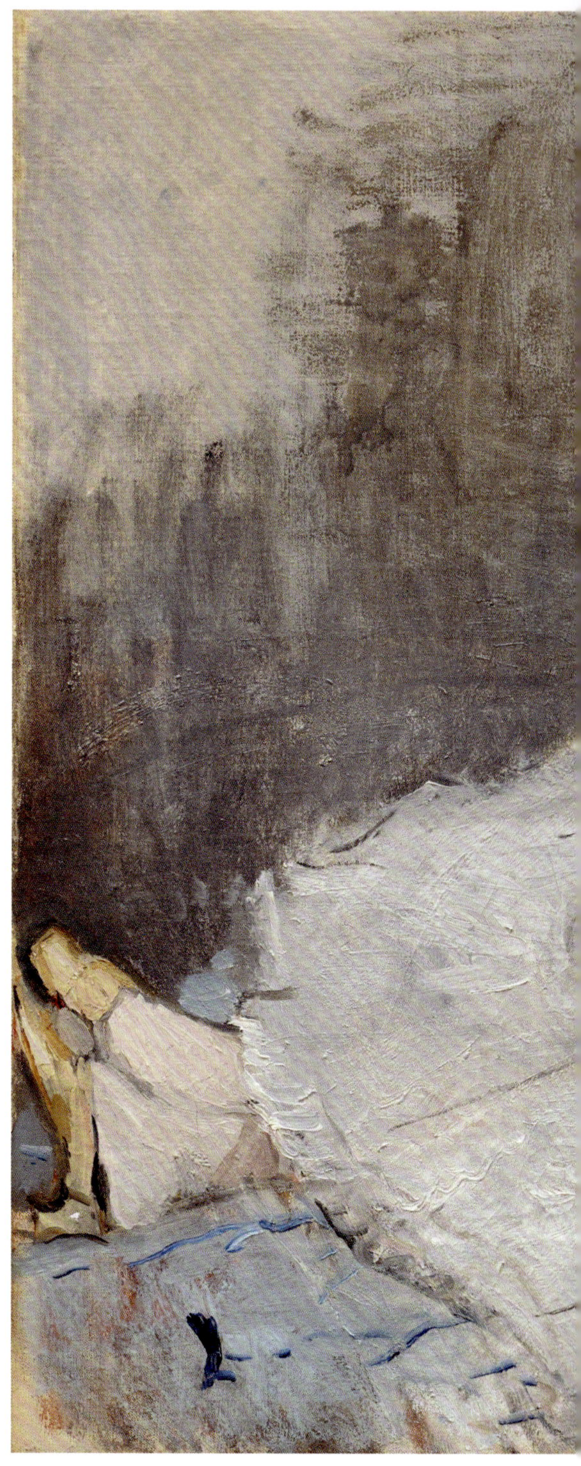

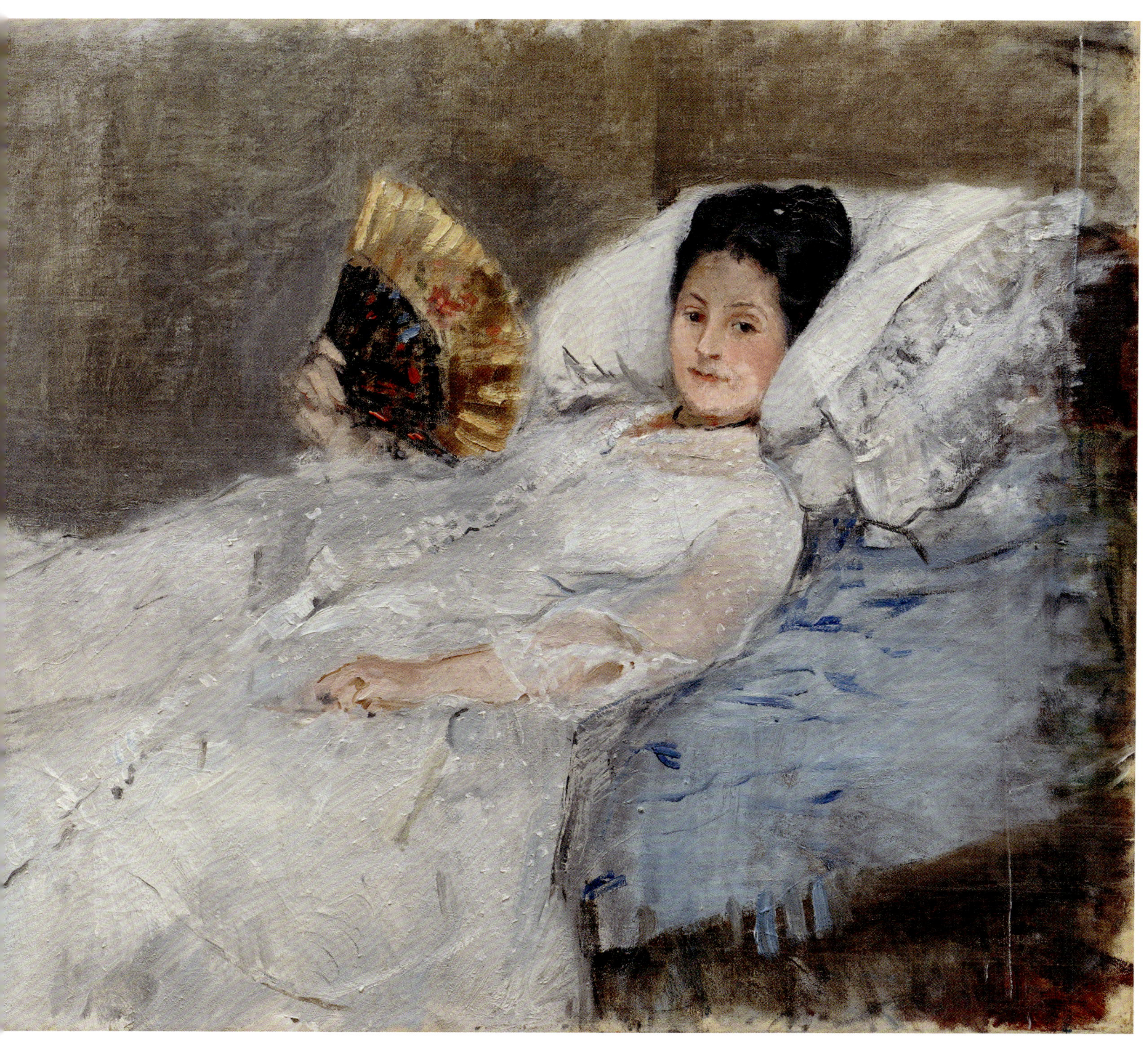

50
Paul Gauguin (1848–1903)
The Little One Is Dreaming, Étude, 1881
Oil on canvas, 59.7 × 74 cm
Inv. no. 190 WH

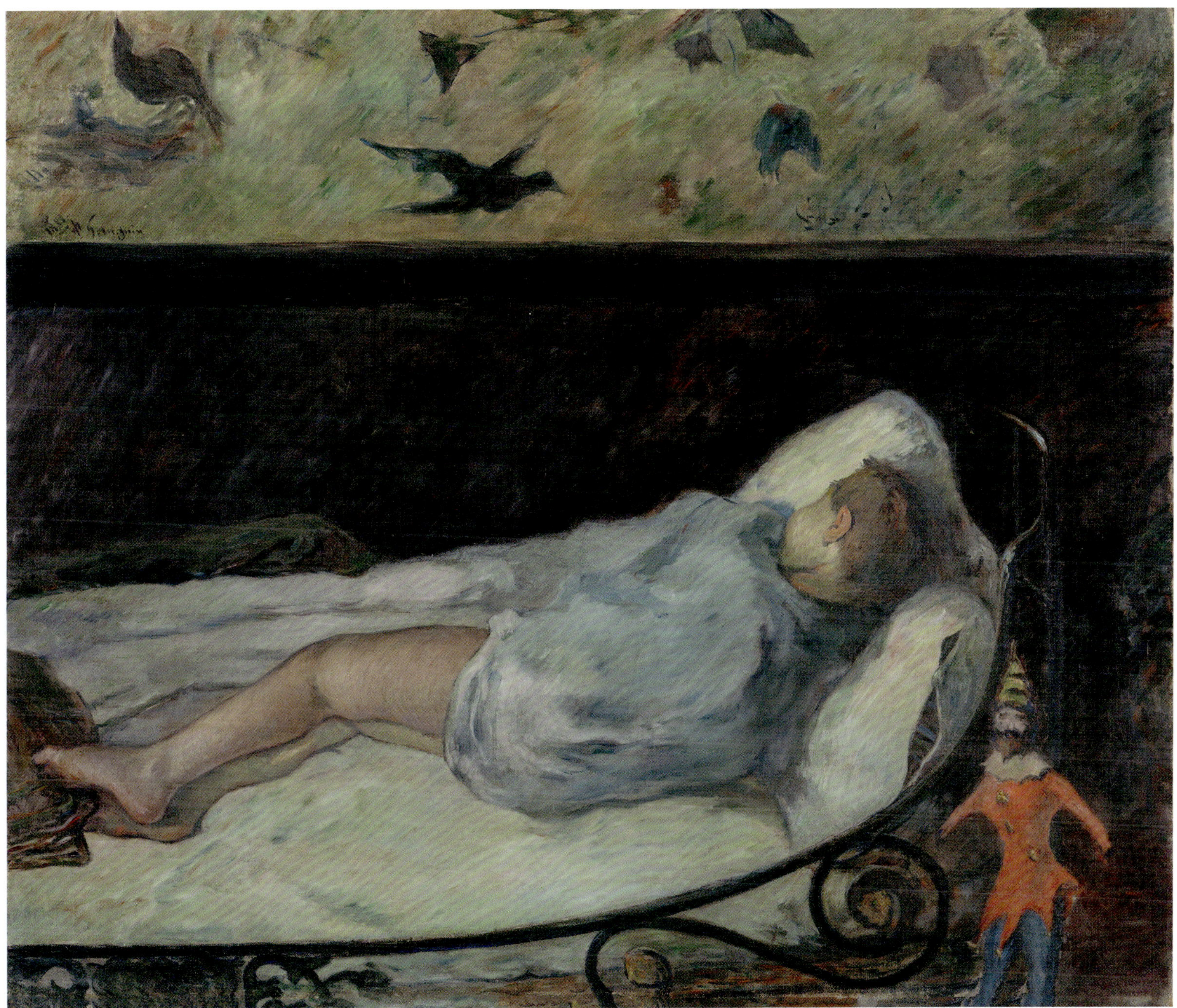

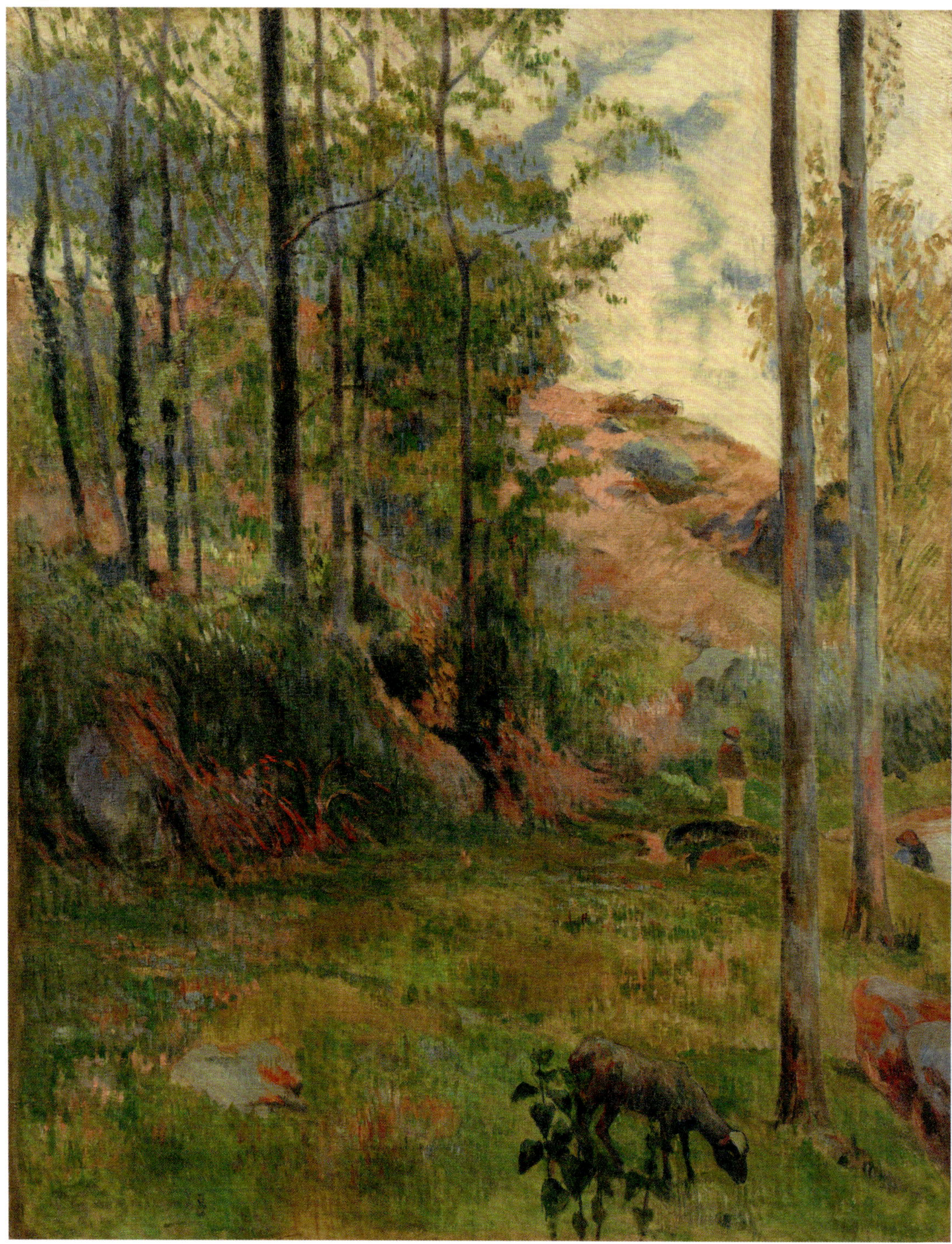

51
Paul Gauguin (1848–1903)
Landscape at Pont-Aven, 1888
Oil on canvas, 92 × 73 cm
Inv. no. 242 WH

52
Paul Gauguin (1848–1903)
Blue Trees (Your Turn Will Come, My Beauty!), 1888
Oil on jute sackcloth, 92 × 73 cm
Inv. no. 254 WH

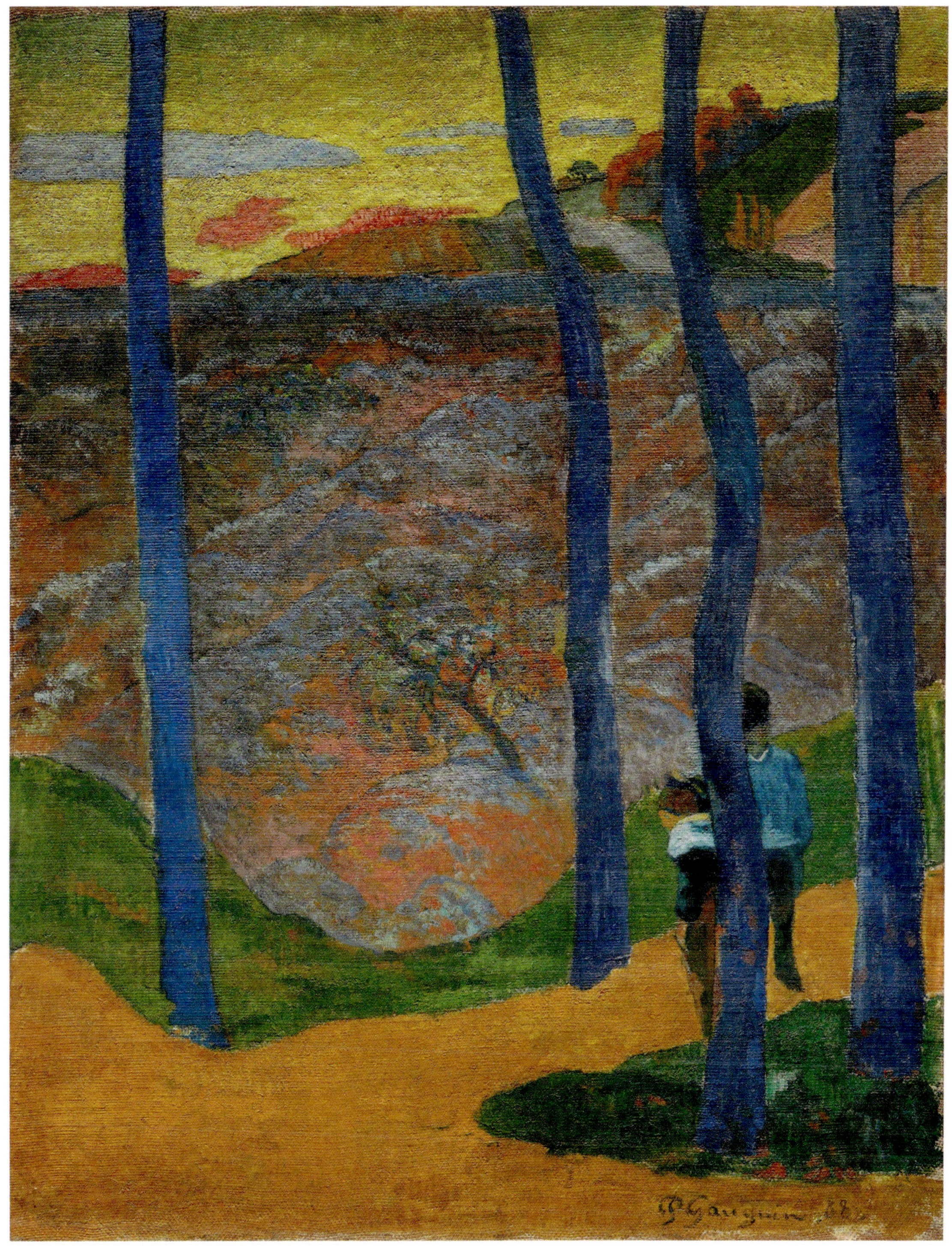

53
Paul Gauguin (1848–1903)
Two Vases with Flowers, c. 1890–91
Oil on jute sackcloth, 65 × 43.5 cm
Inv. no. 243 WH

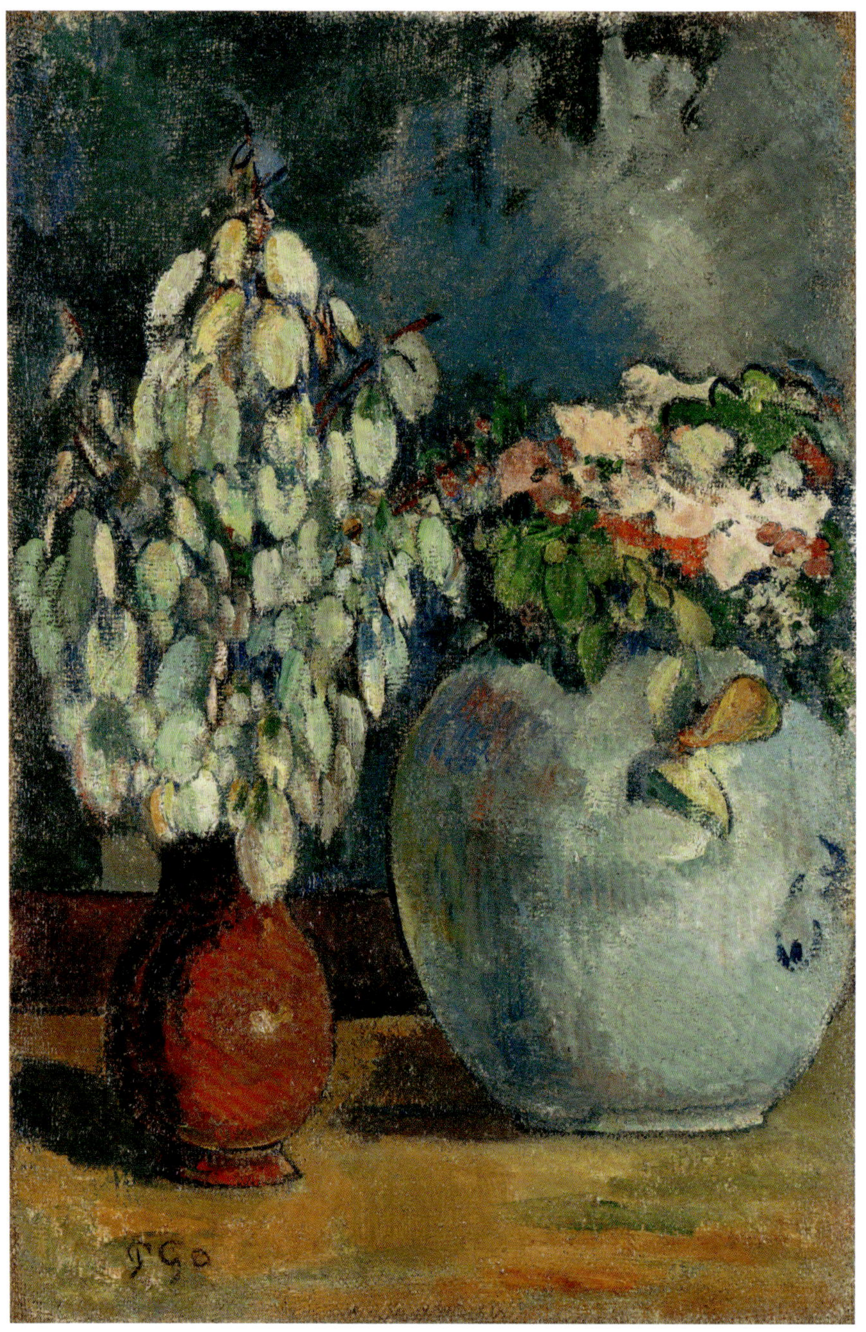

54
Paul Gauguin (1848–1903)
The Wine Harvest, Human Misery, 1888
Oil on jute sackcloth, 72.5 × 92 cm
Inv. no. 223 WH

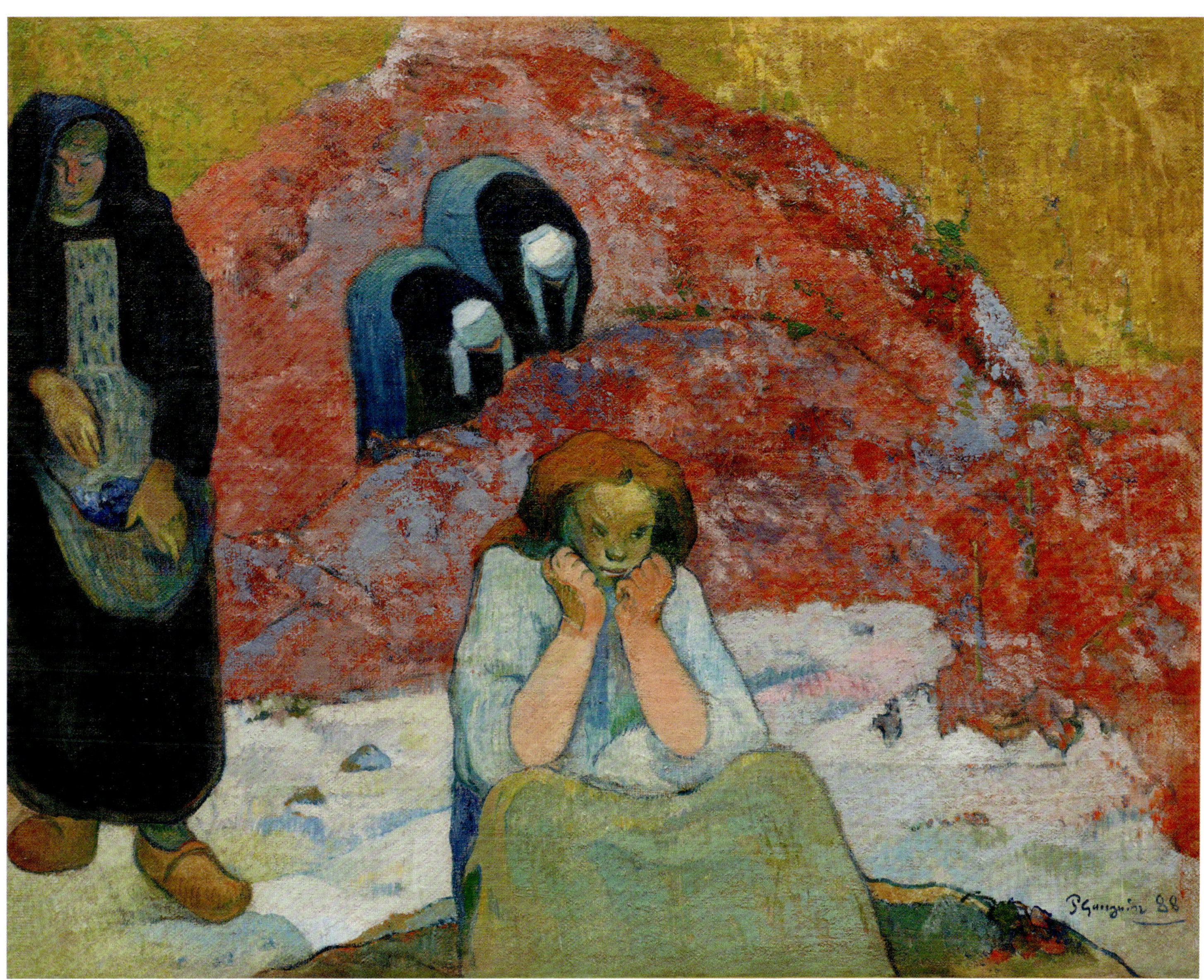

55
Paul Gauguin (1848–1903)
Tahitian Woman, 1898
Oil on sackcloth, 72.5 × 93.5 cm
Inv. no. 225 WH

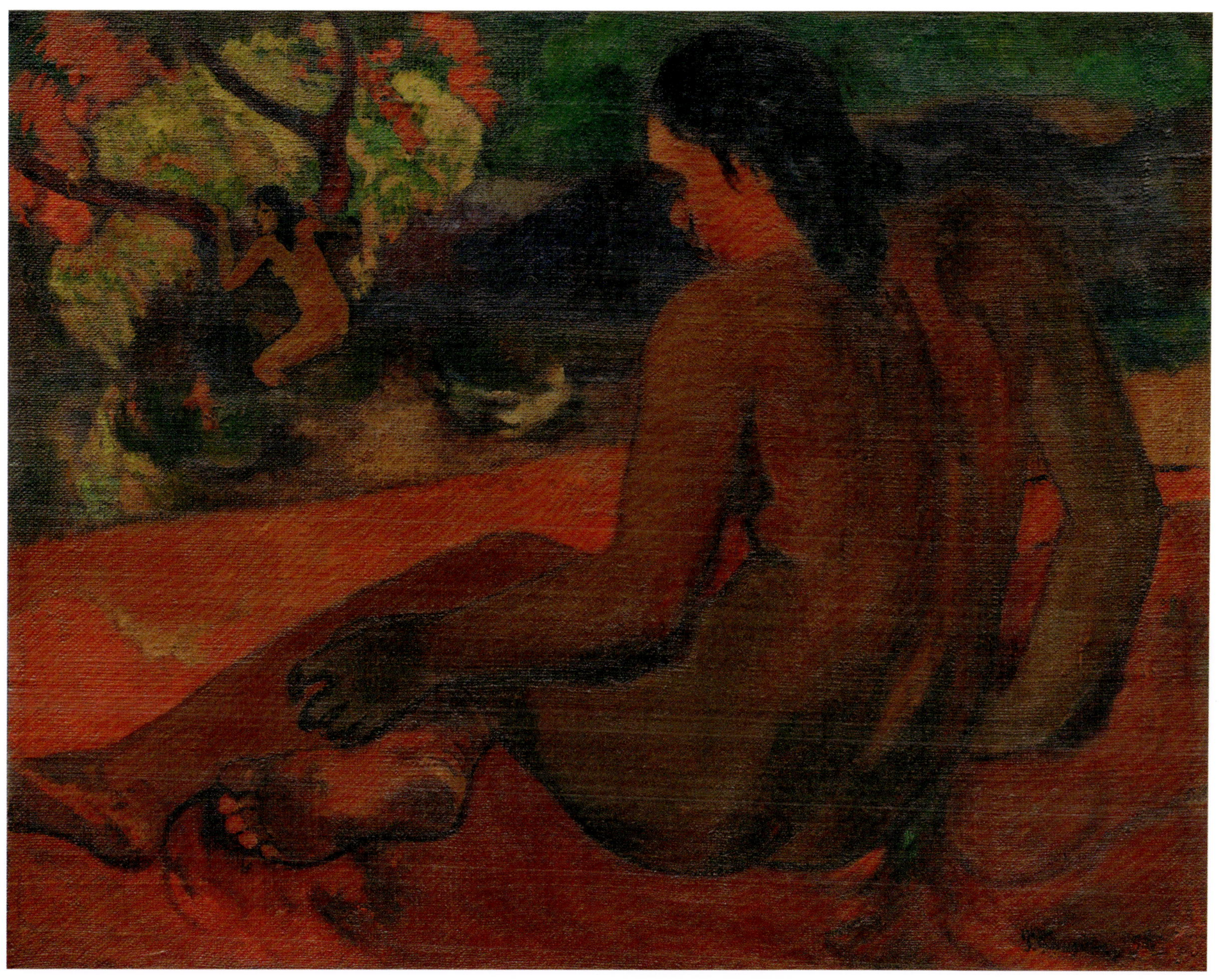

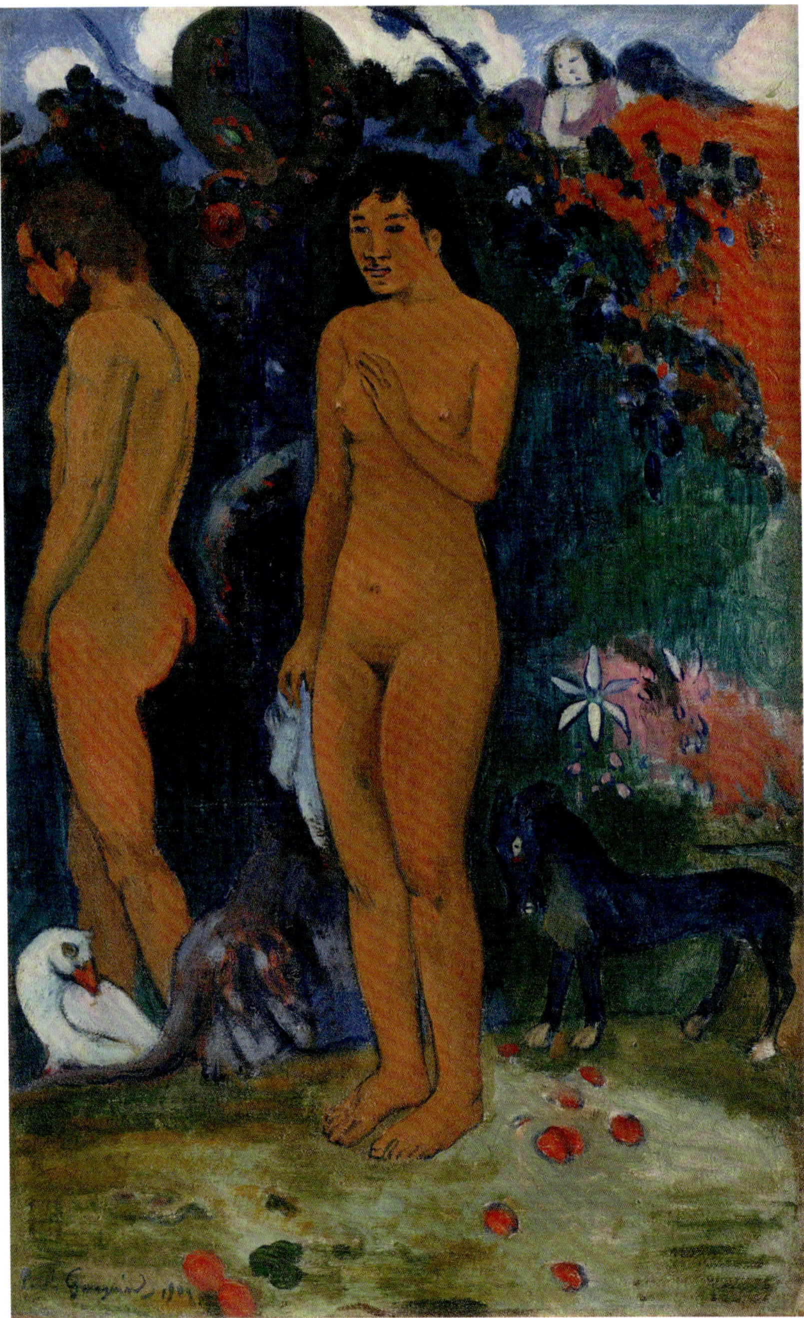

56
Paul Gauguin (1848–1903)
Adam and Eve, 1902
Oil on fustian, 59 × 38 cm
Inv. no. 244 WH

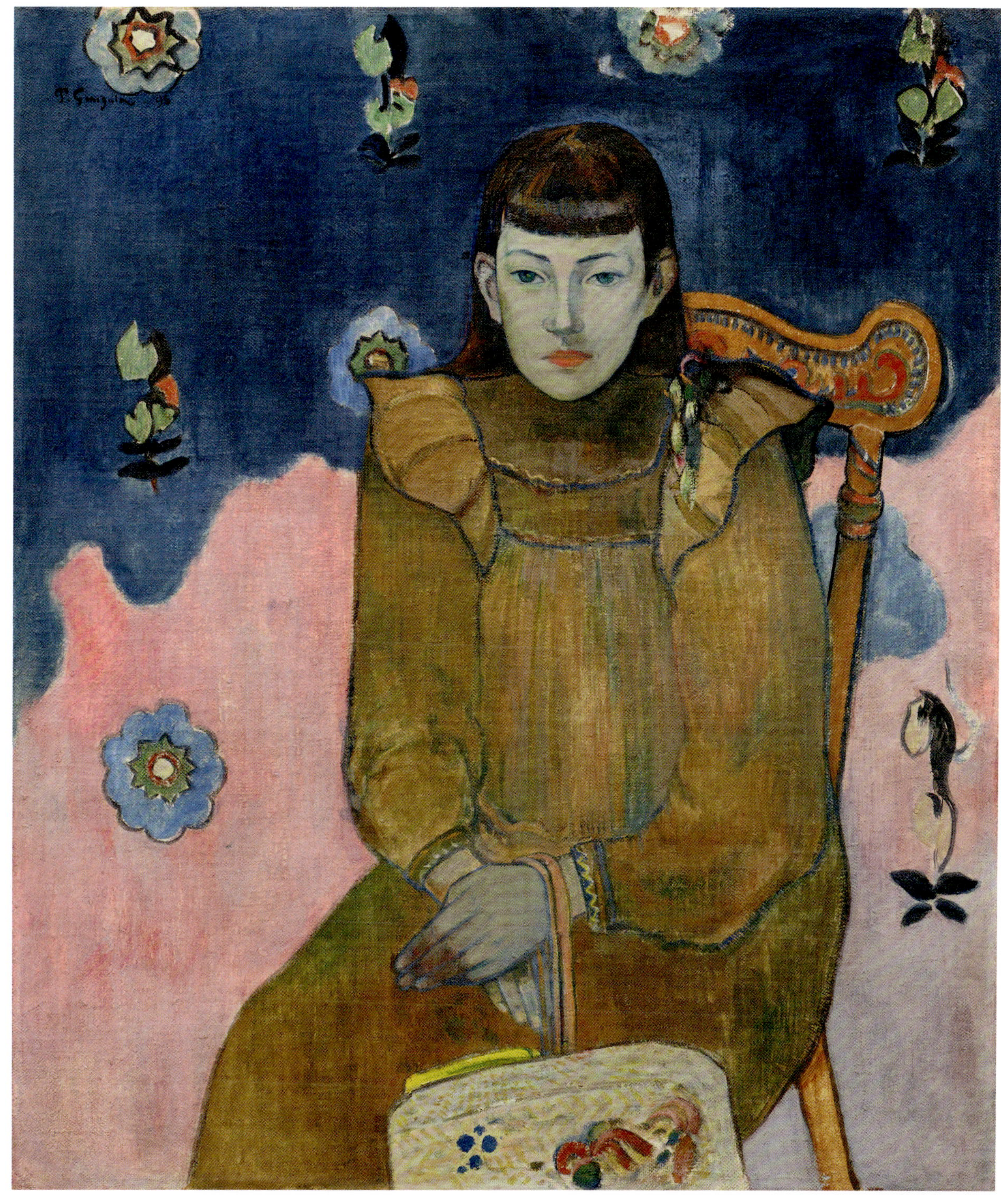

58
Paul Cézanne (1839–1906)
Women Bathing, c. 1895
Oil on canvas, 47 × 77 cm
Inv. no. 234 WH

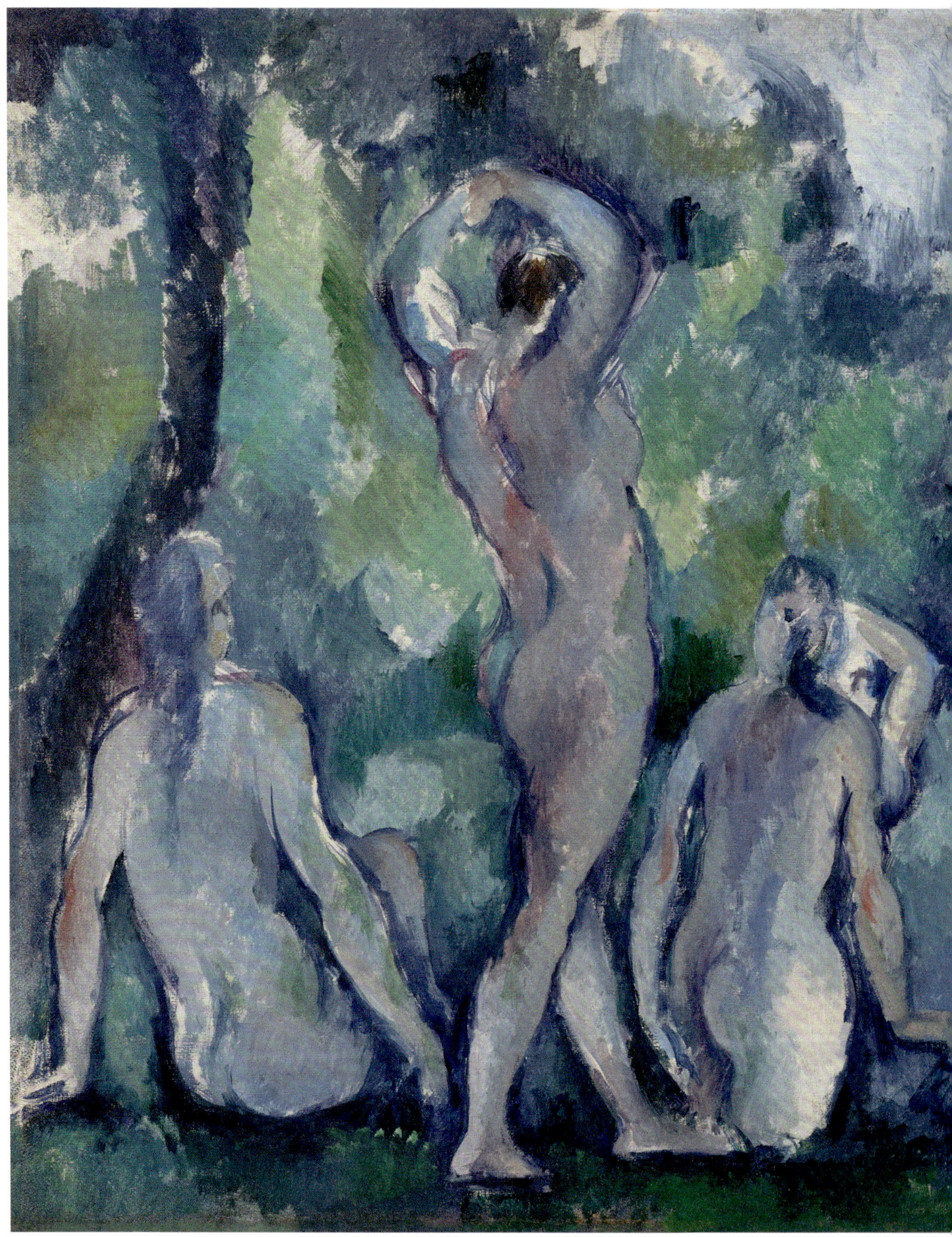

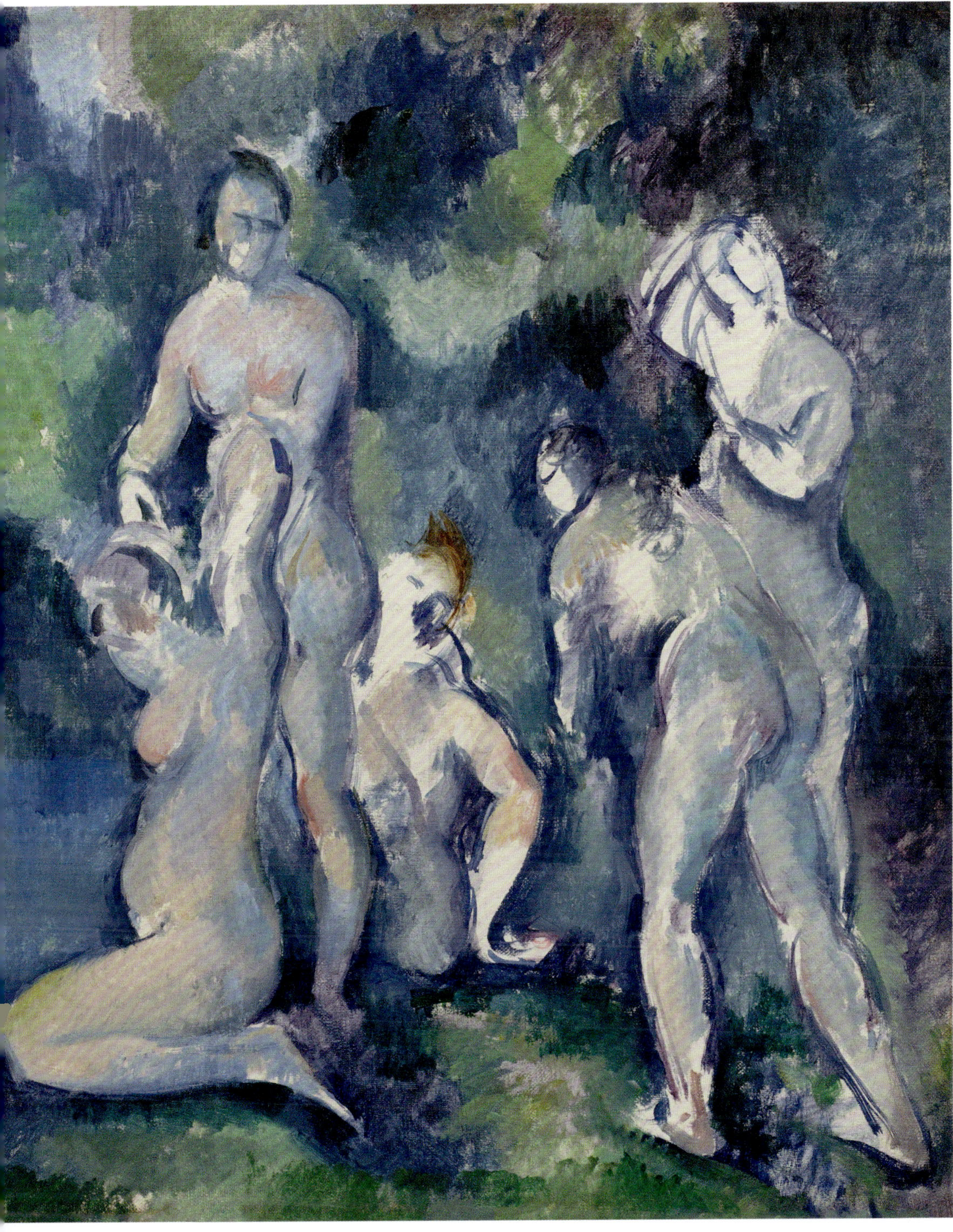

59
Odilon Redon (1840–1916)
Still-life, c. 1901
Oil on canvas, 50 × 73 cm
Inv. no. 285 WH

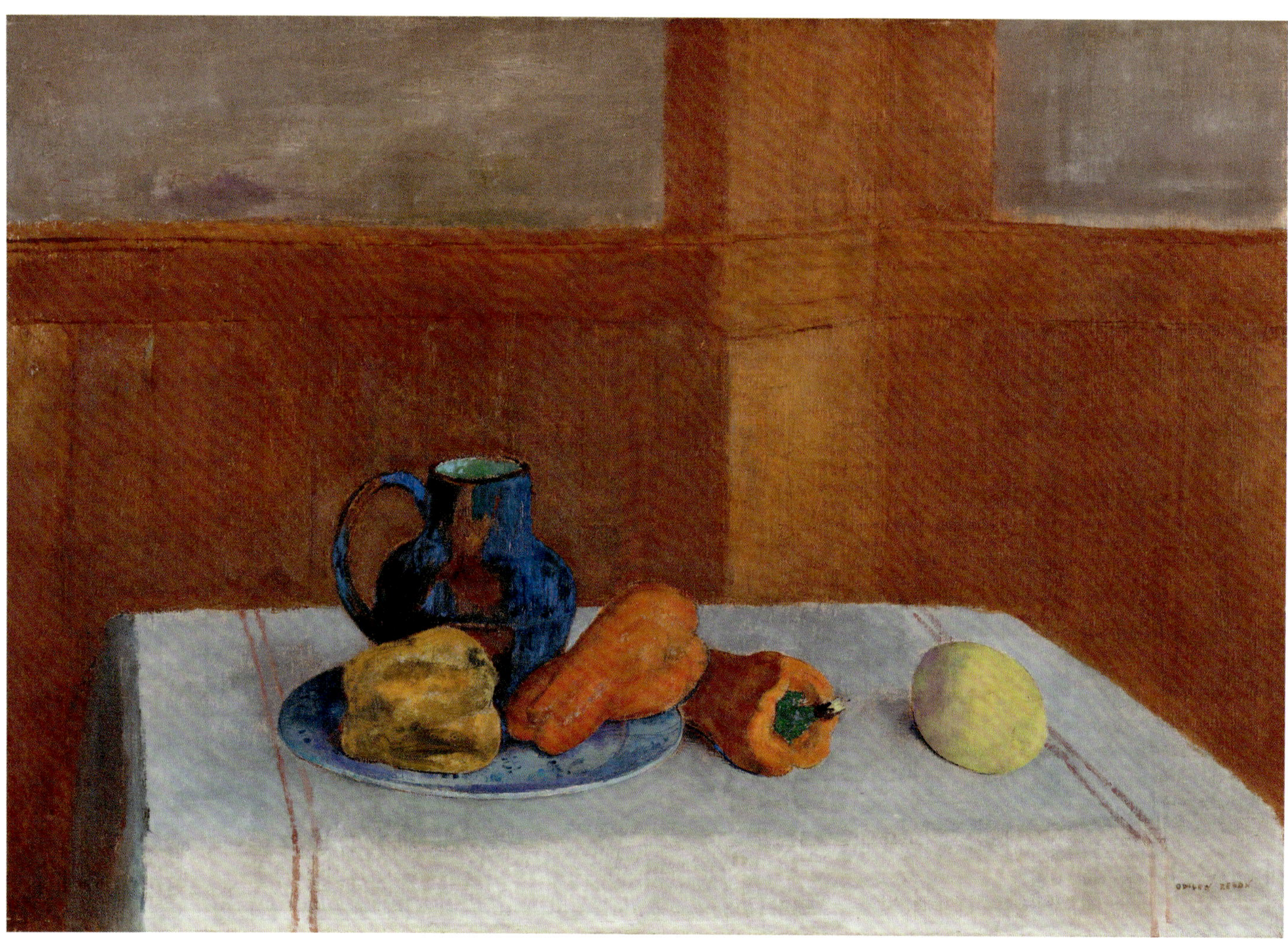

60
Henri Matisse (1869–1954)
Flowers and Fruits, 1909
Oil on canvas, 73 × 60 cm
Inv. no. 259 WH

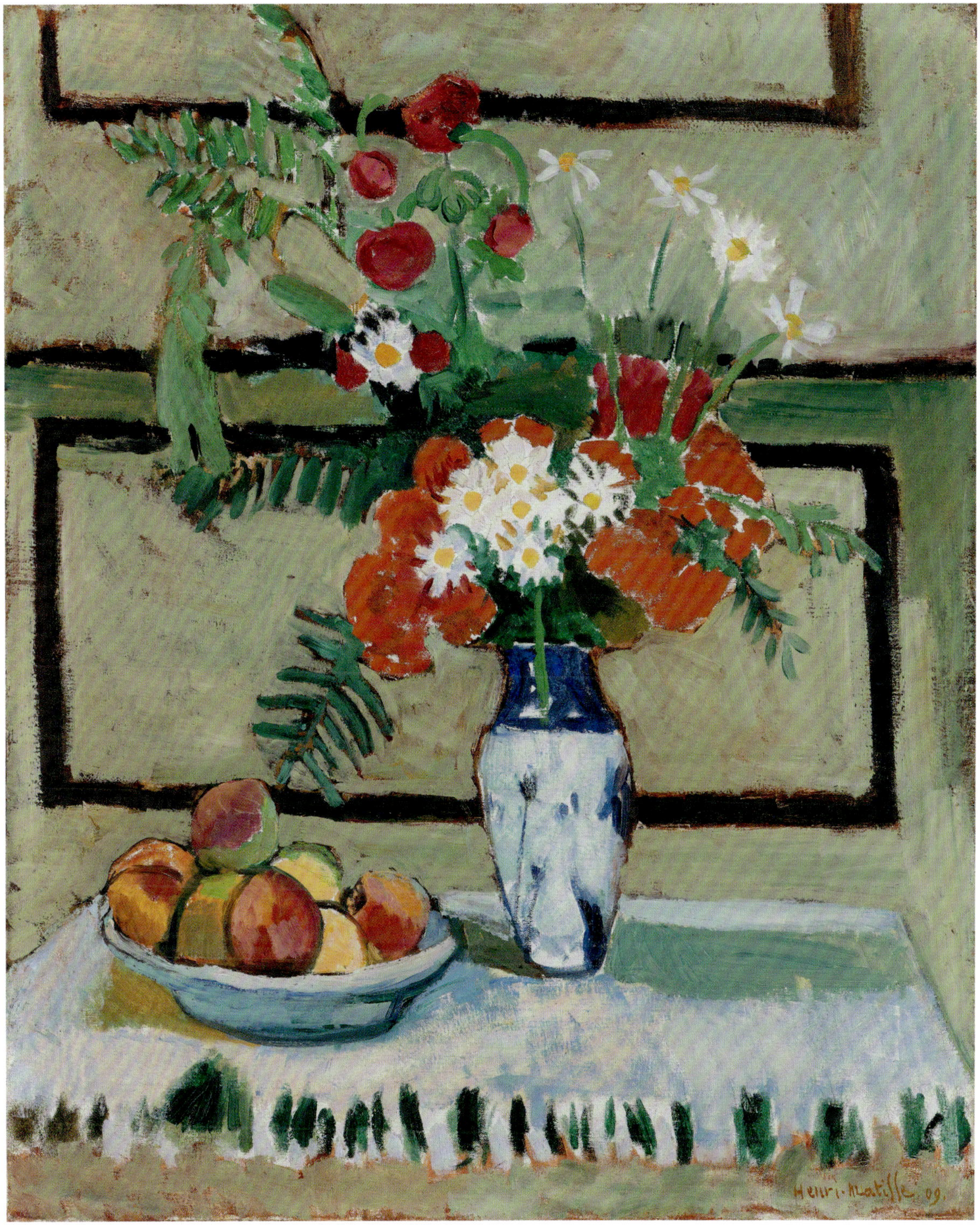

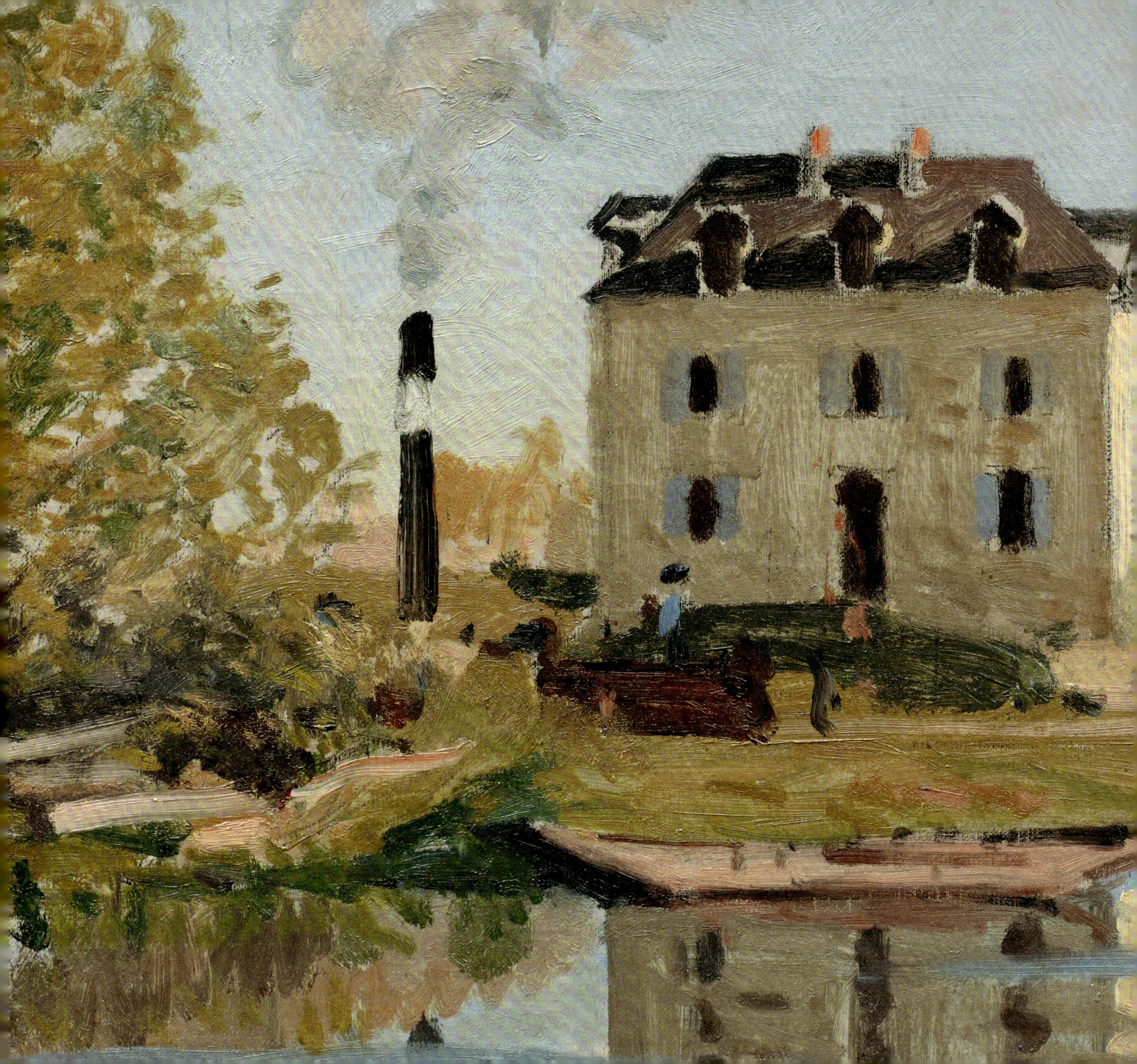

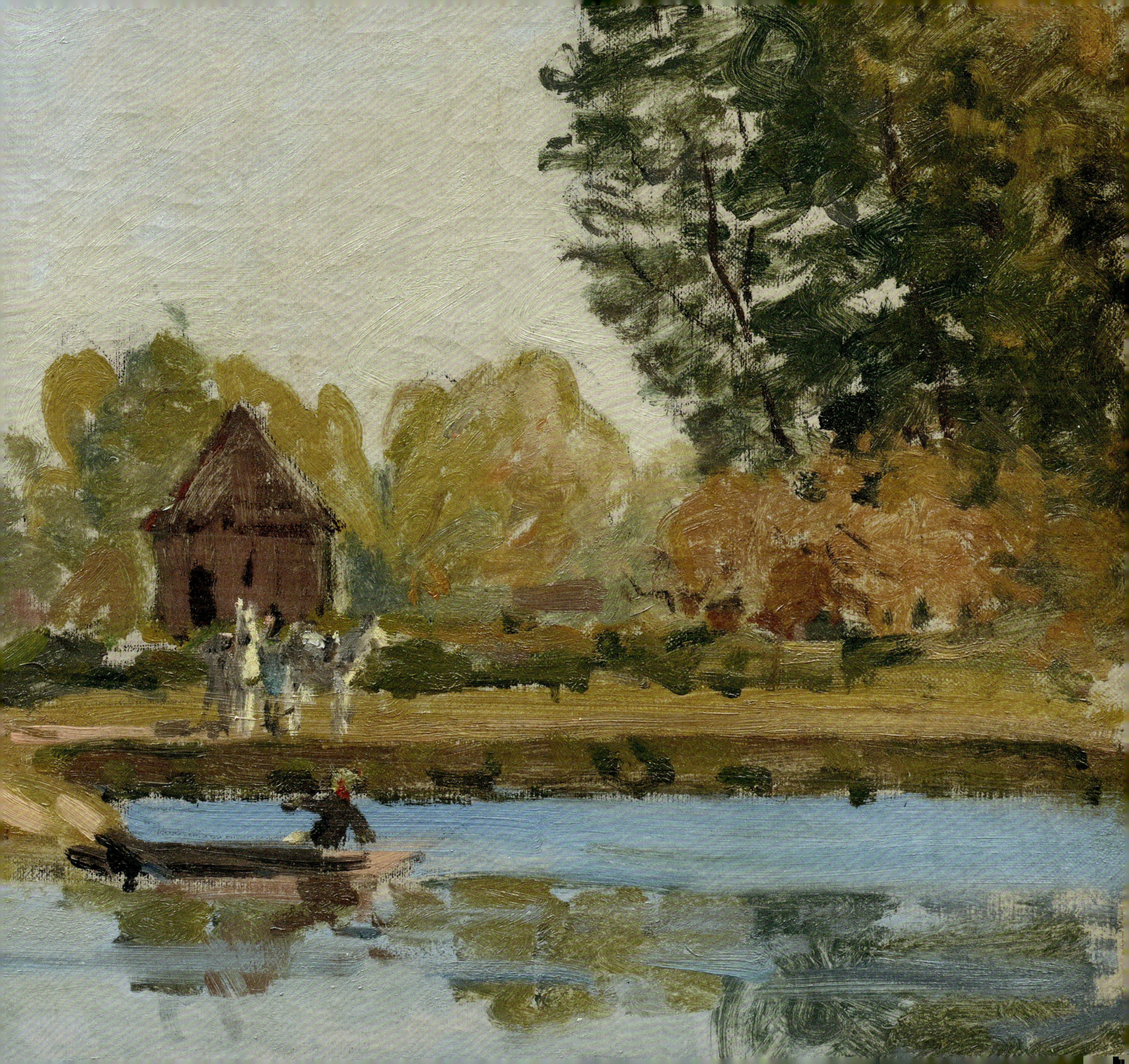

Catalogue Entries

EUGÈNE BOUDIN
(1824–1898)

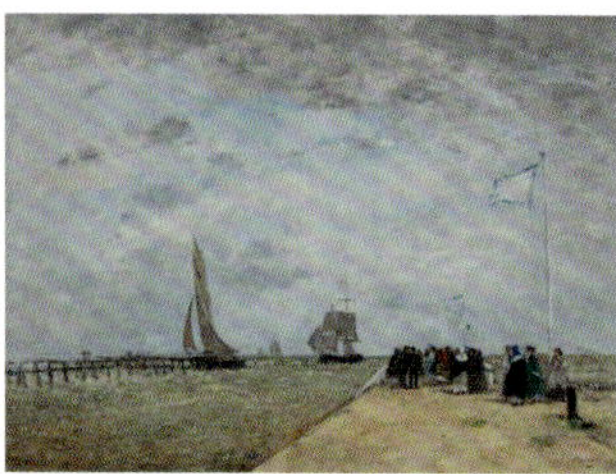

22

The Pier at Trouville, 1867
Oil on canvas, 47 x 64 cm
Inv. no. 185 WH

PROVENANCE: 1867, purchased from the artist (?) by Charles de Bériot, Paris; 11 March 1901, Bériot sale, Hôtel Drouot, Paris; Boussod-Valadon, Paris; 1916, to Wilhelm Hansen

LITERATURE: Schmit 1973, no. 407; Fonsmark et al. 2011, no. 10

Although he showed Monet the importance of painting *en plein air* and even participated in the first Impressionist exhibition in 1874, Boudin belonged to the generation of artists just preceding the movement, his approach closer to that of the naturalists. He carefully observed nature but did not attempt simply to copy it: before starting work on a picture, he decided on its composition, working out viewpoints, areas for emphasis and other important elements, and produced numerous drawn and painted sketches. These were vital parts of the process that led to the final painting.

After discovering Trouville in 1862, Boudin took the resort's beach, pier and harbour as his principal subjects. In the mid-nineteenth century, Trouville became a fashionable seaside resort for the elite. The pier was part of the ritual promenade for wealthy visitors, portrayed here as an undifferentiated group in the distance. Despite Boudin's careful preparation, the picture is permeated with a raw freshness, fulfilling the artist's intention that the finished picture should have the characteristics of a sketch. BA

PAUL CÉZANNE
(1839–1906)

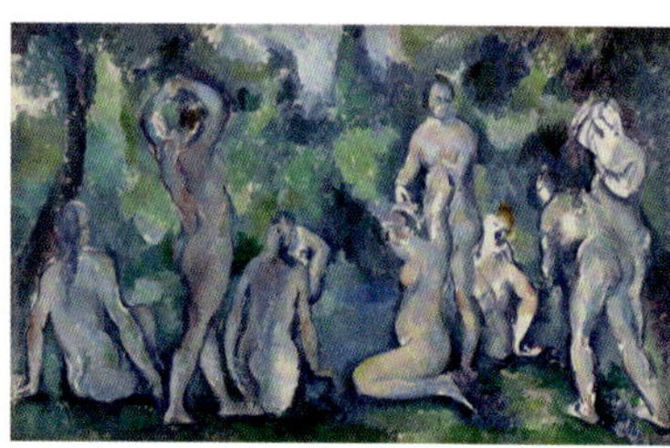

58

Women Bathing, c. 1895
Oil on canvas, 47 x 77 cm
Inv. no. 234 WH

PROVENANCE: Ambroise Vollard, Paris; Alphonse Kann, Saint-Germain-en-Laye; 1918, to Hansen, Heilbuth, Winkel & Magnussen consortium; 1918, to Wilhelm Hansen

LITERATURE: Rewald et al. 1996, no. 751; Fonsmark et al. 2011, no. 12

Although an exhibitor at the first Impressionist exhibition in 1874, employing the Impressionists' colour palette and, like them, working *en plein air*, Cézanne produced work that was essentially different. His ambition was to paint himself into the great classicist tradition as a master of large-scale composition, but in a modern form. Satyrs and nymphs featured in the landscapes he painted outdoors, often in violent situations, unlike the playful bacchanals of Titian or Poussin.

From the third Impressionist exhibition of 1877 onwards, Cézanne explored the gentler motif of bathing. *Women Bathing* is dated to the artist's late period on the combined evidence of the watercolour-like method, the cool palette, and the treatment of the subject. The picture's apparent spontaneity is misleading, however. It was not painted outdoors, nor were the figures based on models in the studio; instead it draws on other pictures, photographs, reproductions of nudes from the Louvre, and Cézanne's earlier drawings and sketches made in the Louvre of work by Michelangelo, Rubens, Delacroix and others. BA

JEAN-BAPTISTE-CAMILLE COROT
(1796–1875)

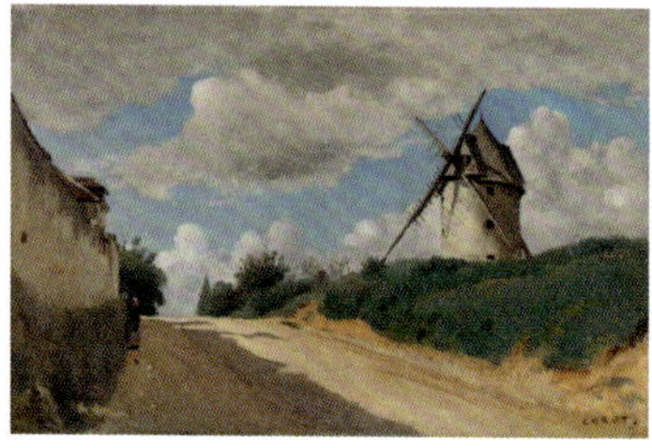

10

The Windmill, c. 1835–40
Oil on canvas, 25 x 39.5 cm
Inv. no. 286 WH

PROVENANCE: *c.* 1910, George Viau, Paris; 1918, to Hansen, Heilbuth, Winkel & Magnussen consortium; 1918, to Herman Heilbuth (50,000 kr.); 1923 (?), transferred to the Danish Landmandsbank; February 1924, to Winkel & Magnussen; 1 May 1925, to Wilhelm Hansen (6,000 kr.).

LITERATURE: Robaut and Moreau-Nélaton 1905, vol. 2, no. 343; Fonsmark et al. 2011, no. 13

Corot had first encountered painting *en plein air* between 1825 and 1828 on his initial visit to Rome, where there was a long-established tradition of sketching in the open air. This provided the basis of landscape paintings to be worked up in the studio for exhibition rather than being seen as finished works of value in themselves. In contrast, Corot started to make *études terminées* (finished studies) directly from the subject, capturing the structure of things rather than the nuances of their surfaces and integrating the sketch directly into the finished work. *The Windmill* is a good representative of this approach.

The picture, painted on the Route de Picardie near Versailles, shows Corot's liking for classical order and monumentality. With its heavy body lit by a moment of direct sunlight and the crisp, delicate lines of its sails, the mill towers above the high horizon. The city wall casts a broad shadow across the road that forms a diagonal axis, creating a natural geometrical structure drawn from the landscape itself. The only figure, a woman, stands in the wall's shadow. BA

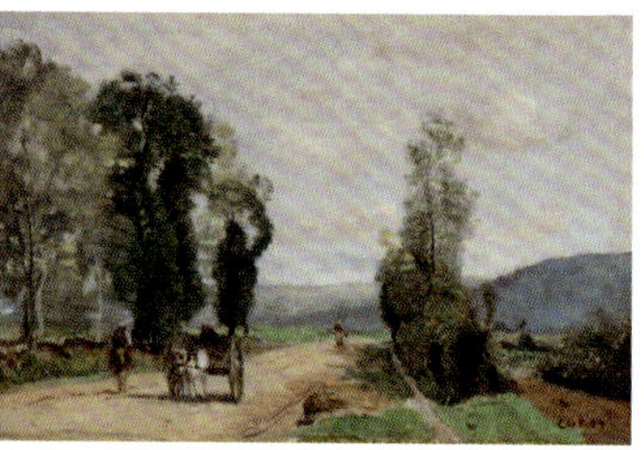

13

Country Road, Côte-d'Or, c. 1840–60
Oil on canvas, 22.5 x 35 cm
Inv. no. 299 WH

PROVENANCE: Alfred II Beurdeley, Paris; 6–7 May 1920, Beurdeley sale, Galerie Georges Petit, Paris; S. Sevadjian, Paris; 1–3 June 1927, Sevadjian sale, Hôtel Drouot, Paris; 1927, to Wilhelm Hansen

LITERATURE: Fonsmark et al. 2011, no. 14

Corot's family came originally from a village in the Côte-d'Or area of Burgundy and he visited the region several times – *Country Road, Côte-d'Or* may be a product of one of these visits. The simple composition employs one of Corot's favourite motifs, a sandy road leading into the picture, animated by a few figures or animals.

Although the exact date of this work is unknown, its style suggests a later date. At the end of the 1840s Corot's style radically changed. Rather than the distinct, sometimes monumental forms of earlier pictures such as *The Windmill* (cat. 10), the mode of representation became more diffuse and restless, with blurred or dissolved outlines, softer colours and loosely sketched vegetation.

The change of style may be understood as a response to the subtle filtering of light through the damp atmosphere, in contrast to the bright light of Italy that had influenced Corot's work in the 1830s and 1840s. However, it can also be seen as a response to contemporary developments in landscape photography in which reflected light dematerialises solid shapes and eats into the shadows and the foliage of trees, giving the surroundings an indistinct, feathery appearance. This misty, poetic depiction of tangible nature is characteristic of the artist's late work. BA

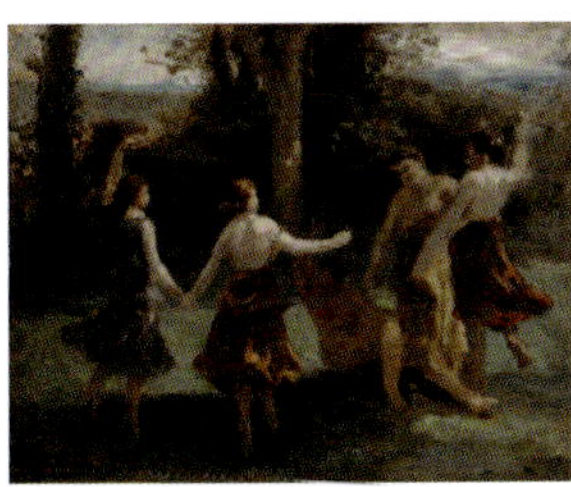

12
Dancing Nymphs, c. 1850
Oil on canvas, 27 x 34 cm
Inv. no. 294 WH

PROVENANCE: until at least 1900, P. A. B. Widener, Philadelphia; to Jos Hessel, then Bernheim-Jeune, then Alphonse Kann, all in Paris; 1918, to Hansen, Heilbuth, Winkel & Magnussen consortium; 1918 (?), to Winkel & Magnussen; between 1925 and 1927 (?), to Wilhelm Hansen

LITERATURE: Fonsmark et al. 2011, no. 16

This oil sketch is closely linked to Corot's *Morning: The Dance of the Nymphs* (Musée d'Orsay, Paris). Exhibited with great success at the 1851 Paris Salon, that picture marked a turning point in Corot's career. He moved away from the classical tradition of landscape painting and towards a more lyrical and atmospheric depiction of the natural world, populated by figures who do not originate from specific mythological or literary tales but are clearly allusions to dance and music.

As in the Salon painting, the group in the present sketch consists of four nymphs – possibly developed from drawings of dancers at the Paris Opéra – dancing around a drunken male figure on the ground. Over the next twenty years, the theme of nymphs pictured in a romantic natural setting appeared with increasing frequency in Corot's work, replacing his more straightforward landscape studies. BA

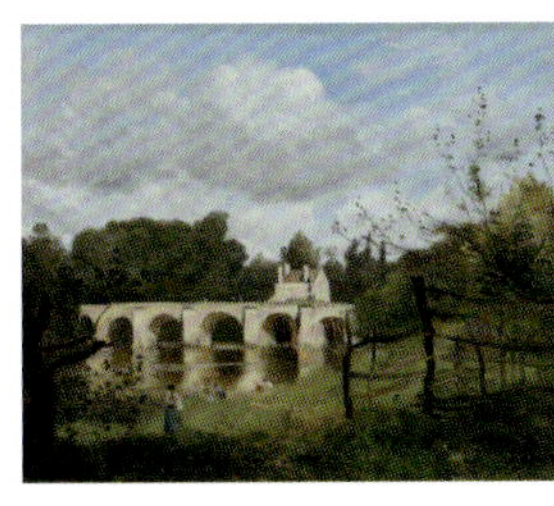

14
The Bridge at Mantes, c. 1850–54
Oil on canvas, 38 x 46 cm
Inv. no. 214 WH

PROVENANCE: Hector Brame, Paris; to Galerie Tempelaere, Paris; December 1897, to Arnold Tripp et Cie; 1918, to Wilhelm Hansen

LITERATURE: Fonsmark et al. 2011, no. 17

Bridges are recurring architectural elements in Corot's landscapes, the earliest of them two views of the grand classical ruins of the Ponte d'Augusto at Narni, near Rome, painted during the artist's first sojourn in Italy between 1825 and 1828. However, this picture of the old Pont de Limay at Mantes – one of at least twenty Corot painted – does not refer back to the monumental grandeur of antiquity, but instead emphasises the human presence in the landscape.

Corot paints a section of the bridge from a slightly elevated viewpoint, obscuring the first three arches and the tollhouse to the right behind a thick growth of trees, while more arches to the left and the course of the river past the bridge are also concealed. This has the effect of taking the bridge out of its context and setting it in a picturesque, poetic landscape. The brightness and rhythmic structure of the bridge contrast with the darker foreground, with its loose, flowing, fleeting brush strokes, framed by a fallen tree and a delicate willow hedge.

People appear at every boundary within the picture – between the shadows of the foreground and the brightness of the middle ground, between meadow and water, and finally on the bridge itself. BA

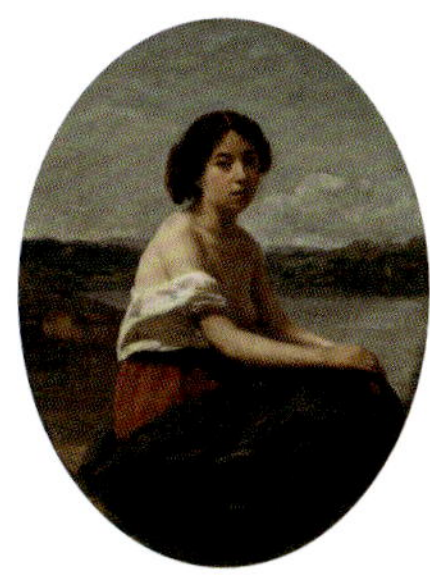

11
Young Italian Woman Seated near a Lake, c. 1850–55
Oil on canvas, 40.5 x 32 cm
Inv. no. 275 WH

PROVENANCE: 27 June 1900, anonymous sale, Paris (3,760 fr.); c. 1910, to George Viau, Paris; 1918, to Hansen, Heilbuth, Winkel & Magnussen consortium; to Herman Heilbuth; between 1923 and 1925, to Wilhelm Hansen

LITERATURE: Robaut and Moreau-Nélaton 1905, vol. 2, no. 664; Fonsmark et al. 2011, no. 18

Corot rarely exhibited pictures in which the figure is given a dominant role, and never between 1840 and 1859. The title of this painting is not Corot's but was added by Alfred Robaut in his 1905 catalogue raisonné – and is misleading in several ways. The girl is not integrated into the landscape but isolated, as if painted in a studio, while the landscape fading into the distance is like a backdrop rather than a real space.

We do not know who sat for the painting and, though the subject is characterised with a portrait-like closeness and intimacy, the work is definitely not a portrait. The three-quarter figure of the young woman, her back brightly lit and her face and bosom in light shadow, dominates the picture, occupying an oddly elevated position above the background. Her indeterminate relationship to the landscape is reflected in an equally ambivalent relationship to the viewer, particularly in the way her body is partly revealed but not flaunted.

As was often the case with his figure paintings, Corot reworked the picture extensively and the oval composition is an adaptation of the original rectangular format. The reworking involved minor changes to the background, but more significant alterations to the woman's appearance – to her face and hair, as well as to her clothing, leaving her almost nude above the waist. The changes efface some of the more specific features of the figure, helping to achieve a more generalised, classical image, possibly modelled on the example of Raphael whom Corot greatly admired and often looked to in his figure paintings.

The meaning of the picture is unclear – it is not a genre painting with features and accessories that might support a narrative. The absence of specific meaning seems to be what Corot was aiming to achieve, drawing on Biblical and allegorical Renaissance models, but without religious or other coded meaning. With its compact pose and outward-looking but distracted gaze, the depiction of the young Italian woman points towards Corot's later female figures, who gradually lose their individual personal character, but acquire their own pictorial reality. BA

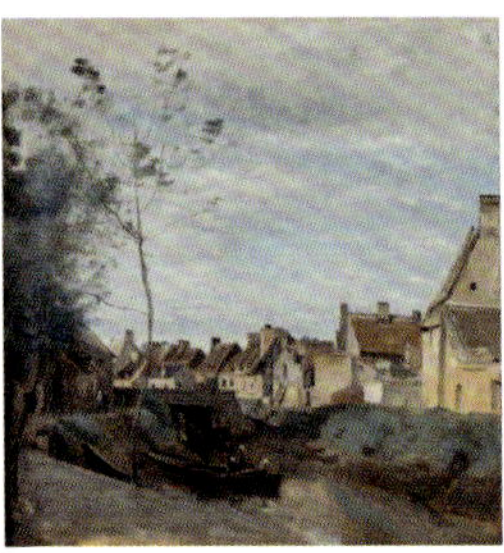

15

The Town of Isigny, Les Hagues, Manche,
c. 1855
Oil on canvas, 34 x 32 cm
Inv. no. 235 WH

PROVENANCE: Louis Sarlin, Paris; 2 March 1918, Sarlin sale, Galerie Georges Petit, Paris (auction not held); 1918, to Herman Heilbuth for Hansen, Heilbuth, Winkel & Magnussen consortium; 1918, to Wilhelm Hansen

LITERATURE: Robaut and Moreau-Nélaton 1905, vol. 2, no. 977; Fonsmark et al. 2011, no. 19

For Corot, subjective experience took precedence over both academic doctrine and objective reality: 'Beauty in art is truth bathed in the impression we have received from looking at nature. I am struck by the sight of a place. While striving for conscientious imitation, I never for one moment lose the emotion that overcame me. Reality is a part of art; feeling completes it.'

Corot's picture of the small town of Isigny gives the impression of having been painted *en plein air* and demonstrates the ease with which he could create the melancholy atmosphere that often dominates his landscapes. A misty, silvery tone pervades the picture, with shadows and reflections minimised. Corot almost ostentatiously demonstrates subjective spontaneity, using broad, loose brushwork as in the silvery-green strokes scattered over the surface of the picture – over roofs, trees and vegetation – and that provide the detail of the river. These brush strokes emphasise the direct nature of the experience rather than capturing a fleeting moment in the manner of the later Impressionists.

As so often in Corot's work, however, it is structure rather than light that unites the elements. The slightly wavy horizontal rhythm of the buildings is broken by a single tree that links earth and sky, while in the cool, green middle ground are a few figures busy in pitch-black boats. Further back on the left bank, a couple walks away from us towards a bridge. Isigny is painted as a string of houses seen from behind, with the river in the foreground. Rather than an objective topographical record, this becomes a kind of pictorial architecture, in which all the details support the total effect. BA

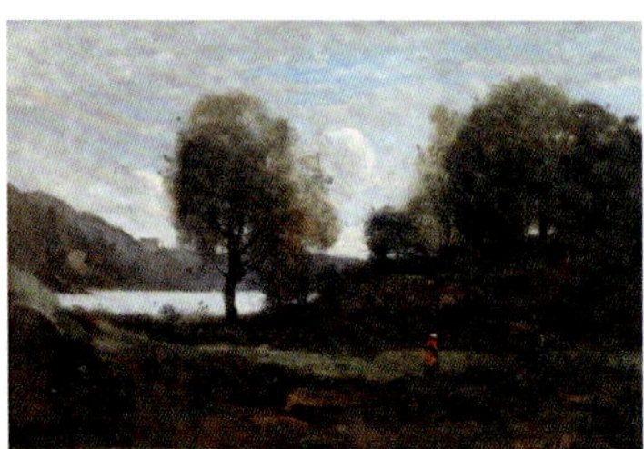

16

Souvenir of a Pond in the Limoges Area,
1855–60
Oil on canvas, 31.5 x 48 cm
Inv. no. 276 WH

PROVENANCE: 1891, Arnold & Tripp, Paris; 1903, to Louis Sarlin, Paris; 2 March 1918, Sarlin sale, Galerie Georges Petit, Paris (auction not held); 1918, to Herman Heilbuth for Hansen, Heilbuth, Winkel & Magnussen consortium; to Winkel & Magnussen; 1919 or 1920, to Herman Heilbuth; between 1923 and 1925, to Wilhelm Hansen

LITERATURE: Robaut and Moreau-Nélaton 1905, vol. 2, no. 1185b; Fonsmark et al. 2011, no. 21

Corot used the term *souvenir* in the titles of almost a fifth of the paintings he exhibited between 1855 and 1874, probably inspired by the painter and theoretician Pierre-Henri de Valenciennes, who advised artists to paint studies from memories of nature or of the works of the great masters. Corot's *souvenirs* may have a starting point in actual landscapes, but stylistically they are more closely related to his imagined, Arcadian landscapes painted in the studio than to the pictures he made *en plein air*.

Pervaded by the silvery tone that characterises Corot's later style, *Souvenir of a Pond in the Limoges Area* gives the impression of being a poetic meditation on a remembered place rather than an accurate study. The bright red and yellow clothing of the woman in the foreground contrasts with the picture's generally sombre colouring, while the white of her head covering connects her to the sunlit building on the horizon on the other side of the pond.

The atmosphere seems to express the pantheistic longing for nature and solitude characteristic of the French Romantic poets: the calm of evening, the melancholy of twilight, the silence of remote valleys, the stillness of lakes. BA

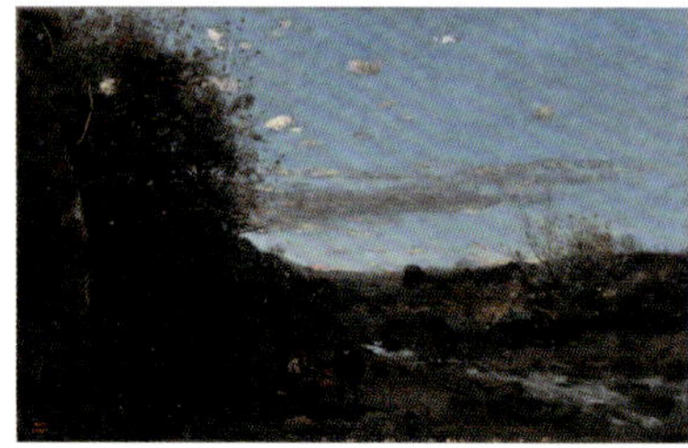

17

Hamlet and the Gravedigger, c. 1870–75
Oil on canvas, 50 x 80.5 cm
Inv. no. 293 WH

PROVENANCE: 26 May 1875, Corot sale, bought by Furtin, Paris (2,930 fr.); George Viau, Paris; 1918, to Hansen, Heilbuth, Winkel & Magnussen consortium; to Winkel & Magnussen; between 1925 and 1928, to Wilhelm Hansen

LITERATURE: Robaut and Moreau-Nélaton 1905, vol. 3, no. 2373, vol. 4, no. 220; Fonsmark et al. 2011, no. 23

The few literary subjects painted by Corot were often inspired by the theatre, and this picture dates from a time when he was a regular theatre-goer. He saw an operatic adaptation of *Hamlet* at the Paris Opéra Comique in March 1868 and reportedly claimed Shakespeare as his favourite poet. Shakespearean subjects proved popular in the nineteenth century, and also inspired Delacroix and Théodore Chassériau among others. Shakespeare's plays were crucial to the development of Romantic drama, which – in Victor Hugo's formulation – combined high and low, comic and tragic, the grotesque and the sublime, epitomised by the graveyard scene in *Hamlet*, with its burlesque dialogue between prince and gravedigger.

However, in Corot's painting it is the landscape rather than the figures that communicates the emotional charge of the scene. The heath – there is no sign of a graveyard, just a single grave – extends bleakly towards the horizon. The leaning bushes and trees, the racing clouds and, not least, the overriding atmosphere of unease in the surface of the picture emphasise the sombre, threatening mood with appropriately theatrical effect. BA

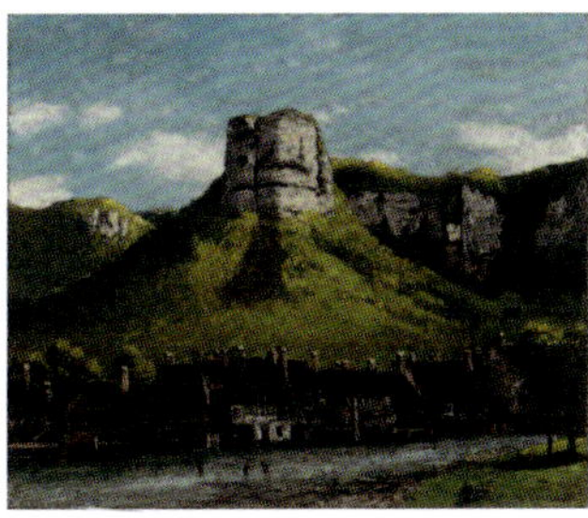

9
*The Wiremakers' Workshops on the
River Loue, near Ornans,* 1861
Oil on canvas, 55 x 66 cm
Inv. no. 186 WH

PROVENANCE: 1916, Wilhelm Hansen

LITERATURE: Fernier 1978, no. 8; Courthion 1985,
no. 1058; Fonsmark et al. 2011, no. 24

In 1855, responding to the rejection of
some of his paintings by the Exposition
Universelle, Courbet exhibited forty pictures
in his 'Pavillon du Réalisme', a temporary
structure built on an adjacent site. These
included his gigantic canvas *The Artist's
Studio* (1854–55; Musée d'Orsay, Paris), in
which Courbet himself is the central figure,
flanked on the left by figures representing
current conflicts and politics, and on the
right by figures, including a nude model
and critics, representing aesthetic ideas.
An ambiguous manifesto, *The Artist's Studio*
exemplifies Courbet's socially committed
work of the late 1840s and early 1850s.
However, the picture on the easel at the
centre of the painting is a landscape, not
immediately identifiable as socially or
politically inspired, and a foretaste of the
artist's future preoccupations.

Although a Realist, Courbet painted
nature in his studio, not *en plein air*. He was
not interested in transient things, nor in the
metaphysical: one should paint only what
one can see. But the content of a work was
something completely different and his
landscapes were neither neutral nor
without political significance. Almost
all his paintings combine the real and
the metaphorical, with his landscapes
influenced by a political attitude that
linked the idea of nature as a source of
freedom and harmony – inspired by the

philosophy of Jean-Jacques Rousseau –
with socialist concepts of freedom and
equality inspired by his friend Pierre-Joseph
Proudhon. Courbet's home town of Ornans
in Franche-Comté was a long way from
Paris, in a region fighting to free itself from
the centralising ambitions of the capital.
Nature and the provinces thus became
symbols of liberation and resistance.

In the foreground of *The Wiremakers'
Workshops,* the dark river that powers the
industry leads the viewer's gaze into the
picture; facing the river, the dilapidated
workshops with their skeletal structure
and dark window apertures block the
eye's movement into the picture but are
themselves dominated by the fortress-like
mountain above. The blurred figures in the
foreground are obviously not masters of
anything but are subject to the inexorability
of nature. Obstacles to the viewer's eye
are a feature of Courbet's landscapes: it
endows nature with a double meaning, on
the one hand as a space for liberation or as
a self-sufficient power – a political symbol
– and on the other as a threat, with nature
and the eternal contrasted with culture
and the temporal. BA

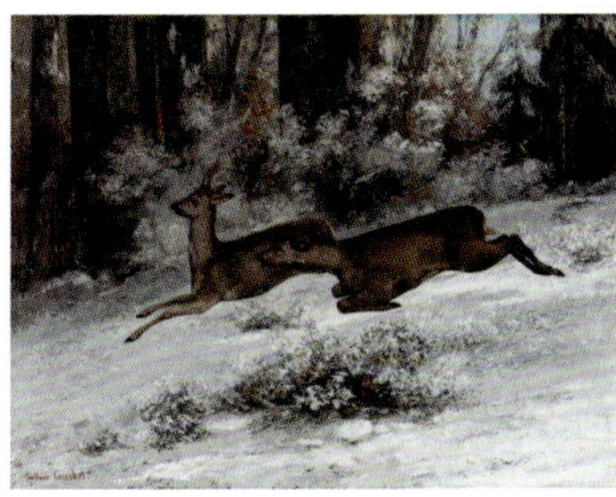

7
*The Ruse, Roe Deer Hunting Episode
(Franche-Comté, 1866),* 1866
Oil on canvas, 97 x 130 cm
Inv. no. 277 WH

PROVENANCE: Jules Paton; 24 April 1883, Paton
sale, Hôtel Drouot, Paris (10,200 fr.); to auctioneer
Léon Tual, Paris; to Drake del Castillo, Paris;
3 November 1917, to Galerie Durand-Ruel, Paris; 1917,
to Bernheim-Jeune, Paris; early 1918 (?), to Herman
Heilbuth, Copenhagen; between 1923 and 1925,
to Wilhelm Hansen

LITERATURE: Fernier 1978, no. 558; Courthion 1985,
no. 551; Fonsmark et al. 2011, no. 25

The Ruse was first exhibited as part of
Courbet's enormous personal exhibition
organised to coincide with the 1867 Paris
Exposition Universelle and held in a
pavilion on the Place de l'Alma, where he
showed some 137 paintings dominated by
landscapes and pictures of animals. This
was Courbet's attempt to find a realistic
and truthful successor to what he saw as
the unreal – or even mendacious –
paintings that dominated the Paris Salon.

Courbet was a keen huntsman and
painted many hunting scenes, and this work
is named after a hunting term – 'le change',
(the ruse) – used to describe the moment
when a fleeing deer deceives the hunter.
Often viewed as merely commercial works,
such paintings can also be interpreted as
allegories of political persecution.

Despite Courbet's commitment to
Realism, this is unmistakably a studio
picture, produced like a traditional figure
painting with the figures painted first and
their surroundings added later. This lack of
integration and the arrested movement
of the deer give the picture a significantly
unreal character. BA

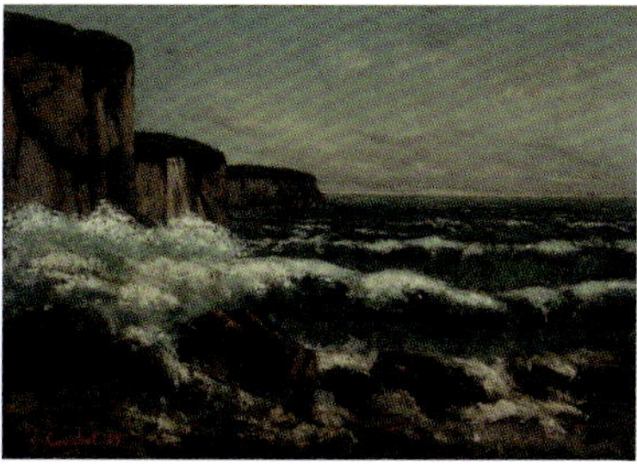

8
The Cliffs near Étretat, 1869
Oil on canvas, 62 x 88 cm
Inv. no. 236 WH

PROVENANCE: Alphonse Kann, Paris; 1918, to
Hansen, Heilbuth, Winkel & Magnussen consortium;
1918, to Wilhelm Hansen

LITERATURE: Fernier 1978, no. 713; Courthion 1985,
no. 685; Fonsmark et al. 2011, no. 26

In August and September 1869 Courbet
spent time at Étretat on the Normandy
coast. The pictures of the sea and the
coast he painted there constituted the
development of one of the principal
themes of his landscapes: self-sufficient
nature in its majestic solitude. A common
element of his sombre sea pictures is
a direct confrontation with nature as a
violent power, with no trace of human life.
Here, the sea appears to be seen from
two viewpoints: in one, the viewpoint is
the upper line of the horizon, overlooking
nature and suggesting Man's superiority;
in the other, the viewpoint is low, with the
sea rising up over the viewer.

This image of nature is not an account
of rhythm or harmony but of the battle
between the sea and the cliffs. The huge
rocks that lie in pieces testify to the
overwhelming strength of the sea. Soon
after Courbet's death, the critic Jules-
Antoine Castagnary interpreted the violent
waves in the artist's sea pictures of 1869 –
in light of the proclamation of the Third
Republic in 1870 – as a metaphor for the
power of the people. BA

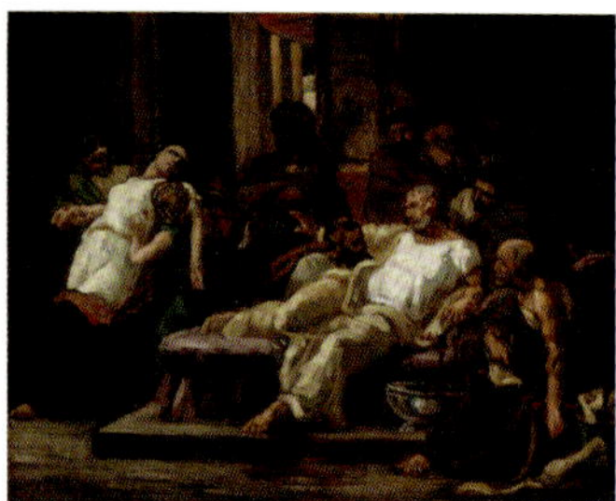

THOMAS COUTURE
(1815–1879)

4

*The Death of Seneca, Sketch,
date unknown*
Oil on canvas, 32 x 40.5 cm
Inv. no. 188 WH

PROVENANCE: 1916, Wilhelm Hansen

LITERATURE: Fonsmark et al. 2011, no. 28

Tacitus' *Annals* provide the source for this oil
sketch. Couture chose the moment when
Seneca – sentenced to death by the corrupt
emperor, Nero – and his wife Paulina have
attempted suicide. Seneca, exhausted by
pain, sends Paulina away to spare her the
sight of his suffering. The philosopher is
supported by grief-stricken companions as
an officer, dark and unyielding, stands in the
centre background.

By making the separation of Paulina
and Seneca – both dressed in white – his
subject, Couture has turned the picture into
a tragic love scene rather than emphasising
the heroism within the episode. Earlier
versions by the Neoclassicists Pierre Peyron
and David had also taken this approach,
and indeed David's *The Death of Seneca*
(1773; Musée du Petit Palais, Paris) provides
a source for both the physical separation
of the main figures and Seneca's gesture as
he orders Paulina to leave. Couture's version,
however, is considerably less theatrical
and more direct: a more intimate, more
bourgeois, less heroic but no less tragic
interpretation than the pre-Revolutionary
works of his predecessors. BA

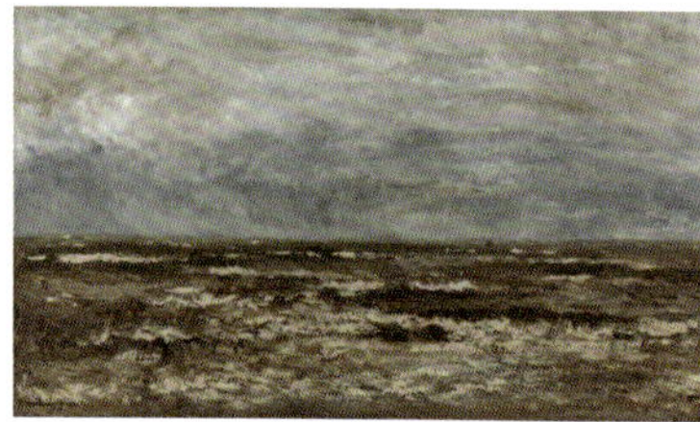

CHARLES-FRANÇOIS DAUBIGNY
(1817–1878)

20

Seascape, Overcast, 1874
Oil on canvas, 83.5 x 147 cm
Inv. no. 189 WH

PROVENANCE: 6–8 May 1878, Daubigny sale,
Hôtel Drouot, Paris (1,360 fr.); James S. Inglis,
New York; 9 March 1910, Inglis sale, New York;
Galerie Tempelaere, Paris; 1916, to Wilhelm Hansen

LITERATURE: Hellebranth 1976, no. 625; Fonsmark
et al. 2011, no. 30

Daubigny realised the Atlantic Ocean's
potential to offer a violent counterpart to
his gentle pictures of the banks of the Seine
and Oise when he visited the Normandy
coast in 1854. He returned frequently,
painting the sea as a distant background
but also producing pictures of dunes,
beaches and the ocean itself. In 1874 he
travelled down the Yonne and the Seine to
Le Havre: this huge canvas, using what was
for Daubigny an unusually wide format, was
one of the works resulting from that journey.

The entire picture seems to express the
endlessness of the huge expanse of water:
from the distant horizon, suggested by two
tiny ships far out to sea, the ocean stretches
towards the land in a rolling motion as the
waves rise and fall. Finally reaching the
shore, it draws itself up to spill out in the left
foreground and to withdraw, flat, to the right.

Daubigny often conveys movement
and changeability by variations in light,
which appear as delicate transitions of
colour in his paint. Here, the dynamic
motion and physical weight of the water
are reflected by the depiction of the sky,
from the dark clouds gathering on the
horizon to lighter ones towards the coastline
where waves crash on the shore. Without
metaphysical overtones or sentiment,
Daubigny presents the cyclical ebb and
flow of the water itself. BA

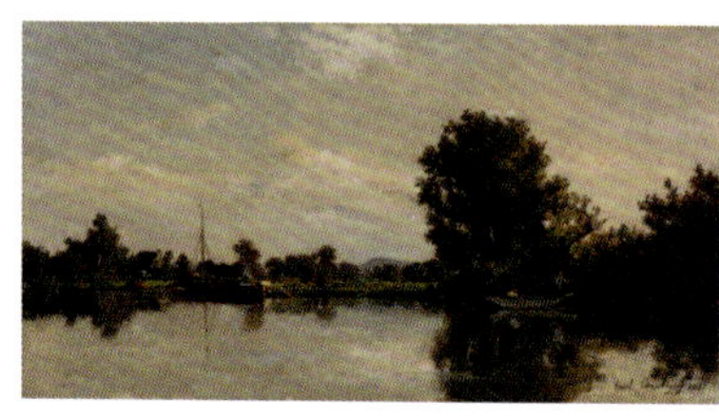

KARL DAUBIGNY
(1846–1886)

21

Boat on the River Oise, 1868
Oil on wood, 30 x 55 cm
Inv. no. 237 WH

PROVENANCE: Isidore Montaignac, Paris;
3–4 December 1917, Montaignac sale, Galerie
Georges Petit, Paris (auction not held); 1917, to
Hansen, Heilbuth, Winkel & Magnussen consortium;
1918, to Wilhelm Hansen

LITERATURE: Fonsmark et al. 2011, no. 31

Karl Daubigny, son and pupil of Charles-
François Daubigny (cat. 20), one of the
leaders of the Barbizon School, followed so
closely in his father's footsteps that his work
seems almost to represent an earlier style
of landscape painting. While the Barbizon
School rejected the fixed paradigms of
landscape painting, it is striking in Karl's work
that the record of a spontaneous impression
created by confrontation with nature has
become instead a form of convention.

This picture represents dusk in a creek on
the river Oise, a landscape already explored
by Théodore Rousseau and which became
almost the personal territory of Karl's father.
Here, it is as if the composition is developed
from a diagram, with the river opening up
on the right-hand side to make way for a
view into the landscape, and the tall trees
rounding off the picture on the left.

With the somewhat heavy and awkward
style, the scenery fails to embody the
emotion the senior Daubigny could bring
to similar subjects. Instead, we have a
pleasant landscape, with two men fishing
from a rowing boat in the foreground
demonstrating how people live in harmony
with nature. Only the large streamlined river
boat – which was to become a recurring
element in the work of Impressionists such
as Sisley and Guillaumin – breaks into the
idyll, anticipating something new. BA

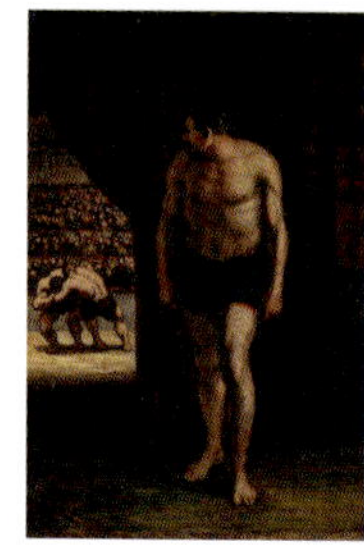

HONORÉ DAUMIER
(1808–1879)

6

The Wrestler, c. 1852
Oil on wood, 42 x 27.5 cm
Inv. no. 278 WH

PROVENANCE: Charles-François Daubigny, Paris;
1878, to Mme Daubigny; 1901, Louis Sarlin, Paris;
2 March 1918, Sarlin sale, Galerie Georges Petit, Paris
(auction not held); 1918, to Herman Heilbuth for
Hansen, Heilbuth, Winkel & Magnussen consortium;
1918, to Herman Heilbuth; 1923, to Reid & Lefèvre,
London (?); between 1923 and 1925, to Wilhelm
Hansen

LITERATURE: Klossowski 1908, no. 178; Fuchs 1927,
pl. 115, p. 40; Fuchs 1930, p. 59; Mandel 1972, no. 56;
Maison 1996, no. I–45; Fonsmark et al. 2011, no. 33

Daumier was one of the few French artists
of the nineteenth century to develop a
contemporary narrative style of painting.
In the tradition of Delacroix and Géricault,
he was interested in contrasts: between the
individual and the masses, movement and
rest, strength and weakness, light and dark.

In *The Wrestler*, Daumier focuses on the
solitary figure in the dimly lit foreground
rather than the spotlit wrestlers performing
in front of the audience. Small differences
between the preparatory sketch and the
finished picture show the artist refining
his representation of this principal figure:
shifted towards the centre, his distance
from the wrestlers in the background has
been reduced, drawing the eye away from
the arena and towards him. In contrast to
the compact, extremely muscular pair in
the background who are almost caricatures,
the solitary wrestler appears defeated. His
body is far from the classical ideal of an
athlete: his legs are too long, his head
too small. BA

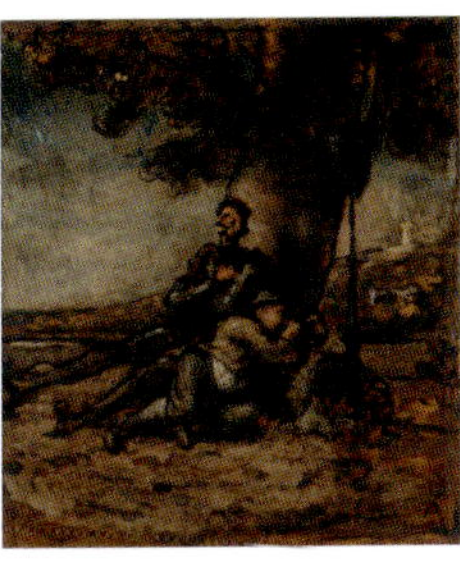

5

***Don Quixote and Sancho Panza
Resting under a Tree, c. 1864–66***
Oil on wood, 42.5 x 38.5 cm
Inv. no. 211 WH

PROVENANCE: 1917, Wilhelm Hansen

LITERATURE: Fuchs 1930, pl. 305b; Mandel 1972,
no. 233; Maison 1996, no. I-173; Fonsmark et al. 2011,
no. 34

Cervantes's *Don Quixote* was Daumier's
favourite subject, with some 29 paintings
and 41 drawings surviving. The knight had
always been popular with French artists
and illustrators, with different generations
emphasising his different aspects – the
lovable, deluded fool in the eighteenth
century, the tragic hero in the nineteenth.
Daumier chose not to reduce him to
a stereotype, instead capturing the
complexity of his character.

Most of Daumier's pictures of Don
Quixote portray the relationship of master
and servant as the pair travel on horse and
mule through a barren landscape. Here,
they have stopped to rest: in a reversal
of what might be expected, the master
watches while the servant sleeps. In the
background, the animals echo their masters'
relationship.

Although it is tempting to see Daumier's
pictures of Don Quixote as psychological
self-portraits, his repeated use of the
character should be understood in a
wider context. His fascination stems from
the knight's situation, trapped between
meaningless reality and dazzling illusion.
Don Quixote embodies the questions that
occupied Daumier as he portrayed his own
times, which he represented repeatedly as
grotesque, distorted theatre or a seductive
phantom. BA

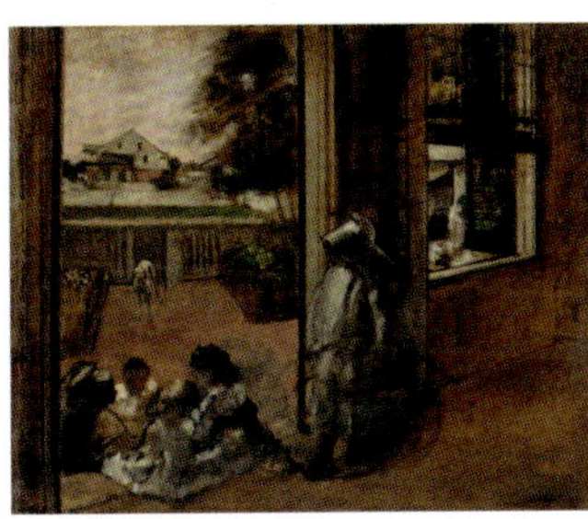

45

***Courtyard of a House (New Orleans,
Sketch), 1873***
Oil on canvas, 60 x 73.5 cm
Inv. no. 238 WH

PROVENANCE: 6–8 May 1918, first Degas sale,
Galerie Georges Petit, Paris (17,600 fr.); to Jos
Hessel for Hansen, Heilbuth, Winkel & Magnussen
consortium; 1918, to Wilhelm Hansen

LITERATURE: Lemoisne 1946, vol. 2, no. 309;
Minervino 1970, no. 346; Fonsmark et al. 2011, no. 40

In 1872 Degas, who was yet to exhibit with
the Impressionists and become successful
as a painter, travelled from Paris to New
Orleans to visit relatives. His mother
was born in the former French colony
where Degas's cousins and brothers were
established cotton traders. Degas spent
six months in New Orleans, during which
time he painted several family portraits
of his cousins and their children, as well as
his uncle's office (*A Cotton Office in New
Orleans*, 1873; Musée des Beaux-Arts de Pau).

This sketch – signed by the artist and
therefore to be considered a finished work
– shows the rear entrance to the house of
Degas's American relatives and a group of
his cousins' and brothers' children sitting
on the step with a black nurse to the left
and a Mastiff in the courtyard. In New
Orleans, Degas painted interiors in subdued
light because problems with his eyesight
prevented him from working in bright light
outdoors. Sketch elements are clearly
visible, including the lines that delineate the
building structures and the sketchiness of
the standing girl's hoop. TL

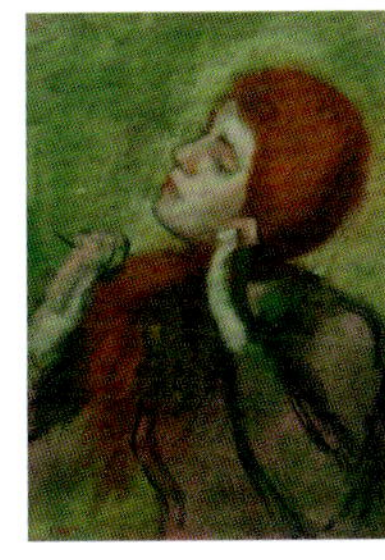

46

Woman Arranging Her Hair, 1894
Oil on canvas, 54 x 40 cm
Inv. no. 290 WH

PROVENANCE: 6–8 May 1918, first Degas sale, Galerie
Georges Petit, Paris; to Galerie Jos Hessel, Paris;
S. Sevadjian, Paris; 22 March 1920, Sevadjian sale,
Hôtel Drouot, Paris; to Galerie Barbazanges, Paris;
between 1923 and 1925 (?), to Wilhelm Hansen

LITERATURE: Lemoisne 1946, vol. 3, no. 1147;
Fonsmark et al. 2011, no. 44

A relatively rare example of an oil painting
from Degas's late career, when pastels
were his preferred medium, this intimate
portrait has many of the qualities of a work
in pastels, with the paint applied in very thin
layers, the brush strokes visible in places.

The young woman is shown in close-up,
her face turned away and her eyes closed,
a pose suggesting introspection. Only the
outlines of her body are sketched in black,
with the rest of the composition built up
entirely with colour. Unlike many of Degas's
toilette pictures, the girl is dressed and there
is no suggestion of a real space nor of the
accessories that frequently take centre
stage in such works.

Women with loose, long hair were
a popular subject around the turn of
the nineteenth century, with artists,
predominantly male, tending either to
dramatise or to romanticise the combing
of hair and other feminine rituals. By
comparison, Degas's approach was more
realistic, yet his central concern was still
to capture the decorative quality of the
movement, with anatomically accurate
reproduction of the hands, for instance,
clearly secondary. ACWI

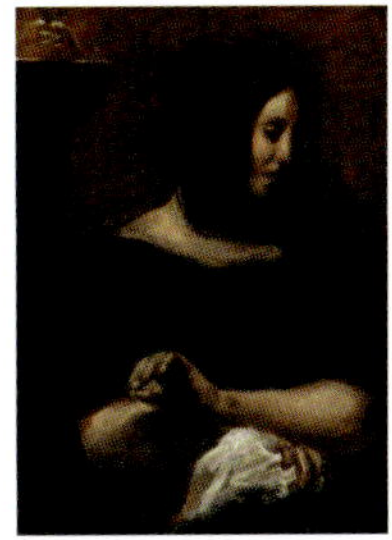

2

George Sand, 1838
Oil on canvas, 78 x 56.5 cm
Inv. no. 280 WH

PROVENANCE: acquired after the artist's death by
Constant Dutilleux, Arras/Paris; 1865, to Dutilleux's
daughter Madame Desavery; 1887, purchased
by P.-A. Chéramy, Paris (500 fr.); 5–7 May 1908,
Chéramy sale, Galerie Georges Petit, Paris (1,350 fr.);
to George Viau, Paris; 1918, to Hansen, Heilbuth,
Winkel & Magnussen consortium; 21 November
1918, to Herman Heilbuth, Copenhagen (35,000 kr.);
between 1923 and 1925, to Wilhelm Hansen

LITERATURE: Robaut 1885, no. 665; Bortolatto 1972,
no. 330; Johnson 1981–89, vols 3–4, no. 233;
Hureaux 1993, no. 297; Fonsmark et al. 2011, no. 47

Delacroix's picture of the writer George
Sand was originally a double portrait:
another part, depicting her lover, the
composer Frédéric Chopin, is in the Louvre.
The fragments were cut from a canvas,
probably unfinished, that showed Sand
listening to Chopin playing the piano. We
do not know why the portrait remained
unfinished, when it was cut up or how the
fragments were originally arranged.

The picture uses a theme that was
central to Delacroix's theory of art, in
which music and painting are closely
related disciplines. Here, he has painted
the experience of music as a frame of
mind through the figure's self-absorbed
posture and her detached expression –
both also features of the portrait of Chopin.
Rather than follow her lover's movements
at the piano, Sand has shut her eyes to
concentrate on listening. TL

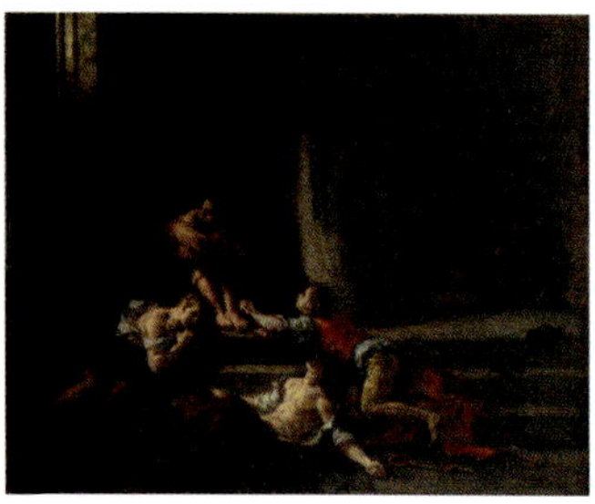

3

Ugolino and His Sons, 1860
Oil on canvas, 50 x 61 cm
Inv. no. 212 WH

PROVENANCE: completed June 1860 for the art dealer Estienne, Paris; January 1887, Hector Brame, Paris (on sale for 30,000 fr.); 1892, to Charles Levesque, Paris; 1916, to Baillehache, Paris; 1917, via Théodore Duret to Wilhelm Hansen

LITERATURE: Robaut 1885, no. 1063; Bortolatto 1972, no. 776; Johnson 1981–89, vols 3–4, no. 337; Hureaux 1993, no. 632; Fonsmark et al. 2011, no. 52

Dante was one of Delacroix's favourite writers. The poet's *Divine Comedy* inspired Delacroix throughout his career: from *The Barque of Dante* (1822; Musée du Louvre, Paris), which made his name, to *Ugolino and His Sons*, painted a few years before his death. Dante recounts that Count Ugolino was condemned to Hell for eating his sons while they were all imprisoned and starving to death. Delacroix depicts an earlier part of the story, when one of the sons throws himself at his father's feet, begging for help. Three sons lie on the steps in front of Ugolino, while a fourth can be glimpsed in the dark right-hand side of the picture. Light falls on the foremost figure's bare chest, highlighting his pale flesh, while his arms are stretched out – an allusion to Christ on the Cross, and thus to the body that, according to Catholic dogma, is eaten during the celebration of the Eucharist.

The Ugolino story attracted two strands of interpretation in Romantic art: one political and the other concerned with aesthetic theory. Politically, the Count was seen as a victim of tyranny – including the despotism of the Church – and the popularity of the subject in the nineteenth century can be linked to liberalism.

Delacroix showed little interest in politics in this latter part of his life, however. In terms of aesthetic theory, conflict between rule-bound classicism and the freedoms of Romantic aesthetics played a prominent role in early nineteenth-century critical debates and *The Barque of Dante* has been seen as Delacroix's youthful declaration of support for a Romantic aesthetic. The Ugolino motif, too, was interpreted as an allegory of the revolt against the tyranny of classicism, and in this context it is significant that the mature Romantic artist chose to revisit *The Divine Comedy*. TL

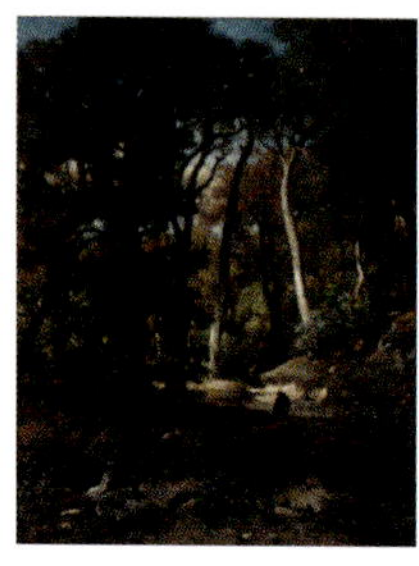

19

A Clearing in the Forest, after 1875
Oil on canvas, 56.5 x 43.5 cm
Inv. no. 241 WH

PROVENANCE: Sommier, Paris; Sommier sale to Durand-Ruel, Paris (?); Isidore Montaignac, Paris; 3–4 December 1917, Montaignac sale, Galerie Georges Petit, Paris (auction not held); 1917, to Hansen, Heilbuth, Winkel & Magnussen consortium; 1918, to Wilhelm Hansen

LITERATURE: Aubrun 1974, no. 134; Aubrun 1982, no. S122; Fonsmark et al. 2011, no. 57

Like Narcisse Diaz de la Peña, Constant Troyon and Théodore Rousseau, Dupré was a central figure of the Barbizon School, which rejected academic painting in favour of recording contemporary personal experience. *A Clearing in the Forest* shows his interest in painting nature and his ability to infuse his work with the spirit of Romanticism. In terms of subject matter, this picture could have been painted in the 1840s, the heyday of the Barbizon School, but the impasto technique indicates that it was produced much later.

The foreground is dark, the overgrown landscape forming an enclosure that contrasts with the lighter clearing at the picture's centre. The clearing represents an ambiguous space in which transformational processes are at play: the glistening foliage there contrasts with the reds and mould-like colours much as the dark forest floor contrasts with the radiant blue sky above. The trees stand like pillars that channel the process of transition – connecting light and dark, sky and ground, and transforming the forest into an almost religious space. The lone man sitting in the clearing links nature with human experience. BA

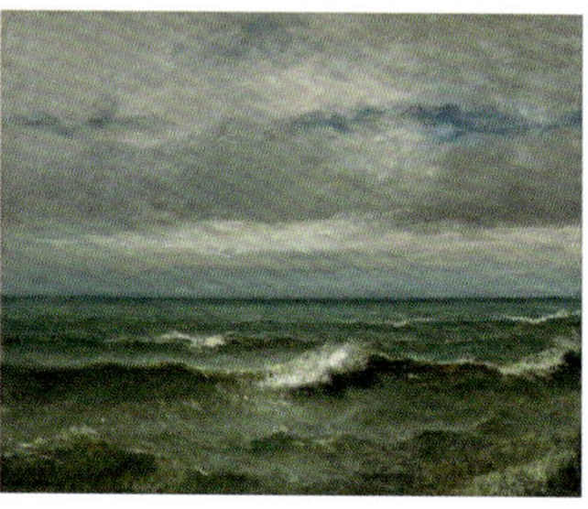

18

The Sea, after 1875
Oil on canvas, 59.5 x 73.5 cm
Inv. no. 222 WH

PROVENANCE: George I. Seney, New York (?); 11 February 1891, Seney sale, New York (?); until at least 1900, P. A. B. Widener, Philadelphia; Tempelaere, Paris (10,000 fr.); 1918, to Hansen, Heilbuth, Winkel & Magnussen consortium; 1918, to Wilhelm Hansen

LITERATURE: Aubrun 1974, no. 572; Aubrun 1982, no. S123; Fonsmark et al. 2011, no. 56

From 1865, Dupré spent his summers at Cayeux-sur-Mer on the Picardy coast. Painted *en plein air* to achieve a kind of realism unattainable in the studio, Dupré's pictures of the coast reveal a deep fascination for the dramatic character of nature, and his ability to convey atmosphere earned him the admiration of the Impressionists.

One of his later seascapes, *The Sea* is almost classical in structure, with the subject reduced to sky and sea, split by the horizon. Clouds glide across the sky and the gentle ripples in the sea move from the left foreground to the right background. A single wave rises and breaks, its white spray like a subdued crescendo in the centre of the water's surface.

The contemporary writer Jules Claretie associated Dupré's seascapes with the artist's exile during the Prussian occupation of Paris in 1870, interpreting his images as symbols of the accidents of war and providing a psychological explanation for the motifs of ships battling the elements and lonely fishing boats dragged onto the shore. Devoid of ships, however, the present work seems to depict the ocean not as a metaphor for destruction but as something stable and ever-present. BA

PAUL GAUGUIN
(1848–1903)

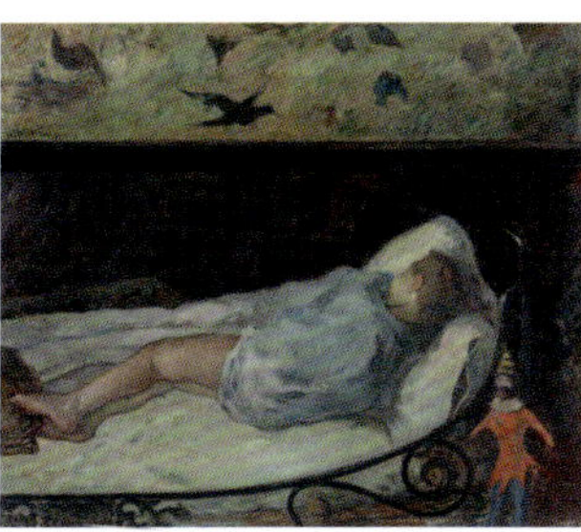

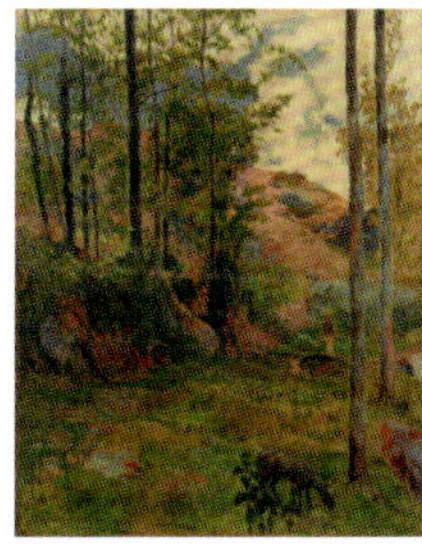

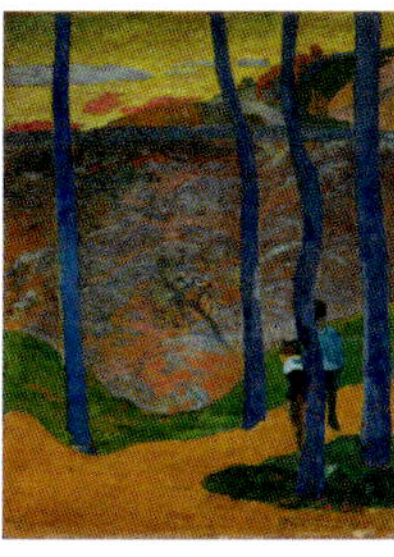

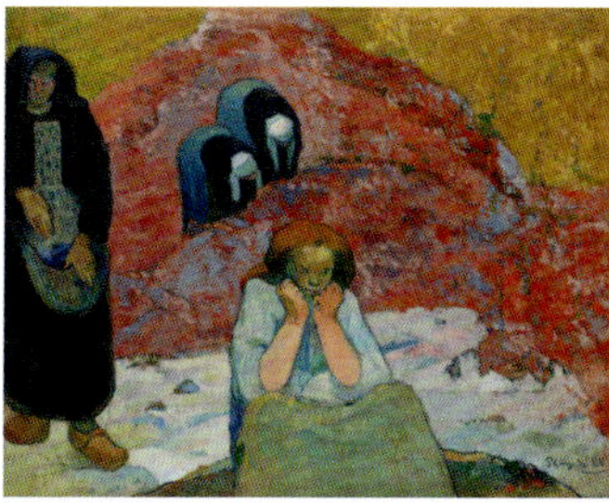

50

The Little One Is Dreaming, Étude, 1881
Oil on canvas, 59.7 x 74 cm
Inv. no. 190 WH

PROVENANCE: Mette Gauguin, Copenhagen;
Konrad Levysohn, Copenhagen; *c.* 1915, returned
to Mette Gauguin; 1916, Wilhelm Hansen

LITERATURE: Wildenstein et al. 1964, vol. 1, no. 52;
Wildenstein 2001, no. 75; Fonsmark et al. 2011, no. 59

Gauguin painted *The Little One Is Dreaming,
Étude* when he was still working as a
stockbroker in Paris. He exhibited it at
the seventh Impressionist Exhibition the
following year, when he became a full-
time artist. Gauguin had met Pissarro who
became a mentor, inviting him to exhibit
with the Impressionists and introducing
him to Cézanne, whose technique of
parallel brush strokes Gauguin adopted.

The child, either Gauguin's son Clovis
or his daughter Aline, lies with his or her
back to us, facing the Cézanne-inspired
wallpaper above the dark dado, its
ethereal pattern of birds representing the
world of fantasy and dreams. The picture
simultaneously evokes two separate
realities: the viewer looking at the sleeping
child and the child's dream.

Although called an *étude,* this is a
finished work and not a preparatory piece
– Gauguin's most ambitious early work,
Étude de nu (Suzanne cousant) from 1880
(Ny Carlsberg Glyptotek, Copenhagen),
was also labelled in this way. The term
might be understood to refer to a musical
étude: a painter's response to a musical
exercise as a means of expression
comparable to Whistler's *Nocturnes,*
painted in the 1870s. A–BF

51

Landscape at Pont-Aven, 1888
Oil on canvas, 92 x 73 cm
Inv. no. 242 WH

PROVENANCE: George Viau, Paris; 1918, to Hansen,
Heilbuth, Winkel & Magnussen consortium; 1918,
to Wilhelm Hansen (15,000 kr.)

LITERATURE: Wildenstein et al. 1964, vol. 1, no. 268;
Sugana 1972, no. 100; Wildenstein 2001, no. 278;
Fonsmark et al. 2011, no. 60

In 1886 Gauguin went to paint at Pont-Aven
in Brittany, in search of an uncorrupted
culture and attracted by the low cost of
living. He returned to Pont-Aven in 1888 to
'imprint upon [his] mind the character of the
landscape and the people', and wrote to
his friend, the painter Émile Schuffenecker:
'I love Brittany. There I can find the wild and
the primitive. When my clogs echo against
the granite, I can hear the muffled, dull and
vigorous tone that I seek in painting.'

He painted *Landscape at Pont-Aven*
shortly after his arrival, probably in March
or April when the trees were about to come
fully into leaf. The picture, framed by a
network of slender tree trunks cut off at
the top, anticipates *Blue Trees (Your Turn
Will Come, My Beauty!)* (cat. 52), painted
towards the end of the same year.

The fine, concise brush strokes suggest
Gauguin's debt to Impressionism but
paradoxically also reflect his awareness
of Pointillism, which he dismissed as the
'ripipoint' movement. It was during this
stay in Brittany that Gauguin abandoned
Impressionist technique and began
painting in planes of non-naturalistic
colour. A–BF

52

*Blue Trees (Your Turn Will Come,
My Beauty!),* 1888
Oil on jute sackcloth, 92 x 73 cm
Inv. no. 254 WH

PROVENANCE: Carl Moll, Vienna; 31 October
1908, to Bernheim-Jeune, Paris; 4 November
1908, to Alphonse Kann, Saint Germain-en-Laye
(2,000 fr.); 11 April 1918, to Hansen, Heilbuth, Winkel
& Magnussen consortium; 1921 at the latest, to
Wilhelm Hansen

LITERATURE: Wildenstein et al. 1964, vol. 1, no. 311;
Sugana 1972, no. 134; Wildenstein 2001, no. 319;
Fonsmark et al. 2011, no. 62

This major work, painted while Gauguin
was staying at Arles with Van Gogh, shows
the strong influence of the Dutch artist.
However, it also reveals the way Gauguin
followed his own 'recipe', using unmixed
colours in complementary pairs – yellow–
blue and red–green. The horizontal lines
in the blue and red clouds of the chrome-
yellow sky contrast with the cobalt-blue
tree trunks, inspired by Japanese wood
engravings, that wend their way up to
disappear over the top edge of the picture.

The dramatic landscape forms the
setting for two figures standing back to
back, half concealed by a tree – a woman
in traditional Arles costume and a man
with his hands deep in his pockets,
uncompromising and threatening. Gauguin
heightened the tension in this work when
he exhibited it at the Salon des XX in
Brussels in 1889 under the ominous title
*Vous y passerez, la belle! (Your Turn Will
Come, My Beauty!).* A–BF

54

The Wine Harvest, Human Misery, 1888
Oil on jute sackcloth, 72.5 x 92 cm
Inv. no. 223 WH

PROVENANCE: purchased from the artist by
Émile Schuffenecker, Paris (300 fr.); Galerie
Arnot, Vienna; 1918, Wilhelm Hansen

LITERATURE: Wildenstein et al. 1964, vol. 1, no. 304;
Sugana 1972, no. 142; Wildenstein 2001, no. 317;
Fonsmark et al. 2011, no. 61

Gauguin was particularly proud of this
major work, painted during his stay with
Van Gogh at the Yellow House at Arles in
1888, and judged it to be his best of the year.
It was inspired by a walk during which the
two artists came across an extraordinary
red vineyard, but the title, as well as the
depiction of women wearing traditional
Breton dress in Provence, suggest a further
symbolic meaning.

In a letter to the painter Émile
Schuffenecker (who was to purchase the
picture), Gauguin described the work: 'Do
you notice in the *Grape Harvest* a poor
disconsolate being? ... It's a woman. Sitting
with her chin resting on her hands, she
thinks of little, but feels the consolation of
this earth ... which the sun inundates in the
vineyard with its red triangle.'

The central figure's pose with her chin
resting on her hands was possibly inspired
by a Peruvian mummy in the Musée
d'Ethnographie du Trocadéro in Paris.
Gauguin reused this motif in several works
often evoking despair. Here, this enigmatic
figure has been interpreted as an allegorical
figure, like Albrecht Dürer's *Melancholia,* or
as a modern fallen Eve. A–BF

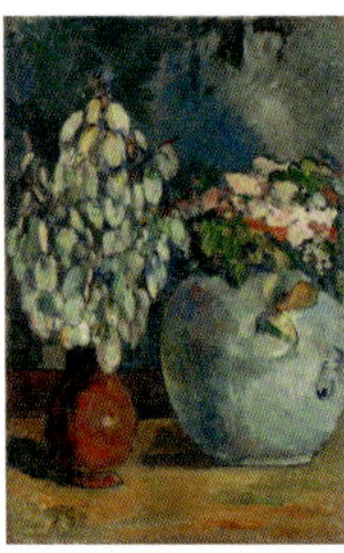

53

Two Vases with Flowers, c. 1890–91
Oil on jute sackcloth, 65 x 43.5 cm
Inv. no. 243 WH

PROVENANCE: George Viau, Paris; 1918, to Hansen, Heilbuth, Winkel & Magnussen consortium; from 1918, Wilhelm Hansen

LITERATURE: Wildenstein et al. 1964, vol. 1, no. 409; Sugana 1972, no. 218; Fonsmark et al. 2011, no. 63

Gauguin first painted flowers early in his career under the influence of Impressionism, but in contrast with the spatial complexity that characterised those works *Two Vases with Flowers* is straightforward in design. Set in a confined space, the vases are seen almost frontally, one slightly forward of the other, a displacement that is emphasised by the shadows they cast. The only element reminiscent of the spatial intricacy Gauguin often built into his pictures is the dark-brown strip, perhaps a frame or a skirting board, above the surface on which the vases stand. Contours are finely drawn and the colour is applied so thinly that the coarse sackcloth shows through in several places.

Nearly all Gauguin's still-lifes can be seen as tributes to Cézanne, and he owned Cézanne's *Still-life with Fruit Dish* (1879–80; Museum of Modern Art, New York) for many years. The bluish wallpaper is reminiscent of Cézanne's work, the simple, balanced composition and the way two similar elements, the vases, are linked. The vase on the right has been painted with the type of parallel brush strokes used by Cézanne, which Gauguin echoed whenever he had that artist's work in mind. A–BF

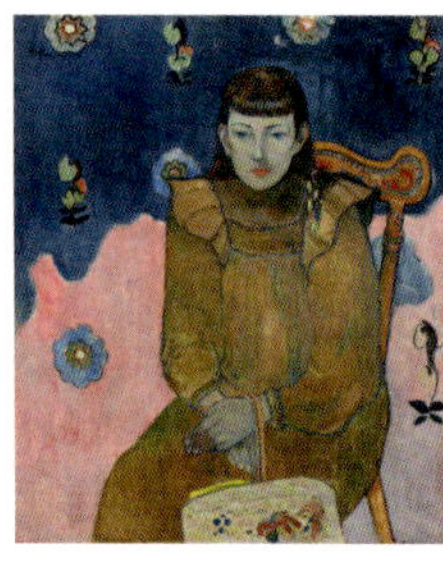

57

*Portrait of a Young Girl
(Vaïte 'Jeanne' Goupil), 1896*
Oil on canvas, 75 x 65 cm
Inv. no. 224 WH

PROVENANCE: Auguste Goupil, Papeete; 1918, to Wilhelm Hansen

LITERATURE: Wildenstein et al. 1964, vol. 1, no. 535; Sugana 1972, no. 376; Fonsmark et al. 2011, no. 64

Gauguin initially hoped to earn an income from painting portraits in Tahiti but only a few commissions materialised, including this one. The sitter is Jeanne Goupil, the nine-year-old daughter of Auguste Goupil, a wealthy lawyer, journalist and politician, and Gauguin's neighbour at the time. Jeanne, also known by her Tahitian name Vaïte, and her family were members of the colonial elite.

Her pale porcelain-like skin and brown dress stand out against the vivid pink and ocean-blue backdrop patterned with floral motifs. Jeanne's impassive expression and bright red-orange lips make her look older than her age. The painting conveys an impression of coolness that is strikingly different from Gauguin's tender depiction of his own child in *The Little One Is Dreaming, Étude* (cat. 50).

In Gauguin's portrait, Jeanne has been interpreted variously as: the antithesis of Polynesian women where the girl is distinct from her Tahitian background, or as a colonist masquerading as a Tahitian wearing a missionary dress with a flower on her shoulder and affecting a native name. A–BF

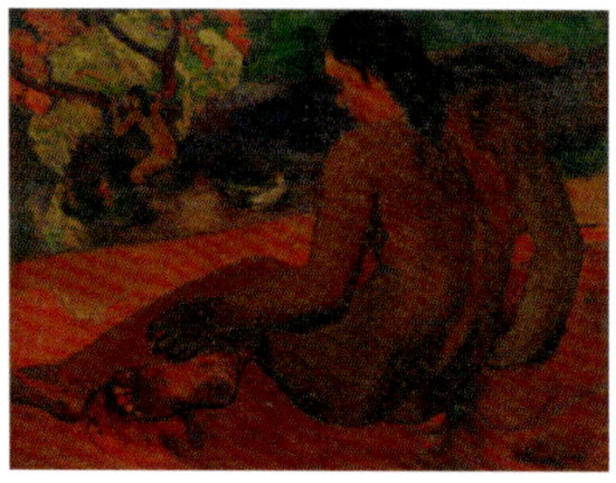

55

Tahitian Woman, 1898
Oil on sackcloth, 72.5 x 93.5 cm
Inv. no. 225 WH

PROVENANCE: Gabriel Frizeau, Bordeaux; 1917 or 1918, via Léon Marseille to Wilhelm Hansen

LITERATURE: Wildenstein et al. 1964, vol. 1, no. 576; Sugana 1972, no. 398; Fonsmark et al. 2011, no. 65

When Gauguin arrived in Tahiti in 1891, he was disappointed to find a French colony instead of the unspoilt paradise he sought. However, in his paintings he represented an imagined Tahiti and his colonial fantasy of the exotic.

In this painting, Gauguin depicted two Tahitian women apparently bathing. Borrowing from traditional motifs from Western art, Gauguin painted the women seen from the back. In the foreground, a figure sits gracefully on the shore while, further in the distance, her companion steps into the water holding on to the branches of a nearby tree.

Gauguin painted this canvas at a time when his work was becoming increasingly self-referential, and the seated figure echoes a figure in *Where Do We Come From? What Are We? Where Are We Going?* (1897; Museum of Fine Arts, Boston), a panorama of life from birth to death which Gauguin described as a summation of his ideas and considered his most important work.

It is one of eight canvases related to *Where Do We Come From? What Are We? Where Are We Going?*, which Gauguin sent to Ambroise Vollard's gallery for exhibition in 1898. These works were then described as 'fragmentary replicas of and studies for' the larger work. The poet and critic André Fontainas complained about the clash between the reds and greens in these works. Gauguin justified his practice: 'Are not these repetitions of tones, these monotonous colour harmonies (in the musical sense) analogous to oriental chants sung in a shrill voice, to the accompaniment of pulsating notes which intensify them by contrast? Beethoven uses them frequently (as I understand it)...' A–BF

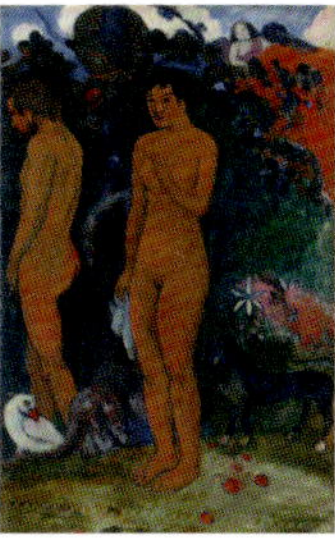

56
Adam and Eve, 1902
Oil on fustian, 59 x 38 cm
Inv. no. 244 WH

PROVENANCE: 1906, Bernheim-Jeune, Paris (?);
1910–11, Galerie Druet, Paris; Alphonse Kann, Saint-
Germain-en-Laye; 1918, to Hansen, Heilbuth, Winkel
& Magnussen consortium; 1918, to Wilhelm Hansen

LITERATURE: Wildenstein et al. 1964, vol. 1, no. 628;
Sugana 1972, no. 441; Fonsmark et al. 2011, no. 66

Eve and her temptation were recurrent
themes in Gauguin's work, and this is one
of his last interpretations of the story,
painted about eighteen months before
his death. At first glance it appears to be a
quite traditional Western representation,
with Adam and Eve standing on either side
of the Tree of Knowledge while the serpent,
coiled around its trunk, offers an apple.
Eve is depicted as a Polynesian woman
and holds the cloth with which she will
cover herself after the Fall of Man. She is
surrounded by animals used as symbolic
figures – a white bird associated with death
and a dark fox that, according to Gauguin,
is 'the Indian symbol of perversion'.

The way Adam is represented, however,
is less conventional. With his brown hair
and beard, he is depicted as a European,
perhaps even a self-portrait by the artist.
Slightly stooping, he faces sideways, as
if he were already leaving the state of
innocence of the Garden of Eden, haunted
by a consciousness of death. In contrast,
Eve, young and robust, stands upright,
unconcerned and pure at the centre of
her world and of the picture.

As is typical for Gauguin, the picture
refers to art from the past, and both Lucas
Cranach's depictions of paradise and the
reliefs of the Borobudur temple in Java, of
which he owned a photograph, may be
sources for Eve's statuesque figure. *Adam
and Eve* can also be seen as a critical
comment on the destruction of Polynesian
culture by the Europeans, a theme Gauguin
returned to in his book *Avant et après*
(*Before and After*) in 1903. A–BF

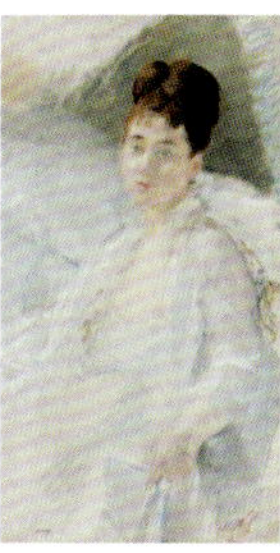

47
*The Convalescent (Portrait of a Woman
in White)*, 1877–78
Charcoal and oil on canvas, 86 x 47.5 cm
Inv. no. 245 WH

PROVENANCE: 20 February 1885, Gonzalès sale,
Hôtel Drouot, Paris (150 fr.); Jeanne Guérard-
Gonzalès, Paris; c. 1914, Galerie Brame, Paris;
Tempelaere collection; 1918, Hansen, Heilbuth,
Winkel & Magnussen consortium; 1918, Wilhelm
Hansen

LITERATURE: Sainsaulieu and Mons 1990, no. 93;
Fonsmark et al. 2011, no. 68

Although not usually regarded as a member
of Manet's school, Gonzalès was his only real
pupil, following him closely in her choice of
subjects and style. On her debut at the Paris
Salon in 1870, critical objections to Manet's
practice were also directed at her. Following
a mixed reaction to her submissions to the
1874 Salon, her painting in oil took on the
crisp lightness of pastel, perhaps showing
the influence of Impressionism. This can be
seen clearly in *The Convalescent*, in which
texture and form are evoked by the way the
colours of light hit different surfaces.

The work has been presented under
the title *Woman in White*. However from
1885, it was exhibited as *The Convalescent*,
a narrative theme that would appeal both
to the public and at the Salon. Features of
the narrative genre are readily apparent:
the model – perhaps the artist's mother or
sister – sits on a soft couch with a blanket
drawn up to her waist and a book dangles
from her left hand. Yet Gonzalès's use of an
unusually tall and narrow format leaves her
little space for the usual additional narrative
features. BA

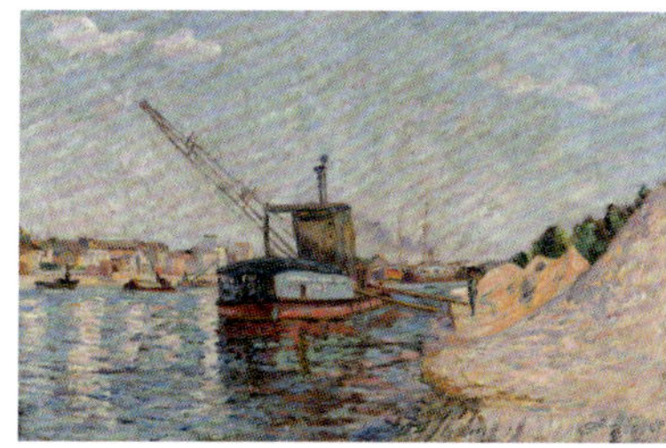

41
Quai de Bercy, Paris, 1885
Oil on canvas, 60 x 92 cm
Inv. no. 265 WH

PROVENANCE: Maurice Leclanché, Paris;
6 November 1924, Leclanché Sale, Hôtel Drouot,
Paris; purchased by Wilhelm Hansen

LITERATURE: Gray 1991, no. 95; Fonsmark et al. 2011,
no. 72

Although Guillaumin, a friend of both
Cézanne and Pissarro and an exhibitor at
the 1863 Salon des Refusés, was a member
of the circle around Manet from which
Impressionism developed, recognition
came slowly to him. This may be explained
by his preferred subjects, typically scenes
from the margins of Paris, where the
expansion of the city was obliterating the
natural landscape. Guillaumin frequently
painted quays, including the Quai de Bercy,
a hub of the wine trade on the eastern edge
of the capital that had only been absorbed
into Paris in 1860. In this work, he depicted
a boat used to extract alluvial sand and
gravel, materials essential to the expanding
construction industry.

The composition of *Quai de Bercy, Paris*
is almost classically calm, with the picture
space extending from foreground to
background. The floating crane dominates
the middle distance like a monument and
also connects the piles of sand to the right
with the buildings lining the waterfront
opposite. However, the stridency of the
colours is anything but calm: Guillaumin,
painting in the intense early morning light,
creates his own complementary harmonies
of orange–red and blue–green, violet and
green, and mauve and yellow, a technique
that fascinated and inspired Van Gogh. BA

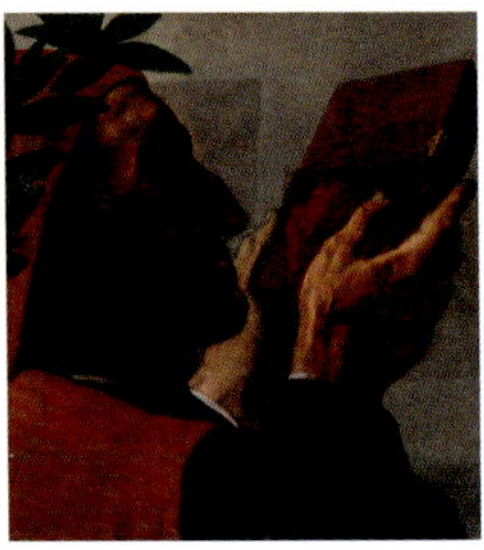

1

*Dante Offering the Divine Comedy
to Homer, c.* 1827 and *c.* 1864–65
Oil on three pieces of canvas mounted
on wood, 38 x 35.5 cm
Inv. no. 248 WH

PROVENANCE: 13 October 1866, bought from the
artist by Etienne-François Haro, Paris; 6–7 May 1867,
Ingres sale, Hôtel Drouot, Paris (1,480 fr.); Haro, Paris;
30–31 May 1892, Haro sale, Paris, bought back or
withdrawn; 30 April–3 May 1897, Haro sale, Galerie
Sedelmeyer, Paris; Edgar Degas, Paris (?); 26 March
1918, first Degas sale, Paris; Bernheim-Jeune; 1918 (?),
Wilhelm Hansen

LITERATURE: Wildenstein 1954, no. 171; Camesasca
1971, no. 121; Ternois 1980, no. 204; Fonsmark et al.
2011, no. 80

Ingres was commissioned in 1825 to paint
a ceiling in the Louvre (then the Musée
Charles X). *The Apotheosis of Homer*
represents the poet enthroned as a deity
and being crowned with a laurel wreath
before an antique temple. He is surrounded
by the so-called Homeridae, the heirs to
the Homeric tradition in music, literature,
drama, sculpture and painting. Dante,
positioned halfway between antiquity
and modernity, represents the continuity
between them. Ingres returned to the
subject in 1842–55 and in 1864–65.

*Dante Offering the Divine Comedy
to Homer*, collaged from three pieces
of canvas, is part of a group of small
oil paintings but its position within the
chronology is uncertain. The fragments
may originate from sketches and studies
for the Louvre commission, dating from
1826–27, but cut out and remounted when
Ingres was working on his final version
in 1864–65. Whatever their origin, these
collages must be considered as works in
their own right. BA

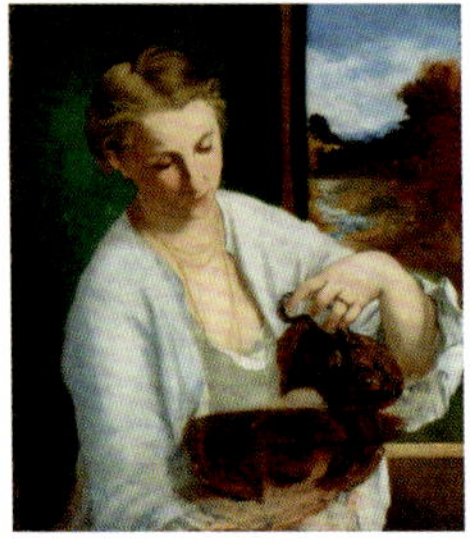

23

*Woman with a Jug (Suzanne Leenhoff,
later Manet), c.* 1858–60
Oil on canvas, 61 x 54.5 cm
Inv. no. 282 WH

PROVENANCE: after the artist's death to Suzanne
Manet; 1894, Madame M. Laurent-Cély, Asnières;
Madame L.-C. Fougery, Buc, Yvelines; between 1923
and 1925, to Wilhelm Hansen

LITERATURE: Duret 1902, no. 15; Tabarant 1931,
no. 24; Jamot and Wildenstein 1932, vol. 1, no. 23;
Orienti and Venturi 1967, no. 21; Orienti 1970, no. 21;
Rouart and Wildenstein 1975, vol. 1, no. 20; Orienti
and Pool 1985, no. 21; Fonsmark et al. 2011, no. 84

One of the great innovators of modern
painting, Manet was nevertheless deeply
rooted in the art of the past, incorporating
elements from the major European
traditions and genres. Underlying his
approach were two ambitions: to claim
a sort of ownership of the past, and to
create a new kind of painting that referred
to masterpieces of the past but radically
refreshed their forms and subject matter.
This would be necessary, he felt, if art
were to function as an interpreter of the
contemporary world.

In *Woman with a Jug*, one of his earliest
paintings, the motif of a woman pouring
water into a bowl suggests a genre picture,
and yet there is no contextualising narrative.
Her light clothing suggests a morning
toilette, but this is contradicted by her
jewellery. Jug and bowl are unfinished and
there is a striking contrast between the
woman's beautifully executed left hand
and her right, which is only sketched in.

The model was Suzanne Leenhoff.
Manet and Leenhoff lived together from
1860, marrying in 1863 – the ring on her left
hand has prompted an interpretation of
the painting as an engagement picture.

However, this is more likely to be one of
the painting's many historical references.
The main motif – a woman pouring water
from a jug into a bowl – was an accepted
emblem of the virtue of moderation.

The positioning of the figure between
interior and exterior is familiar from
Venetian Renaissance art, alluding
specifically to Titian's *Woman with a Mirror*
(*c.* 1515; Musée du Louvre, Paris), which
Manet knew well. The model for a woman
pouring water with her left hand is the
standing woman with a pitcher in Titian's
Pastoral Concert (*c.* 1509; Musée du Louvre,
Paris), which was also used in Manet's
scandalous *Le Déjeuner sur l'herbe* (1863;
Musée d'Orsay, Paris). Thus all the details
evoke art-historical sources but – unlike
Le Déjeuner sur l'herbe – both theme and
composition avoid confrontation with the
spectator. The classical illusion of the
picture space is maintained and it is only
at the bottom, where the unfinished hand
does not support the bowl, that the illusion
is broken. BA

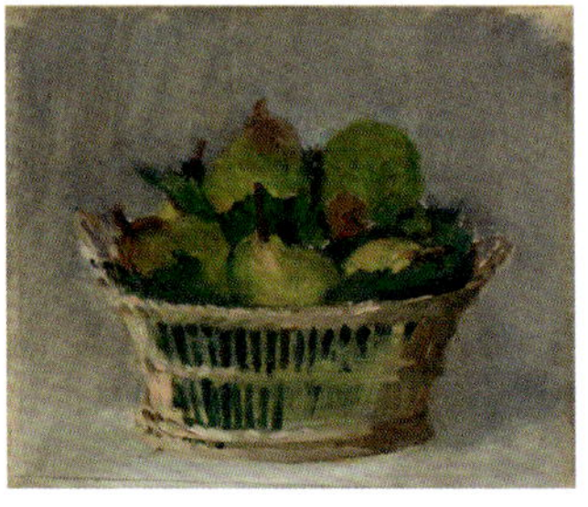

24

Basket of Pears, 1882
Oil on canvas, 35 x 41 cm
Inv. no. 197 WH

PROVENANCE: 1883, inventory of Manet's estate;
4–5 February 1894, Manet sale, Hôtel Drouot, Paris,
sold to Albert Robin, Paris (500 fr.); Théodore Duret,
Paris; 1916, to Wilhelm Hansen

LITERATURE: Duret 1902, no. 309; Tabarant 1931,
no. 340; Jamot and Wildenstein 1932, vol. 1, no. 413;
Orienti and Venturi 1967, no. 321A; Orienti 1970,
no. 325A; Rouart and Wildenstein 1975, vol. 1,
no. 354; Orienti and Pool 1985, no. 321A;
Fonsmark et al. 2011, no. 88

Still-life was a genre greatly valued by
Manet ('A painter can say all he wants with
fruit or flowers or even clouds,' the dealer
Ambroise Vollard recorded him as saying)
and it accounted for almost a fifth of his
work. *Basket of Pears* is one of a group of
later pictures in which a single type of fruit
is represented in a basket or on a dish at the
centre of the canvas. Here the basket forms
a delicate frame around the green pears on
their bed of vine leaves. The painting was
probably done in a single session, with light,
precise brush strokes. The still-life asserts
itself as something with a life of its own,
providing a purely visual pleasure without
an allegorical or secondary meaning.

Manet painted *Basket of Pears* during
the last summer of his life. His enjoyment
of the visual has been seen as connected
with his anxiety about losing the world –
an anxiety that can also be read into the
still-life motif in the artist's last great work,
A Bar at the Folies-Bergère (Courtauld
Gallery, London), also painted in 1882,
in which a vase of flowers and a dish of
oranges are given a direct and tangible
place in a world of mirrors. BA

HENRI MATISSE
(1869–1954)

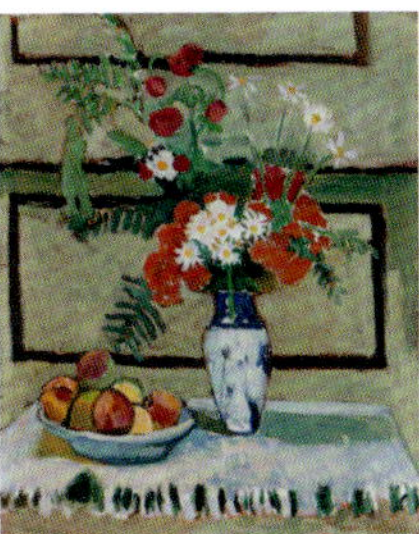

60
Flowers and Fruits, 1909
Oil on canvas, 73 x 60 cm
Inv. no. 259 WH

PROVENANCE: 1909, purchased from the artist by
Galerie Bernheim-Jeune (?); 1909, to Alphonse
Kann, Saint Germain-en-Laye (?); 11 March 1918, to
Hansen, Heilbuth, Winkel & Magnussen consortium;
to Galerie Barbazanges, Paris (?); 1922 (?), to
Wilhelm Hansen

LITERATURE: Carrà 1982, no. 531; Fonsmark et al.
2011, no. 91

In his 1908 book *Notes of a Painter*, Matisse
criticised Impressionist attempts to record
nature, extolling simplicity and clarity in
opposition to the seduction of transient
sensation. The point of painting, according
to Matisse, was not the imitation of nature
but the transformation of perception,
achieved by balancing the structure of a
picture rather than by focusing on specific
feelings. The drama and action of the
picture were not in its subject matter, but
in its form. Thus from 1908 to 1910 Matisse's
work concentrated on the ornamental, the
decorative line and the plane.

The interplay between space and the
two-dimensional picture plane, between
illusion and decoration, forms the basis
for the explosive colour and majestic
arrangement of *Flowers and Fruits*. The
subject is presented frontally and in parallel
with the surface of the picture, and the
background represents both a real room
and a decorative grid. BA

CLAUDE MONET
(1840–1926)

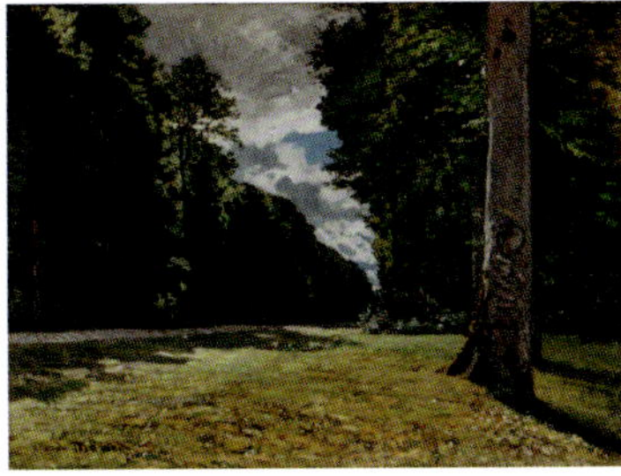

25
*The Chailly Road through the Forest
of Fontainebleau*, 1865
Oil on canvas, 97 x 130.5 cm
Inv. no. 250 WH

PROVENANCE: February 1869, probably sent by
Frédéric Bazille to Monet in Le Havre in a vain
attempt to sell; 1873, bought from the artist by
Durand-Ruel, Paris (700 fr.); 1873, to Jean-Baptiste
Faure, Paris, then back to Durand-Ruel, Paris (?);
c. 1891, Henri Rouart, Paris; 9–11 December 1912,
Rouart sale, Galerie Manzi-Joyant, Paris; back
to Durand-Ruel, Paris; 25 March 1918, to Émile
Duval-Fleury, Paris, for Hansen, Heilbuth, Winkel &
Magnussen consortium; 1918, to Wilhelm Hansen

LITERATURE: Wildenstein 1996, vol. 2, no. 57;
Fonsmark et al. 2011, no. 92

Monet stayed at Chailly, near Fontainebleau,
from April to October 1865, painting a series
of forest scenes in preparation for a very
large but never completed painting of an
alfresco luncheon, undoubtedly in response
to Manet's *Le Déjeuner sur l'herbe* (1863;
Musée d'Orsay, Paris). Monet's intention was
to confront Manet's studio painting and
its web of art-historical references with a
contemporary and objective interpretation
of the subject based on studies *en plein air*.

The broad, open foreground of this
picture gives the impression of an empty
stage waiting for characters to arrive. The
shadowy path on the left-hand side creates
a contrast with the striking wedge of clouds
and sky in the background, while the broad
tree trunk in the right foreground focuses
attention on the empty, stage-like space.

Monet represents a civilised route
through the forest, suggesting a destination
for an excursion. In contrast to the Barbizon
School's contemplations of unspoiled
nature, Monet gives us nature as a backdrop
for the pleasures of the bourgeoisie. BA

26
Seascape, Le Havre, c. 1866
Oil on canvas, 43 x 59.5 cm
Inv. no. 264 WH

PROVENANCE: 1878, purchased from the artist
by Victor Chocquet, Paris; to his widow; 1 April
and 5 July 1899, Chocquet sale, Galerie Georges
Petit, Paris; to Pinto, then Félix François Depeaux,
Rouen; 1 June 1906, Depeaux sale, Galerie Georges
Petit, Paris; to George Viau, Paris; 1918, to Hansen,
Heilbuth, Winkel & Magnussen consortium;
21 November 1918, to Herman Heilbuth (20,000 kr.);
20–21 February 1924, American Art Galleries auction,
New York; Galerie Barbazanges, Paris (?); before
1925, to Wilhelm Hansen

LITERATURE: Wildenstein 1996, vol. 2, no. 72;
Fonsmark et al. 2011, no. 93

For Monet, brought up on the coast at
Le Havre and with two of his teachers –
Eugène Boudin (cat. 22) and Johan Barthold
Jongkind – painters of marine scenes, water
and the sea occupied a special place in his
life and work. Monet was certainly aware
that paintings of the sea represented an
under-exploited niche in the art world
and therefore offered a possible career
opportunity. However, the sea also provided
opportunities for painting *en plein air*
where nature is at its most changeable
and atmospheric.

Although he was influenced in
technique by the sea paintings of Manet,
Whistler and Courbet, and by the Japanese
woodcuts he had collected from the age
of sixteen, Monet retained a dramatic,
narrative element in many of his seascapes.
In the present work, however, this is reduced
to the tiny ships, while the sea, radically
simplified, is itself the subject, a study in
tonality with a complex interplay of green,
grey-blue and white with accents of orange,
dark brown and pale pink. Where the sky is
open and without material weight, Monet's
brush strokes are equally insubstantial,
merging into one another. By contrast,
clouds and sea are given a physical
presence with thick, rapid, sketchy brush
strokes.

The sea here is interpreted not as a
solid mass but as a vibrating, tangible
surface. The illusion of spatial depth is only
sporadically suggested by the decreasing
size of the brush strokes and the tiny dark
boats on the horizon. In style and subject
matter, this study of reflected light on
moving water foreshadows Monet's later
paintings of his water garden at Giverny. BA

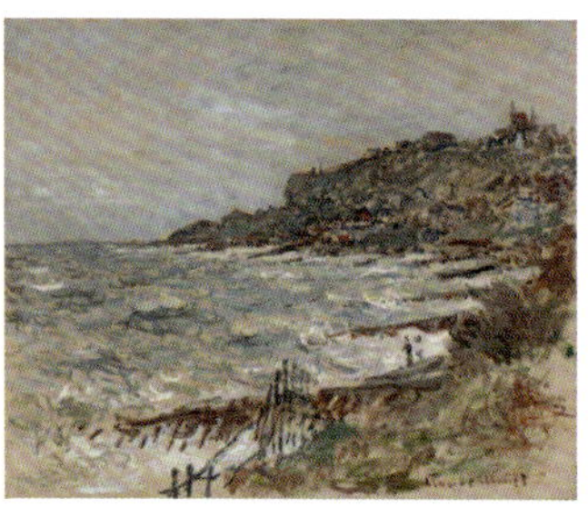

27

*The Cliff near Sainte-Adresse, Overcast,
c. 1881*
Oil on canvas, 60 x 73 cm
Inv. no. 283 WH

PROVENANCE: *c.* 1880, Durand-Ruel, Paris; 1899,
to Paul Gallimard; between 1923 and 1925,
to Wilhelm Hansen

LITERATURE: Wildenstein 1996, vol. 2, no. 689;
Fonsmark et al. 2011, no. 94

This painting dates from near the start of a
period of seven years during which Monet
worked almost exclusively on the Channel
coast. Executed rapidly and with relatively
few brush strokes, the work is, unusually,
a picture produced *en plein air* without
any later modification, its loose, sketchy
character reflecting the immediacy of the
experience.

Although Sainte-Adresse had become
a holiday resort for the wealthy inhabitants
of Le Havre, Monet shows the rugged,
unspoiled character of the coast. Nothing
has been done to conceal the ordinariness
of the late summer day. The sky is painted
with light, broad strokes; the sea with light,
sweeping strokes; the land with smooth, flat
strokes that follow its contours. Everything
is sketchily reproduced, including the two
figures who stand at the edge of the beach,
apparently oblivious to the energy of the
sea before them.

There is a kind of harmony between sea,
sky and land and the composition is without
hierarchy, with no centre or areas of intense
focus. This is an early example of the kind
of rough coastal landscape picture that
Monet continued to produce throughout
the 1880s. BA

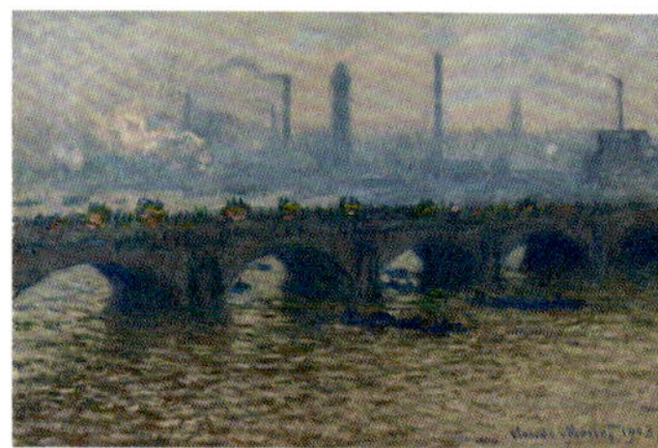

28

Waterloo Bridge, Overcast, 1903
Oil on canvas, 65.5 x 100.5 cm
Inv. no. 198 WH

PROVENANCE: December 1905, purchased from
the artist by Durand-Ruel, Paris; March 1906, to
Bernheim-Jeune, Paris; 1916, to Wilhelm Hansen

LITERATURE: Wildenstein 1996, vol. 2, no. 1561;
Fonsmark et al. 2011, no. 95

Monet's late work is dominated by series of
pictures of the same subject in changing
light and weather conditions. The most
extensive of these were painted in London
where Monet came to paint in early 1900.
He attempted to capture the changing
light of the city through the mist or fog,
which delighted him. He wrote to his wife
Alice: 'Early this morning there was an
extraordinary fog, completely yellow; I think
I did not too bad an impression of it; it's
always beautiful.'

Above all, the misty atmosphere of
London provided what Monet called the
enveloppe, the light or atmosphere through
which everything is perceived. In *Waterloo
Bridge, Overcast*, the light from the sky and
its reflections could be read as the subject
of the painting, though the bustling life of
the city – barges on the Thames, buses and
pedestrians on the bridge, factory chimneys
contributing to the smog – fills the canvas.
The foreground and the bridge itself are
relatively clear, while beyond the bridge
the city's industrial life is seen in the misty
blue distance against a pink sky.

The London pictures were usually
finished in the studio rather than while
Monet was in the city, a process that could
take up to two years. In his search for an
ever more truthful representation of what
he had seen, he distanced himself further
and further from it. BA

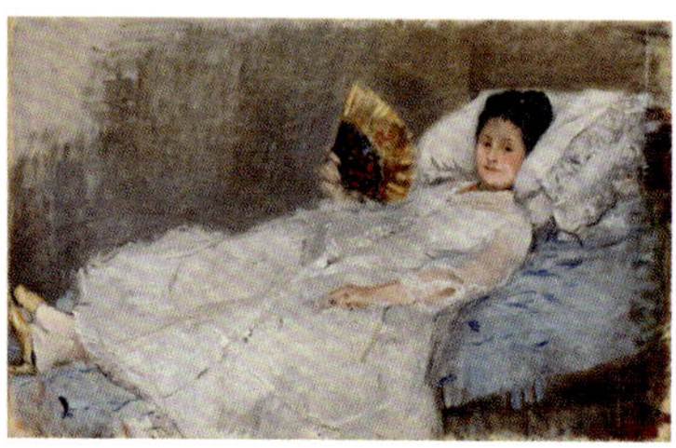

49

*Woman with a Fan (Portrait of
Madame Marie Hubbard)*, 1874
Oil on canvas, 50.5 x 81 cm
Inv. no. 200 WH

PROVENANCE: Marie Hubbard, Paris; 1895, to her
son Gustave-Adolphe Hubbard, Paris (?); Alfred
Stevens, Paris; M. Aulard (auctioneer); 23 December
1910, to Galerie Durand-Ruel, Paris; 1912, to Galerie
Bernheim-Jeune, Paris; 1916 (?), to Wilhelm Hansen

LITERATURE: Angoulvent 1933, no. 122; Bataille and
Wildenstein 1961, no. 33; Clairet et al. 1997, no. 33;
Fonsmark et al. 2011, no. 97

Although Morisot's style shares the
vocabulary of the Impressionists in
representing the ephemerality of
perception, she used her sketch-like
mode of painting as much to evoke the
psychological qualities of her subjects as
to capture nature. Contemporary critics
admired this ability, praising the nervy
sensitivity of her work.

Morisot had a close and complex
relationship with Manet over several
years from their meeting in late 1867 or
1868, modelling for fourteen pictures
and marrying his brother Eugène in 1874.
However, unlike Manet who did not take
part in the Impressionist exhibitions, Morisot
was heavily involved and participated in
seven out of the eight shows, only being
prevented from exhibiting once due to
illness following the birth of her daughter.

Morisot's unconventional portrait of
Marie Hubbard looks like a direct response
to Manet's depiction of women: the
reclining pose, the coloured fan contrasting
with the almost monochrome shades
of the rest of the picture, and the sitter's
direct look are all hallmarks of Manet's
pictures. However, Morisot's portrait does
not feature the challenging indifference

that characterises Manet's early, modern,
erotic and more or less openly provocative
women, such as the famous *Olympia* (1863;
Musée d'Orsay, Paris).

Hubbard, a friend of Morisot's mother
and the wife of a senior civil servant, is
sinking comfortably into the cushions
beneath her head, and all the picture's
features seem to be subordinate to this
state of relaxation. The model is idly cooling
herself with a silk fan and is dressed in
a diaphanous loose-fitting kimono and
slippers – clothing exclusively reserved
for the private sphere. These evoke quite
a different intimacy from that of *Olympia*.
Similarly, the interplay between the model's
gaze and that of the artist and observer is
not hierarchical, as it is between the woman
and the (presumably) male observer of
Olympia. The artist's gaze is returned with
a friendly smile, emphasising the fact that
the staging of Madame Hubbard as a
demi-mondaine is playful, without erotic
charge. BA

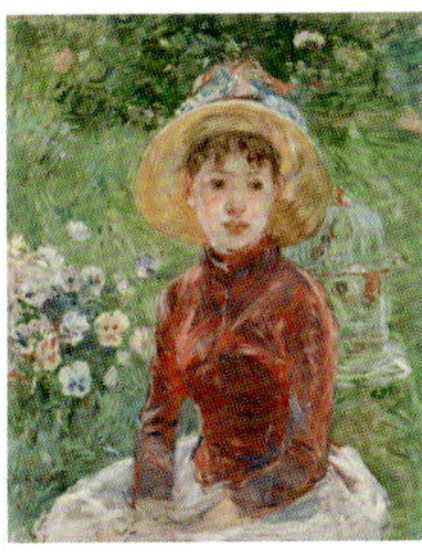

48
*Young Girl on the Grass, the Red Bodice
(Mademoiselle Isabelle Lambert)*, 1885
Oil on canvas, 74 x 60 cm
Inv. no. 251 WH

PROVENANCE: 1896, George Viau, Paris; 4 March 1907, Viau sale, Galerie Durand-Ruel, Paris; repurchased or withdrawn by Viau (?); 1918, to Hansen, Heilbuth, Winkel & Magnussen consortium; 1918, to Wilhelm Hansen (20,000 kr.)

LITERATURE: Angoulvent 1933, no. 247; Bataille and Wildenstein 1961, no. 173; Clairet et al. 1997, no. 177; Fonsmark et al. 2011, no. 98

In *Young Girl on the Grass*, the seventeen-year-old Isabelle Lambert is shown in a garden, halfway between the private indoor space and an external social space. The girl occupies the middle of the picture, her face framed by the dynamic, rotating brush strokes of her straw hat and red jacket. She is surrounded by the whirling, green environment – an insubstantial space characteristic of Morisot's work. Although the model is slender and girlish, her jacket is tight-fitting and adult; despite dominating the painting, she seems almost absent, looking dreamily out but not at the viewer. The caged bird can be interpreted as the traditional metaphor for innocence, while the pansies in the background are an emblem of love, suggesting the sitter is between two worlds, on the cusp of a new period of her life.

Unlike her male contemporaries, who portrayed the domestic spaces occupied by women as alien and exotic, Morisot depicted the private female world as familiar rather than the subject of fantasy. BA

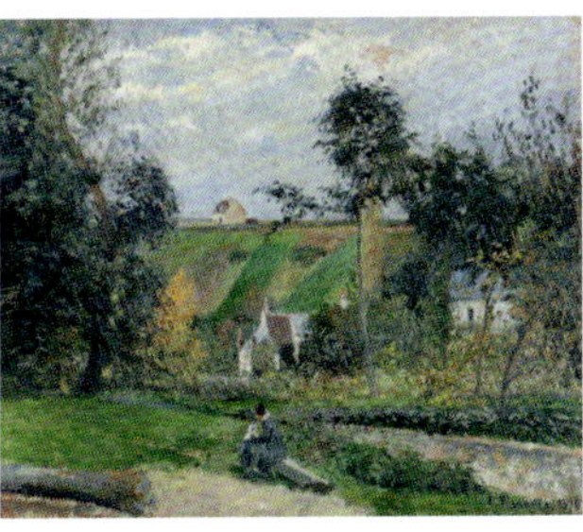

29
*By St Anthony's Brook, The Hermitage,
Pontoise*, 1876
Oil on canvas, 54 x 65 cm
Inv. no. 260 WH

PROVENANCE: Durand-Ruel, Paris (?); Galerie Barbazanges, Paris (?); between 1923 and 1924, to Wilhelm Hansen

LITERATURE: Pissarro and Venturi 1939, no. 348; Fonsmark et al. 2011, no. 99

In 1866–68 and again in 1872–81 Pissarro lived at Pontoise (then a small town about 30 km north-west of Paris), accompanied at times by Cézanne and Gauguin. The young artists of the so-called 'Pontoise School' were starting to use the experimental techniques of the Barbizon School to paint what were then artistically undiscovered areas of France. For Pissarro – leader of the school – light, the seasons and the daily rhythm of life constituted the starting points for his work.

This brook in a village near Pontoise was a favourite subject for Pissarro. In the foreground, a young woman sits with her face turned away from the viewer, leaning towards a small child. Although the figures are suggested by just a few brush strokes, Pissarro convincingly reproduces such details as the woman's flowing blue dress and pinned-up black hair, and her pose suggests maternal affection. The landscape rises behind the figures. The colouring in the middle distance is mainly shades of green, though individual leaves or whole tree trunks glow in warm, golden-orange tones suggesting the rapid approach of autumn. ACWI

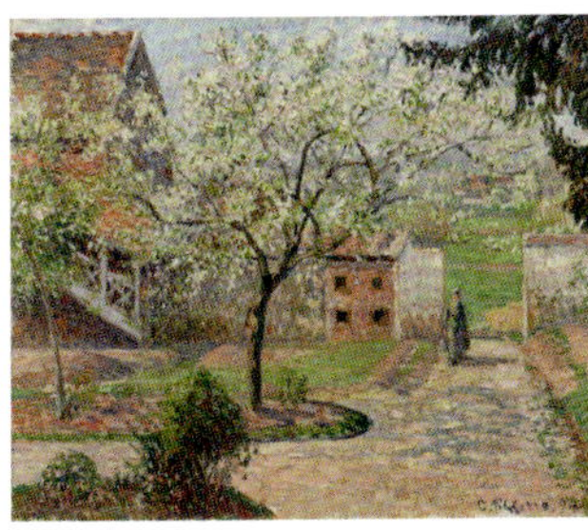

31
*Plum Trees in Blossom, Éragny
(The Painter's Home)*, 1894
Oil on canvas, 60 x 73 cm
Inv. no. 267 WH

PROVENANCE: Maurice Leclanché, Paris; 6 November 1924, Leclanché sale, Hôtel Drouot, Paris; Wilhelm Hansen

LITERATURE: Pissarro and Venturi 1939, no. 877; Fonsmark et al. 2011, no. 100

Pissarro moved to Éragny, to the north-west of Paris, in 1884, living there until his death in 1903. The area was to become his principal source of inspiration. This picture shows the view from his house: on the left-hand side is part of the barn that he had converted into a studio.

The pictorial space in the background is defined by the studio and the wall; in the foreground and middle distance it is primarily the vegetation that creates depth and perspective. The dark green of the branches in the top right-hand corner is matched in the bushes diagonally across. Despite the tight composition, the painting provides a luminous depiction of the fertility of spring, the blossom-covered crown of the plum tree at its centre extending over most of its width. The brush strokes are mainly horizontal or vertical, following natural lines, but a sense of the tree's constant movement is produced by the many-angled strokes that make up the shiny paint layer of the crown.

Although Pissarro rejected Neo-Impressionist Pointillism, this painting has touches of the technique. Pissarro could not embrace Pointillism because the style took him too far from the foundation of his art – nature. ACWI

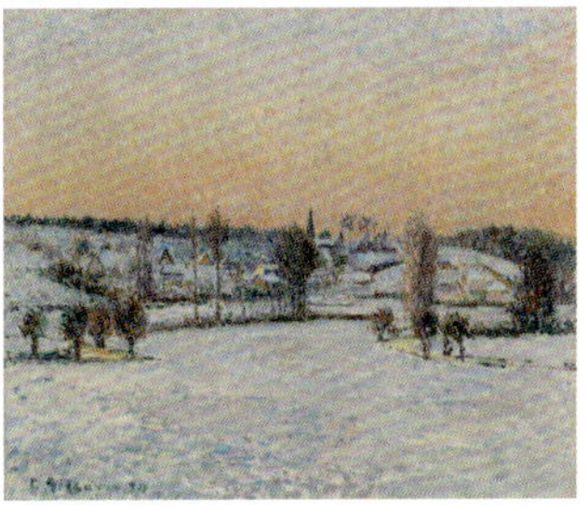

30
Snowy Landscape, Éragny, Evening, 1894
Oil on canvas, 54.5 x 65 cm
Inv. no. 201 WH

PROVENANCE: J. Landau; 24 May 1910, Landau auction; 1916, to Wilhelm Hansen

LITERATURE: Pissarro and Venturi 1939, no. 869; Fonsmark et al. 2011, no. 101

Few Impressionist painters painted *en plein air* during the cold days of winter, and besides, Pissarro suffered throughout his life from an eye condition that forced him to stay indoors for long periods. As a result he had to find his subjects close to home, as in this winter landscape, painted from the second floor of his house and studio at Éragny. Many of his winter pictures record the atmospheric effect of snow on the colours of the landscape, as here, where the pink and gold of the sky just before a snowfall are captured with great precision.

The picture space is structured through variations in colour and the width of the brush strokes, which establish perspective. The snowy foreground is painted in dense, broad strokes while the brush strokes in the middle ground are smaller. The golden sky behind the village opens up with broader, less dense strokes. Furthest away from the viewer, the sky is orange-red, gradually becoming lighter and finally taking on the same blue and white shades as the foreground. The artist's use of colour thus creates a kind of enclosed space into which the viewer looks.

Pissarro considered winter to be the most colourful season and he found the light of high summer cold. Many of his winter pictures – and this landscape in particular – are suffused with colours and warmth. ACWI

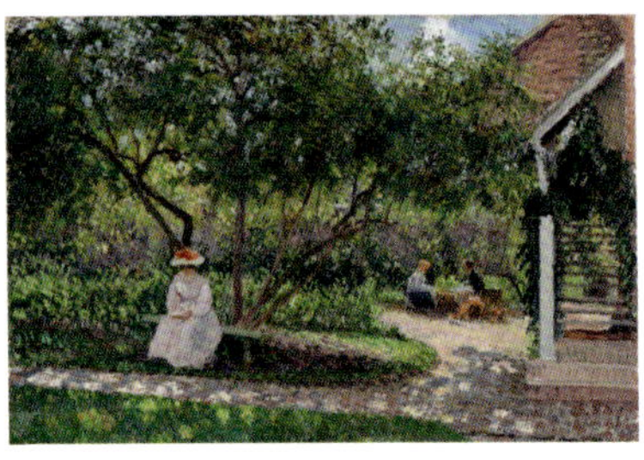

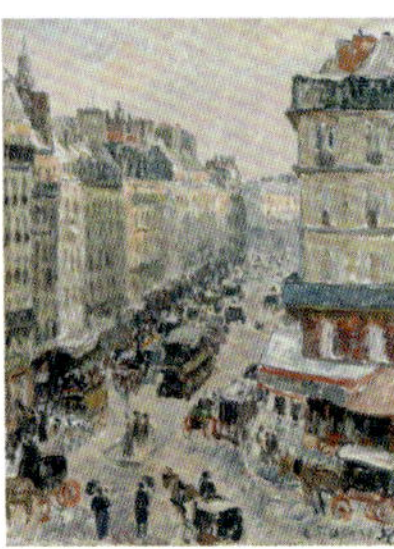

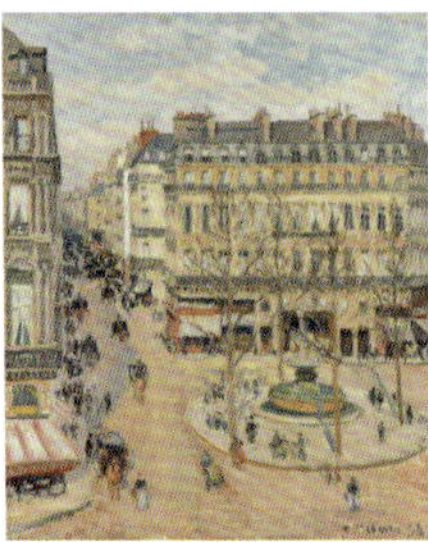

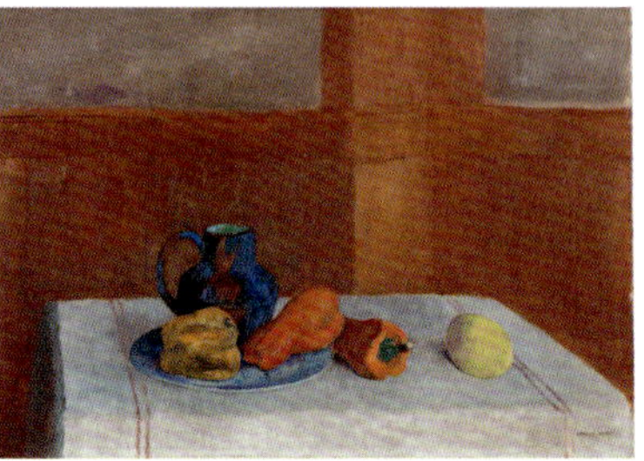

32
A Corner in the Garden, Éragny, 1897
Oil on canvas, 65.5 x 81 cm
Inv. no. 202 WH

PROVENANCE: 1 September 1897, acquired from the artist by Galerie Durand-Ruel, Paris; 25 March 1898, to Duval-Fleury, Paris; probably from here, at the latest in 1921, to Wilhelm Hansen

LITERATURE: Pissarro and Venturi 1939, no. 1011; Fonsmark et al. 2011, no. 102

Late in life, as his failing eyesight made it more difficult to paint in the open air in the countryside, Pissarro continued to find inspiration in his house and garden at Éragny (see cats 30, 31). The changing weather, light and seasons remained his focus but were now depicted in this more intimate context. Here Pissarro paints a corner of his luxuriant garden on a summer afternoon. Paths provide a simple diagonal emphasis and structure while also suggesting that the garden extends beyond the apparently arbitrary and therefore surprising curtailment of the pictorial space. Three figures are incorporated into this image of calm repose.

The dominant green tones contrast with the paths on which the trees cast plum-coloured shadows broken up by brighter patches of sunlight – all characteristic Impressionist elements. Although it is not one of Pissarro's more experimental works, the painting shows a mastery of the representation of the summer sun's mild glow that could only have been attained through long study of the changing light. ACWI

33
Rue Saint-Lazare, Paris, 1897
Oil on canvas, 35 x 27 cm
Inv. no. 300 WH

PROVENANCE: May 1897, acquired from the artist by Durand-Ruel, Paris (?); Félix François Depeaux, Rouen; 31 May–1 June 1906, Depeaux sale, Galerie Georges Petit, Paris; 30 June 1921, Depeaux sale, Hôtel Drouot, Paris; S. Sevadjian, Paris; 1–3 June 1927, Sevadjian sale, Hôtel Drouot, Paris; (?), Wilhelm Hansen

LITERATURE: Pissarro and Venturi 1939, no. 981; Fonsmark et al. 2011, no. 103

In the last ten years of his life, Pissarro painted some eleven series of cityscapes including two sets depicting the area around the Gare Saint-Lazare in Paris. This area had been radically remodelled by Baron Haussmann's urban redevelopment and became an important source of inspiration for the Impressionists, including Monet who painted the Gare Saint-Lazare series between 1876 and 1877. However, Pissarro was not primarily interested in representing modern life but in capturing changing effects of light and weather in the city. Pissarro tended to record views from hotel rooms, explaining the elevated viewpoint of such cityscapes.

Though carefully worked, the brush strokes' sketchiness suggests that the picture was painted quickly and gives it a sense of the movement and life of the city streets. Pissarro varies the number and density of the layers of paint, from thick blotches to thin strokes through which the canvas can be seen. Spots of colour punctuate and enliven the greyness of the atmosphere. ACWI

34
Morning Sun in the Rue Saint-Honoré, Place du Théâtre Français, 1898
Oil on canvas with underlying drawing in black crayon, 65.5 x 54 cm
Inv. no. 261 WH

PROVENANCE: 26 April 1898, acquired from the artist by Durand-Ruel, Paris; between 1923 and 1924, Wilhelm Hansen

LITERATURE: Pissarro and Venturi 1939, no. 1020; Fonsmark et al. 2011, no. 104

Painted from a window at the Hôtel du Louvre, this is one of a series of fifteen pictures of this part of Paris by Pissarro, his intention not to paint a detailed and accurate record, but to capture an impression of the urban scene at a particular moment. In a letter to his son Lucien, Pissarro enthusiastically reported: 'I have found a room at the Grand Hôtel du Louvre with a splendid view … I am delighted to be able to try to do those streets of Paris that one tends to call ugly, but that are so silvery, so luminous and so lively … It's completely modern!'

The sketched main lines of the composition are combined with a wealth of fine detail. In the foreground, for instance, a woman's red hat, white apron and shopping basket are suggested with a few strokes.

The sense of calm contrasts with many contemporary representations of the hectic modern city. Soft colours and Pissarro's sketch-like technique give an air of timelessness, as if the artist's atmospheric paintings of everyday life in country towns, with their slow pace and traditional ways, had influenced his representation of the capital. ACWI

59
Still-life, c. 1901
Oil on canvas, 50 x 73 cm
Inv. no. 285 WH

PROVENANCE: 23 April 1925, sale, Hôtel Drouot, Paris; purchased by Collection Hodebert/ Galerie Barbazanges; May 1925 at the latest, to Wilhelm Hansen

LITERATURE: Berger 1964, no. 234; Wildenstein and Lacau St Guily 1996, no. 1381; Fonsmark et al. 2011, no. 106

Although a contemporary of the Impressionists, Redon had no sympathy with their ideas and worked in a kind of artistic isolation until he met Gauguin in 1886, when he found common ground with the Symbolists. This led to changes in his practice. In place of his bizarre, hallucinatory black-and-white charcoal and print visions of the 1880s, in the 1890s colour became significant and Redon switched to working in pastels, watercolours and oils. His new work contributed to the advent of Fauvism and earned him Matisse's admiration.

Still-life belongs to these later works but is an unusual subject for Redon, whose other such pictures are dominated by flower motifs. The level of realism is also uncharacteristic, though the picture echoes other Symbolist works in the play of the complementary blue and gold.

In this period Redon used colour to suggest the spiritual and magical, like Baudelairean 'correspondences' between the objects or colours of the material world and the ideas, truths or feelings that lie beyond it. His use of colour also has more conventional connections, both to the Christian tradition dating back to the Middle Ages and to Eastern religious imagery, where colours have spiritual significance and power, such as the blue and gold here. BA

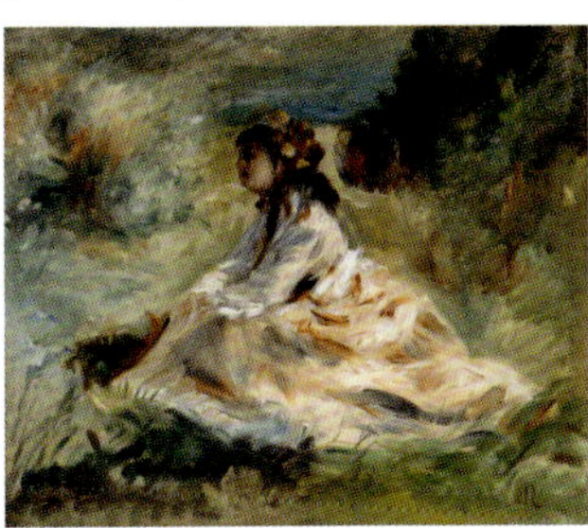

42
Woman in a Meadow (Lise Tréhot), c. 1868
Oil on canvas, 29 x 34.5 cm
Inv. no. 204 WH

PROVENANCE: by 1916, Wilhelm Hansen

LITERATURE: Daulte 1971, vol. 1, no. 35; Fonsmark et al. 2011, no. 107

A contemporary figure in a landscape was a core motif for the later Impressionists – Manet's *Le Déjeuner sur l'herbe* (1863; Musée d'Orsay, Paris) is the best known and Monet's unfinished canvas of the same title perhaps the most ambitious example (see cat. 25), and both were extremely contentious. This little oil sketch is an example of Renoir's characteristic use of this motif, revealing a spontaneous delight in beauty and abandonment to the act of painting, which is just as strong a motivation for him as the pleasure of portraying people in harmony with their surroundings.

Renoir approached figure painting in a much more sensual manner than his contemporaries and introduced it into modern history painting in a relaxed way, apparently untroubled by theory. This comes over clearly in rapid sketches such as *Woman in a Meadow*. Here, the young woman – Lise Tréhot, Renoir's lover and favourite model, then aged twenty – is seen from slightly below, as if Renoir were sitting or lying when he painted her using soft flowing brush strokes. She sits in a relaxed pose, her face barely lit and her wide flowing dress merging with the golden ground and into the enclosing landscape. BA

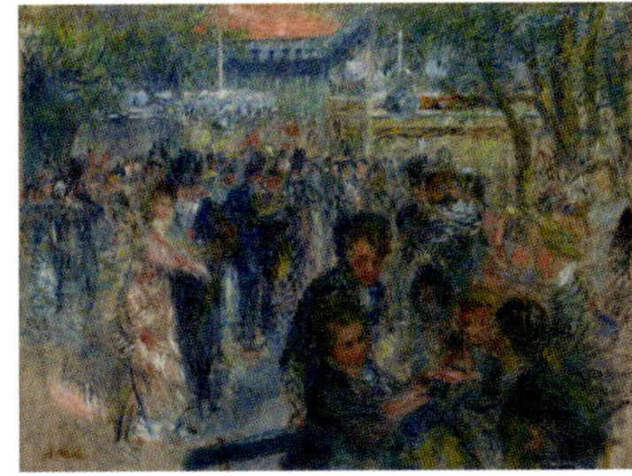

44
Le Moulin de la Galette, Sketch, 1875–76
Oil on canvas, 65 x 85 cm
Inv. no. 271 WH

PROVENANCE: Prince de Wagram, Paris; 1912, Marczell von Nemès, Budapest; 18 June 1913, Nemès sale, Galerie Manzi-Joyant, Paris (17,100 fr.); M. Levesque, Paris; Ambroise Vollard, Paris; 1916, Christian Tetzen-Lund, Copenhagen; Galerie Barbazanges, Paris (?); presumably between 1924 and 1925, Wilhelm Hansen

LITERATURE: Daulte 1971, vol. 1, no. 207; Fezzi 1972, no. 247; Fonsmark et al. 2011, no. 108

In 1875 Renoir set to work on *Dance at Le Moulin de la Galette* (1876; Musée d'Orsay, Paris), his most ambitious work of the mid-1870s, for which he made several sketches including the present work. Le Moulin de la Galette was a popular dance garden and restaurant in Montmartre, where on Sundays local working-class people, artists and students came to dine and dance in the garden. Renoir decided to make the garden the subject of his large-format painting, a monument to the lives of ordinary young people, in contrast with works such as Manet's *Music in the Tuileries Gardens* (1862; National Gallery, London), in which the protagonists are the Parisian upper middle classes.

Dance at Le Moulin de la Galette has no main character – the figures represent Renoir's circle of friends and models, as well as working-class revellers. A group in the foreground attracts our attention but is also part of the flowing rhythm of figures bound together by the soft light and stippled glints that fall through the foliage. The figures themselves form the landscape, and Renoir clearly intended their absorption in the dance as well as the surroundings to embody the carefree and joyful atmosphere.

This quick sketch comes very close to the finished composition now in the Musée d'Orsay. Isolated brush strokes hint at forms and indicate directions and reflections of light in an almost abstract way. However, the composition in the sketch is more compressed, with the result that the foreground group is more dominant and becomes part of a dynamic interplay on the diagonal with the dancing couple on the left. BA

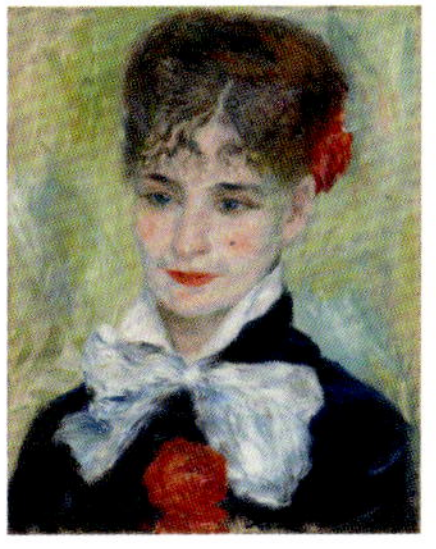

43
Portrait of a Romanian Lady (Madame Iscovesco), 1877
Oil on canvas, 41 x 33 cm
Inv. no. 205 WH

PROVENANCE: Galerie Barbazanges, Paris; by 1916, Wilhelm Hansen

LITERATURE: Daulte 1971, vol. 1, no. 258; Fezzi 1972, no. 300; Fonsmark et al. 2011, no. 109

Renoir was deliberately working as an innovative *modern* painter during the 1870s when he experimented not only with pictures of contemporary life but also with portraits, a genre usually tightly constrained by convention. This picture of Madame Iscovesco is one of his bolder experiments in colour, with its contrasts between the deep violet-blue of her dress, the crimson tones of her lips and the roses and the lemon-yellow background – a combination also seen in the woman's hair and even on her face, where her yellowish complexion with its violet shadows is heightened with the white paint that became the core of Renoir's palette.

Nothing is known about Renoir's model for this picture. With her narrow, sharp features, she does not represent what we think of as the artist's ideal beauty. It is possible that she was a paid model, in which case Renoir could risk experimenting with stark colour contrasts and the coarse, physical modelling of the face. Whatever the circumstances, the contrast between the way the woman's presence fills the painting and her introspective, almost self-absorbed expression is striking. BA

ALFRED SISLEY
(1839–1899)

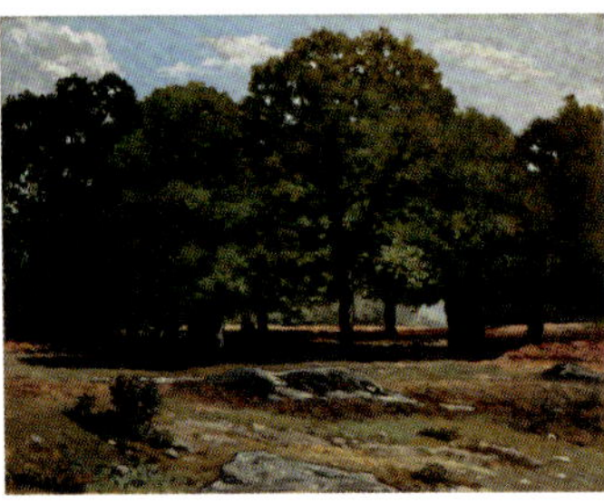

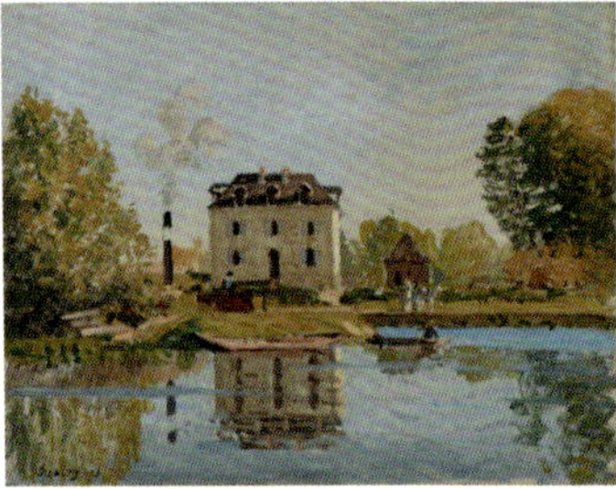

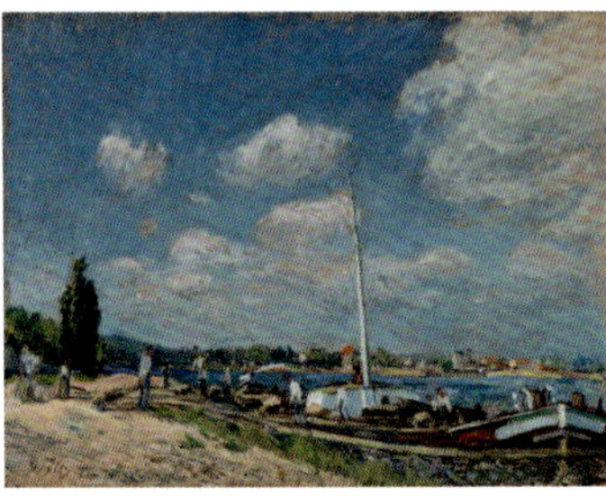

35
*Line of Chestnut Trees at
La Celle-Saint-Cloud*, 1865
Oil on canvas, 50.5 x 65.5 cm
Inv. no. 262 WH

PROVENANCE: 1914, Galerie Durand-Ruel, Paris;
after 1923 and before 14 November 1924, to
Wilhelm Hansen

LITERATURE: Daulte 1959, no. 2; Fonsmark et al. 2011,
no. 121

Sisley was a member of the Impressionists'
inner circle, having met both Monet
and Renoir when they were students of
Charles Gleyre in the early 1860s. Like
them, he was fascinated by the landscapes
of the Barbizon School. Their common
background can clearly be seen if *Line of
Chestnut Trees at La Celle-Saint-Cloud* is
compared with Monet's *The Chailly Road
through the Forest of Fontainebleau* (cat. 25):
both works are painted with broad, dense,
Courbet-inspired brushwork and use the
dark palette characteristic of the later
Impressionists' early landscapes.

The title of Sisley's work refers to
a wooded area west of Paris that was
popular for excursions from the city, but
a closely related painting in the Musée
du Petit Palais, Paris, was first exhibited as
The Edge of the Forest of Fontainebleau.
Both paintings may therefore represent
the Forest of Fontainebleau where Sisley
painted with Monet and Renoir in the mid-
1860s. The present painting may be a study
for the larger picture of the two, though its
confident composition and high degree
of finish suggest it is a work in its own right.
As two interpretations of the same subject,
the pictures are early examples of the
serial works that came to dominate Sisley's
oeuvre and those of other Impressionists. BA

36
*The Flood, Banks of the Seine, Bougival,
1873*
Oil on canvas, 50 x 65.5 cm
Inv. no. 253 WH

PROVENANCE: c. 1873, acquired from the artist
by Edgar Degas; 26 March 1918, Degas collection
auction at Galerie Georges Petit, Paris (15,000 fr.);
to Galerie Trotti for Hansen, Heilbuth, Winkel &
Magnussen consortium; 21 May 1918, to Wilhelm
Hansen (15,000 fr.)

LITERATURE: Daulte 1959, no. 89; Fonsmark et al.
2011, no. 122

In the 1870s Bougival, now a western suburb
of Paris, was a popular leisure destination
made accessible by the expansion of the
railway network. Sisley had moved from
Paris to Louveciennes, along the Seine
just west of Bougival, in 1871, and painted
a series of pictures of the area in which the
river in flood dominates the composition.

The painting's subject is not the
destructive effect of a flood but its
structural pictorial potential. The water
surface forms a broad horizontal band,
while the small factory building and
chimney on the far side create vertical
lines that are extended by reflection. The
reflections establish a formal stability
reminiscent of Corot, and it is perhaps
this that attracted Degas, its first owner,
who was not otherwise interested in
Impressionist landscape painting but did
have a weakness for Corot's early Italian
landscapes.

Unlike the other Impressionists, Sisley
took a fundamentally graphic approach
to landscape painting, planning his
compositions in drawings before he painted
them *en plein air*. This meant he could work
more spontaneously in front of the subject,
as here, where he has apparently used a
wide brush to apply a pale blue underlay
to the whole surface and to sketch the
buildings, trees and their reflections. This
planned spontaneity mirrors the content
of the picture, where the reflections, still
and timeless in the water, are contrasted
with the ephemerality of autumn leaves,
smoke rising from the chimney and the
man gliding past in his boat. BA

37
Unloading Barges at Billancourt, 1877
Oil on canvas, 50 x 65 cm
Inv. no. 273 WH

PROVENANCE: Pontremoli, Paris; 11 June 1924,
Pontremoli sale, Paris; Étienne Bignou, Paris;
between 1924 and 1925, Wilhelm Hansen

LITERATURE: Daulte 1959, no. 274; Fonsmark et al.
2011, no. 123

Sisley anticipated artists such as Seurat,
Signac and Guillaumin in painting scenes
of industrial development. Unlike them,
however, he was not interested in glorifying
the landscape of work. Billancourt, on
the right bank of the Seine in south-west
Paris, had a harbour for barges and some
industry. Most of the views Sisley painted
showed the industrial landscape from
a distance, but in *Unloading Barges at
Billancourt* he chose a closer viewpoint.

The barge pushes its bow into the right
corner to anchor the composition; the
foreground is viewed from a very low angle,
giving the boat monumental presence. The
panoramic view of the red-roofed town
on the far bank provides a line of coloured
accents that contrast with the staccato
rhythm of the white-shirted men unloading
the barges onto barrows in the foreground.

These working men occupy a small part
of the picture in comparison with the wide,
high sky – dense blue with scudding clouds
– over the low horizon. As an Impressionist,
Sisley was fascinated by light and equally
by the sky, insisting that it 'is never just a
backdrop … It gives the picture depth not
simply through its successive planes (for
the sky has planes, just like the earth), but
through its form and its relationship to
the whole effect or to the picture's
composition – it gives it movement.' BA

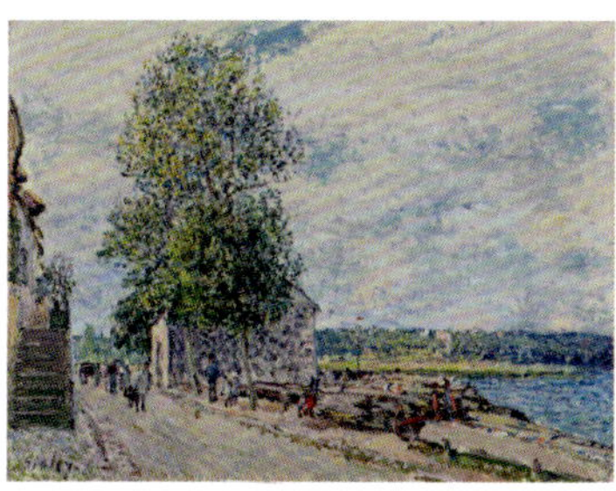

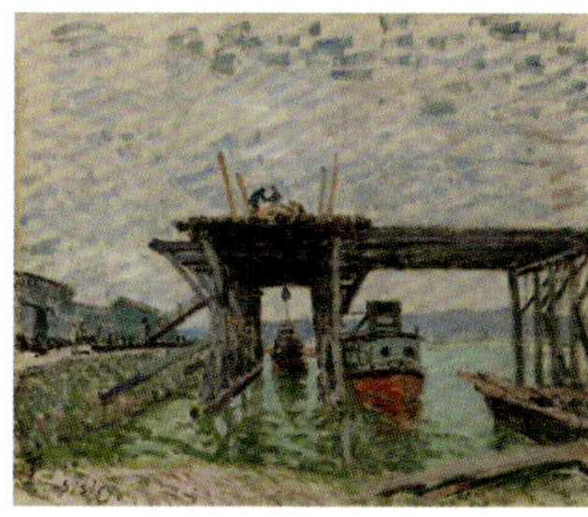

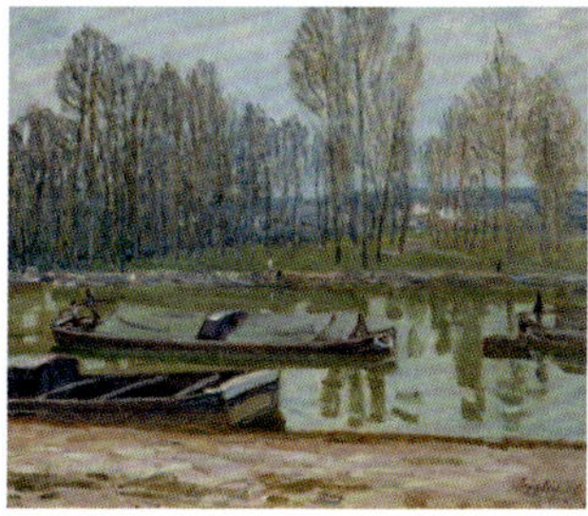

38

September Morning near Saint-Mammès and the Veneux-Nadon Hills, 1884
Oil on canvas, 54 x 72.5 cm
Inv. no. 269 WH

PROVENANCE: Jean-Baptiste Faure, Paris; 1 March 1900, Durand-Ruel, Paris; 14 November 1924, Wilhelm Hansen

LITERATURE: Daulte 1959, no. 551; Fonsmark et al. 2011, no. 124

It was at Sisley's home town of Saint-Mammès that he began his practice of painting the same subject from different angles. Saint-Mammès, where the confluence of the rivers Seine and Loing imparted a special atmosphere to the riverside moorings, particularly inspired him. In this painting, the river acts as a backdrop to the village street. Two tall trees cut the picture in two, with the right-hand side depicting the view towards the town of Veneux-Nadon on the horizon. It was characteristic of Sisley to give his pictures titles that refer not only to the geographical situation of the subject, but also to the time of day, the season, or weather conditions, indicating that he wanted to capture these fleeting effects as much as the specific physical aspects of the landscape.

A preparatory sketch shows Sisley trying to capture the view in a compact composition formed from the steps of the building to the left, the tree and the vertical lines of the building behind it, which frame and anchor the other lines. However, the finished picture shows no sign of planning and instead gives an impression of spontaneity. Brush strokes are free and almost experimental, from the dynamic, directional lines on the road to the chaotic whirling movements in the sky that give the picture's surface its restless character. BA

39

The River Boat Garage, 1885
Oil on canvas, 46 x 56 cm
Inv. no. 230 WH

PROVENANCE: Léon Daudet, Paris; 17 December 1903, Durand-Ruel, Paris; 22 November 1906, Paul Rosenberg, Paris; 1918, Wilhelm Hansen

LITERATURE: Daulte 1959, no. 582; Fonsmark et al. 2011, no. 125

Everyday life along the banks of the river was a constant source of fascination for Sisley. Around 1885 he painted a series of pictures centred on boat building and repair. This example, painted from an uncompromisingly frontal viewpoint, records the monumentality of the wooden structures in the riverscape, animated by the barge entering the shed from the back and the men busy on the roof. For a long time, the subject was misunderstood as a bridge under construction.

The picture takes its tone from the balance of the blue–pink sky, the green river water with its pale surface reflections, the violet hills in the background and the pink earth in the foreground, the whole bathed in a misty light derived from the unpainted canvas, which can be seen behind the sparse brushwork. As an Impressionist *par excellence*, Sisley was interested above all in capturing the diffusion of light and the movement of air. BA

40

Barges from Berry on the Loing Canal in Spring, 1896
Oil on canvas, 54 x 65 cm
Inv. no. 231 WH

PROVENANCE: 1 May 1899, Sisley sale, Galerie Georges Petit (4,600 fr.); Adolphe Tavernier, Paris; 6 March 1900, Tavernier sale, Galerie Georges Petit (5,150 fr.); Marquise Arconati-Visconti, Paris; Bernheim-Jeune, Paris; Prince de Wagram, Paris; 1918, Wilhelm Hansen

LITERATURE: Daulte 1959, no. 847; Fonsmark et al. 2011, no. 126

During the last twenty years of his life Sisley became increasingly reclusive, rarely visiting Paris and not participating in discussions about the Symbolist and Post-Impressionist artists' challenge to Impressionism. However, Monet's serial pictures were clearly a source of inspiration. In 1891 Sisley painted two pictures of haystacks, presumably with Monet's paintings of haystacks from 1890–91 in mind. In 1893–94 he painted a series of pictures of Moret-sur-Loing's medieval cathedral, probably inspired by Monet's pictures of Rouen Cathedral from 1892 and 1893.

Monet was pushing observational analysis to the point where objective observation turns into purely subjective painting – thus engaging with the concerns of the Symbolists and Neo-Impressionists. By contrast, Sisley's serial painting – often featuring rivers and canals – was a way of analysing a subject from different viewpoints and angles rather than a process of experimentation with the means of expression.

Barges from Berry on the Loing Canal in Spring is composed in strips running parallel to the picture plane: the canal bank and the canal with low barges emphasising the weighty movement of the water, with open woodland beyond, and further away still a town bounded on the horizon by a range of hills.

Despite its title, the picture is infused with a subdued and luminous winter clarity, captured with soft brush strokes. Its simplicity should not imply that it is a symbolic, subjective work. The contrast between the horizontal canal and the skeleton-like poplars is one Sisley had recorded in his earlier pictures of the Loing Canal: the painting's origin – as ever with Sisley – is nature itself. BA

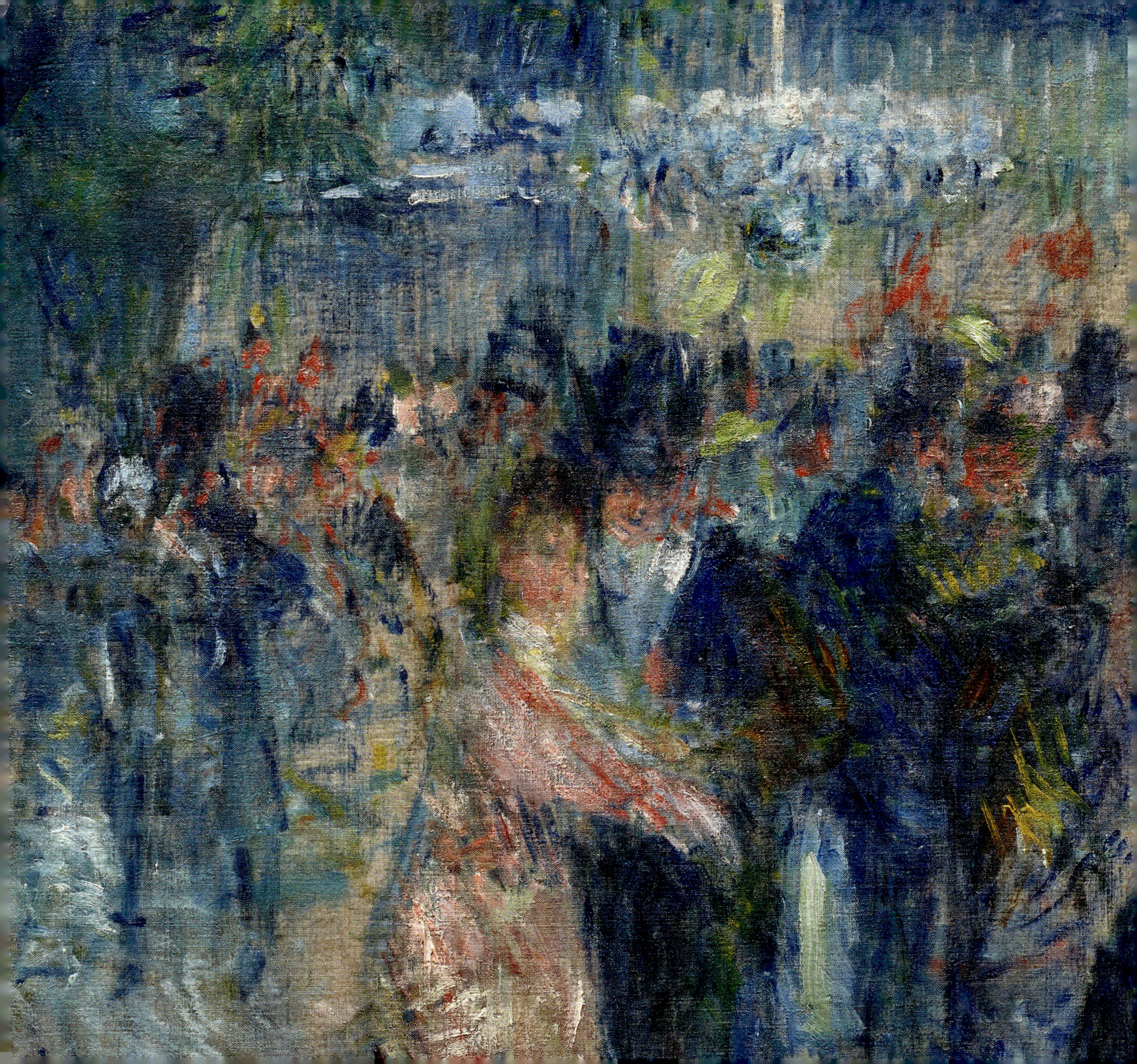

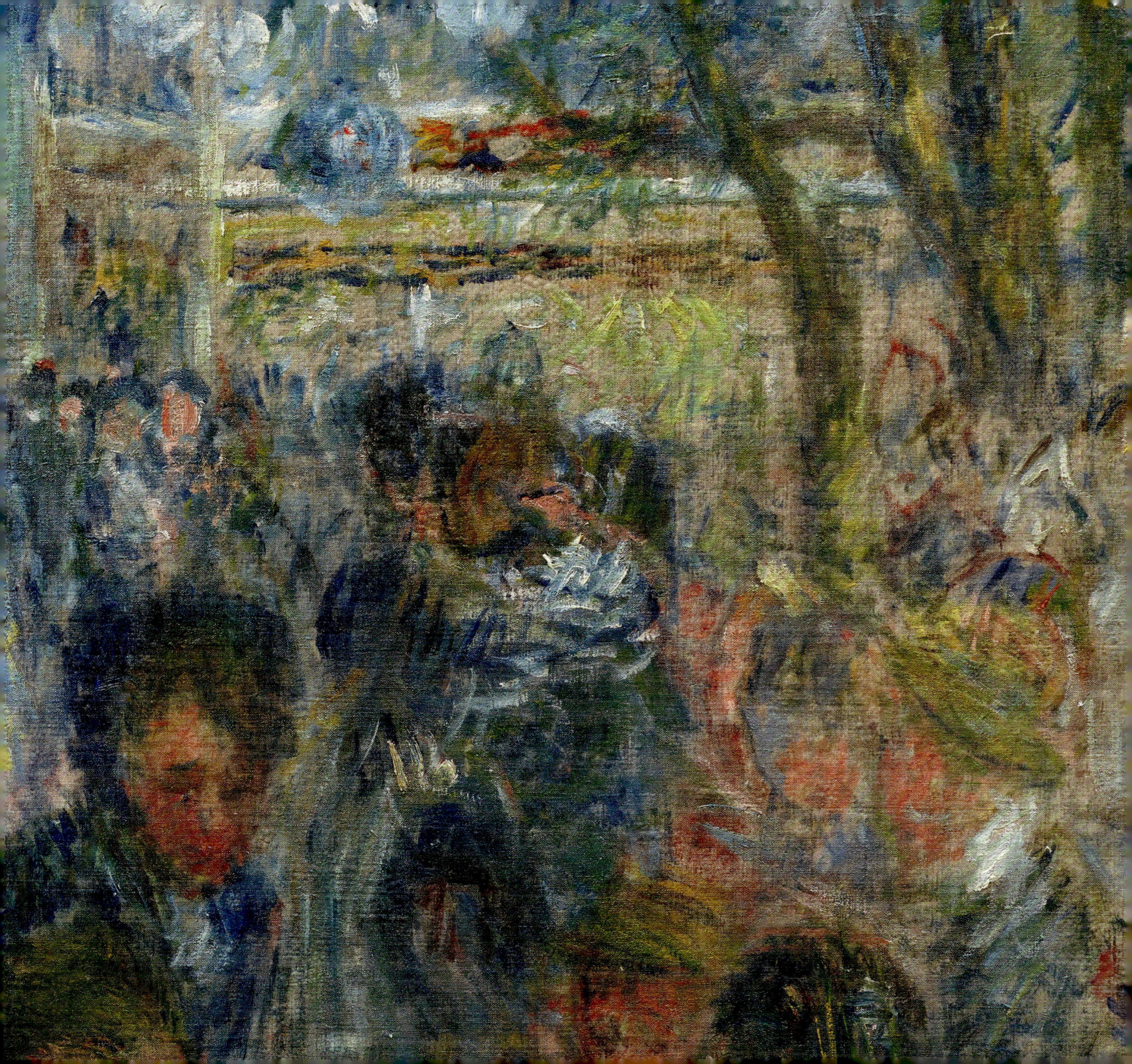

Endnotes

An Introduction to Wilhelm Hansen's Collection of French Art at Ordrupgaard
Anne-Birgitte Fonsmark (pages 13–23)

With the exception of its two closing paragraphs, this essay was first published by Hatje Cantz Verlag, Ostfildern, in the catalogue French Art at Ordrupgaard *(2011). The original text is copyright © Hatje Cantz Verlag, Ostfildern; Ordrupgaard, Copenhagen; and the author, 2011. It is reprinted here in an abridged version by kind permission of the three copyright holders.*

1 See former Hafnia staff member Erik Schøller Larsen (March 2000); the information, presented by Ernst Jonas Bencard, can also be found in Leo Swane, *Etatsråd Wilhelm Hansen og hustru Henny Hansens malerisamling: katalog over kunstværkerne på Ordrupgaard*, Copenhagen, 1954, p. 11.

2 Haavard Rostrup, *Franske malerier på Ordrupgaard*, Copenhagen, 1978, pp. 18 and 10.

3 Ordrupgaard Archive (abbreviated as 'OA' in subsequent entries), nos 137 WH and 389.

4 Anne-Birgitte Fonsmark, 'Wilhelm Hansen's Collection of Danish Art at Ordrupgaard', in Birgitte Anderberg and Thomas Lederballe (eds), *Ordrupgaard: Danish Art from the Century of the Golden Age*, Copenhagen, 1999, pp. 6–23.

5 See Rostrup, *Franske malerier på Ordrupgaard*, 1978, and Anderberg and Lederballe, *Ordrupgaard: Danish Art*, 1999.

6 OA, summary of capsule 2, p. 17.

7 Letters from Wilhelm Hansen to Henny Hansen (abbreviated as 'WH' and 'HH' in subsequent entries), 3 and 4 January 1893, OA, capsule 3.

8 See Rostrup, *Franske malerier på Ordrupgaard*, 1978, p. 17.

9 See Karl Madsen (intr.), *Fransk malerkunst fra det nittende aarhundrede*, exh. cat., Statens Museum for Kunst, Copenhagen, 1914.

10 Letter from Tyge Møller, Paris, to Helge Jacobsen, Ny Carlsberg Glyptotek, 29 January 1916, Ny Carlsberg Glyptotek archive, Copenhagen.

11 Ibid.

12 Klas Fåhræus to WH, 19 September 1918, OA, capsule 1.

13 WH to HH, 22 September 1916, OA, capsule 6. He also mentions exercising self-control: 'Courbet's self-portrait – (you remember the photograph I had of that) – is wonderful, but I did not buy it, the price will have to fall a lot before I can think of purchasing it.'

14 WH to HH, 20 September 1916, OA, capsule 6.

15 See Anne Distel, *Impressionism: The First Collectors*, New York, 1990, pp. 57ff.

16 Théodore Duret to WH, 4 October 1916, OA, capsule 2.

17 Rostrup, *Franske malerier på Ordrupgaard*, 1978, p. 24.

18 Ibid.; Théodore Duret to WH, 8 November 1917, OA, capsule 2, p. 6.

19 WH to HH, 14 February 1919, OA, capsule 6.

20 The art dealer Asta Møller to Helge Jacobsen, 1 February 1919, Ny Carlsberg Glyptotek Archive, Copenhagen.

21 WH to HH, 14 March 1919, OA, capsule 6.

22 WH to HH, 9 November 1919, OA, capsule 6.

23 Rostrup, *Franske malerier på Ordrupgaard*, 1978, p. 26.

24 Distel, *Impressionism*, 1990, p. 39.

25 See letter from Claire Durand-Ruel Snollaerts, 2 July 1997, Wildenstein Institute, Paris.

26 See Ann Dumas et al., *The Private Collection of Edgar Degas*, exh. cat., The Metropolitan Museum of Art, New York, 1997–98.

27 Rostrup, *Franske malerier på Ordrupgaard*, 1978, p. 27.

28 On this subject, see Per H. Hansen and Søren Mørch, *Den Danske Bank*, Copenhagen, 1997, inter alia p. 240.

29 WH to HH, 19 September 1922, OA, capsule 6.

30 WH to HH, 23 September 1922, OA, capsule 6.

31 This is clear from the letter from Frederik Poulsen to the attorney L. Zeuthen, 2 February 1923; see Mikael Wivel, *Ordrupgaard: udvalgte værker*, Copenhagen, 1993, p. 38.

32 Léonce Bénédite negotiated and selected works on Matsukata's behalf, probably on the basis of a contract to spend a fixed amount, namely 1,500,000 francs.

33 Hansen as quoted by Kai Borchsenius in the feature article in the daily newspaper *Politiken*, 14 September 1943; see Wivel, *Ordrupgaard: udvalgte værker*, 1993, p. 37, note 43, and Rostrup, *Franske malerier på Ordrupgaard*, 1978, p. 34.

34 WH to HH, 23 January 1924, OA, capsule 6; reference is made inter alia to the list of the OA, *Résumé of Sale*, by Andrea Rygg Karberg and Ernst Jonas Bencard, 1998, pp. 57ff.

35 See Ernst Jonas Bencard's investigation of WH's inventory cards of the collection of French art (in OA); the periodical *Samleren* in its issue of June 1925 carried an article entitled 'The Recovery of the Ordrupgaard Collection'.

36 See Bencard's investigation of WH's inventory cards for the collection of French art (in OA).

37 Richard R. Brettell and Anne-Birgitte Fonsmark, *Gauguin and Impressionism*, exh. cat., Ordrupgaard, Copenhagen; Kimbell Art Museum, Fort Worth, 2005–06, no. 41.

38 Rostrup, *Franske malerier på Ordrupgaard*, 1978, p. 26.

'A wartime price': Collecting French Painting in Copenhagen
Anna Ferrari (pages 25–31)

1 Their French collection consisted of 156 works in 1922 before Hansen sold part of it to pay his debt to the Danish Landmandsbank. See Anne-Birgitte Fonsmark on pp. 18–20 of the present catalogue.

2 Théodore Duret published *Les Peintres impressionnistes: Claude Monet, Sisley, C. Pissarro, Renoir, Berthe Morisot* in Paris in 1878, followed by *Histoire des peintres impressionnistes: Pissarro, Claude Monet, Sisley, Renoir, Berthe Morisot, Cézanne, Guillaumin* in Paris in 1906, a copy of which Hansen owned. Camille Mauclair published *L'Impressionnisme: son histoire, son esthétique, ses maîtres* in Paris in 1904.

3   Ann Dumas, 'Introduction', in Ann Dumas and Michael E. Shapiro (eds), *Impressionism: Paintings Collected by European Museums*, exh. cat., High Museum of Art, Atlanta; Seattle Art Museum; Denver Art Museum, 1999, pp. 12–27, p. 22.

4   Shchukin started collecting works by Monet in 1898, before buying paintings by Degas, Cézanne, Gauguin, Van Gogh, Matisse and, eventually, Picasso. By the time the First World War broke out, he owned 51 Picassos, the largest collection in the world. Morozov favoured Bonnard, Gauguin and especially Cézanne but also collected works by Monet, Renoir and Picasso. Both collections were confiscated during the Russian Revolution and are today divided between the Pushkin Museum of Fine Arts in Moscow and the Hermitage Museum in St Petersburg.

5   Anne Distel, *Les Collectionneurs des impressionnistes: amateurs et marchands*, Paris, 1989, p. 239.

6   Other Danish collectors, such as the tobacco manufacturer Heinrich Hirschsprung (1836–1908) and his wife Pauline (1845–1912), focused exclusively on Danish art from the nineteenth and early twentieth centuries. The Hirschsprungs started collecting in 1866 and gave their collection to the Danish nation in 1902. Their collection was opened to the public in 1911.

7   Quoted in Flemming Friborg, 'The Clash of Generations: Carl and Helge Jacobsen's Views on Art', in Flemming Friborg et al., *Ancient Art to Post-Impressionism: Masterpieces from the Ny Carlsberg Glyptotek, Copenhagen*, exh. cat., Royal Academy of Arts, London, 2004, pp. 22–25, p. 24. See also Kristof Glamann, *Beer and Marble: Carl Jacobsen of New Carlsberg*, Copenhagen, 1996, p. 124.

8   Görel Cavalli-Björkman, 'The Reception of Impressionism in Scandinavia and Finland', in Dumas and Shapiro, *Impressionism*, 1999, pp. 91–96, p. 91.

9   Ibid.

10 Friborg in Friborg et al., *Masterpieces from the Ny Carlsberg Glyptotek*, 2004, pp. 22–25, p. 24.

11 Of the 40 artists whose work Hansen collected before 1922, 33 were represented in the 1914 French art exhibition. The best-represented artists at the exhibition were Delacroix, Corot, Manet, Monet, Renoir, Sisley, Gauguin and Cézanne, who were also those most featured in Hansen's collection, except for Delacroix whose works were unavailable to buy, according to Duret.

12 His collection included German and Dutch seventeenth-century works, and Danish drawings from the seventeenth century onwards. See Kasper Monrad (ed.), *Henri Matisse: Four Great Collectors*, exh. cat., Statens Museum for Kunst, Copenhagen, 1999, p. 166.

13 Malcolm Gee, 'Johannes Rump', *Grove Art Online*, accessed 8 November 2019.

14 These included Courbet's *Three Young Englishwomen by a Window* (1865); Manet's *The Absinthe Drinker* (1859) and *The Execution of the Emperor Maximilian* (1867); Sisley's *Inundation: The Ferry of the Île de la Bac* (1872) and *The Furrows* (1873); Monet's *Shadows on the Sea: The Cliffs at Pourville* (1882); and Gauguin's *Landscape from Tahiti with Four Figures* (c. 1893). See the catalogue of works from the Glyptotek in Friborg et al., *Masterpieces from the Ny Carlsberg Glyptotek*, 2004.

15 Jacobsen bought David's *Portrait of the Comte de Turenne* (1816); Corot's *In Deep Thought* (1850–60); Delacroix's *The Death of Charles the Bold at the Battle of Nancy* (1828) and *Young Lioness* (1832); Daumier's *Before the Judge* (1850–60); Millet's *Cutting the Cabbage* (c. 1853) and *Woman Sewing* (c. 1853); Courbet's *Self-portrait* (c. 1853); Manet's *Portrait of Madame Isabelle Lemonnier* (1879–82); Degas's *Dancers in the Foyer* (c. 1880–90) and *Dancers in Red Skirts* (c. 1884); Cézanne's *Self-portrait* (1885–86) and *Nature morte* (1879–82); Renoir's *Young Girls* (c. 1877); Toulouse-Lautrec's *Portrait of Monsieur Delaporte* (1893); and Van Gogh's *Portrait of 'Le Père Tanguy'* (1887). Helge Jacobsen donated his collection of French art to the Glyptotek in 1927.

16 Tetzen-Lund later dispersed his collection, and, as it was never fully catalogued, its exact extent is unknown; see Monrad, *Matisse: Four Great Collectors*, 1999, p. 137. Until now, little has been known about Tetzen-Lund's collection but recent research at the Statens Museum for Kunst, Copenhagen, is uncovering new material. See Dorthe Aagesen, 'Christian Tetzen-Lund, Johannes Rump and Danish Collections of Modern French Art, 1900–25', conference paper presented at 'The Sergei Shchukin Collection: History, Impact and International Context', Boris Vipper Memorial Conference, Pushkin Museum of Fine Arts, Moscow, 11–13 September 2019. Accessed 3 December 2019.

17 Hans Edvard Nørregård-Nielsen, 'A Dynasty of Brewers and Collectors', in Friborg et al., *Masterpieces from the Ny Carlsberg Glyptotek*, 2004, pp. 10–13.

18 Géraldine David, 'Is Art Really a Safe Haven? Evidence from the French Art Market During the First World War', Université Libre de Bruxelles, CEB Working Paper, no. 14/025, October 2014, p. 10.

19 Ibid.

20 Ibid., p. 21.

21 'La personne qui possédait ce portrait avant la guerre en demandait 80 mille francs, mais il me semble que vous devriez l'avoir présentement entre 30 et 50 mille francs.' Théodore Duret to WH, 4 October 1916, OA. Hansen did not buy this painting and it is today in the Staatliche Kunsthalle Karlsruhe.

22 Duret to WH, 6 July 1917 and 8 November 1917, OA.

23 For example, Courbet's *The Cliffs near Étretat* (cat. 8) and Cézanne's *Women Bathing* (cat. 58) belonged to the important collector Alphonse Kann, and Monet's *The Chailly Road through the Forest of Fontainebleau* (cat. 25) had been owned by Jean-Baptiste Faure and then Henri Rouart, two early amateurs of Impressionism.

24 Rolf Hobson, Tom Kristiansen, Nils Arne Sørensen and Gunnar Åselius, 'Introduction: Scandinavia in the First World War', in Claes Ahlund (ed.), *Scandinavia in the First World War: Studies in the War Experience of the Northern Neutrals*, Lund, 2012, p. 18.

25 Émile Duval-Fleury, a Parisian director of a branch of Hansen's insurance company Hafnia, helped Hansen and his consortium with logistics, safely storing newly purchased works before organising transport to Copenhagen via Switzerland where they were shown in two exhibitions at the Musée d'art et d'histoire in Geneva in 1918 ('Exposition d'art français', 15 May to 23 June, and 'Exposition de tableaux anciens et modernes: Collection de M. le conseiller d'état Hansen à Copenhague', 9 to 22 December). See Rasmus Kjærboe, 'Collecting the Modern: Ordrupgaard and the Collection Museums of Modernist Art', PhD thesis, Aarhus University, 2016, pp. 367–69.

26 Dorthe Aagesen, 'The Avant-garde Takes Copenhagen', in Dorthe Aagesen et al., *The Avant-garde in Danish and European Art, 1909–19*, exh. cat., Statens Museum for Kunst, Copenhagen, 2002–03, pp. 152–71.

27 Hobson et al. in Ahlund, *Scandinavia in the First World War*, 2012, p. 30.

28 See Anne-Birgitte Fonsmark on p. 14 of the present catalogue.

29 Hobson et al. in Ahlund, *Scandinavia in the First World War*, 2012, p. 23. See also Bjarne Søndergaard Bendtsen, 'Making Sense of the War (Denmark)', in Ute Daniel, Peter Gatrell, Oliver Janz, Heather Jones, Jennifer Keene, Alan Kramer and Bill Nasson (eds), *1914–1918 Online. International Encyclopaedia of the First World War*, issued by Freie Universität Berlin, 13 September 2017.

30 Aagesen, *The Avant-garde in Danish and European Art*, 2002–03, p. 168.

31 Arsène Alexandre, 'Offensive et Défensive de nos Collections', *La Renaissance de l'art français et des industries de luxe*, April 1918, pp. 1–2, p. 1.

32 Aagesen et al., *The Avant-garde in Danish and European Art*, 2002–03, p. 164.

33 Romy Golan, *Modernity and Nostalgia: Art and Politics in France between the Wars*, New Haven, 1995, pp. 28–30.

34 Marianne Wirenfeldt Asmussen, *Wilhelm Hansen's Original French Collection at Ordrupgaard*, Copenhagen, 1993, p. 56.

Selected Bibliography

Catalogues and Exhibitions of the Ordrupgaard Collection

Birgitte Anderberg and Thomas Lederballe (eds), *Ordrupgaard: Danish Art from the Century of the Golden Age*, Copenhagen, 1999

Richard R. Brettell and Anne-Birgitte Fonsmark, *Gauguin and Impressionism*, exh. cat., Ordrupgaard, Copenhagen; Kimbell Art Museum, Fort Worth, 2005–06

Pierre Curie and Anne-Birgitte Fonsmark (eds), *Le Jardin secret des Hansen: la collection Ordrupgaard*, exh. cat., Musée Jacquemart-André, Paris, 2017

Anne-Birgitte Fonsmark et al., *French Art at Ordrupgaard: Complete Catalogue of Paintings, Sculptures, Pastels, Drawings and Prints*, Berlin and Stuttgart, 2011

Thomas Lederballe and Rebecca Rabinow (eds), *The Age of Impressionism: European Paintings from Ordrupgaard*, Copenhagen, exh. cat., Walters Art Museum, Baltimore; The Metropolitan Museum of Art, New York; Museum of Fine Arts, Houston, 2002

Karl Madsen, *Malerisamlingen Ordrupgaard, Wilhelm Hansens samling: malerier, akvareller, pasteller, tegninger af franske kunstnere*, Copenhagen, 1918

Haavard Rostrup, *Franske malerier på Ordrupgaard*, Copenhagen, 1978

Haavard Rostrup, *Histoire du Musée d'Ordrupgaard, 1918–78: d'après des documents inédits*, Copenhagen, 1981

Petr Šámal (ed.), *French Impressionism: Masterpieces from the Ordrupgaard Collection*, exh. cat., Národní Galerie, Prague, 2019

Leo Swane, *Etatsråd Wilhelm Hansen og hustru Henny Hansens malerisamling: katalog over kunstværkerne på Ordrupgaard*, Copenhagen, 1954

Paul Lang, *Impressionist Treasures: The Ordrupgaard Collection*, exh. cat., National Gallery of Canada, Ottawa, 2018

Paul Lang and Martha Degiacomi, *Trésors impressionnistes: la collection Ordrupgaard*, Fondation Pierre Gianadda, Martigny, 2019

Marianne Wirenfeldt Asmussen, *Wilhelm Hansen's Original French Collection at Ordrupgaard*, Copenhagen, 1993

Mikael Wivel, *Ordrupgaard: udvalgte værker*, Copenhagen, 1993

General Publications

Dorthe Aagesen et al., *The Avant-garde in Danish and European Art, 1909–19*, exh. cat., Statens Museum for Kunst, Copenhagen, 2002–03

Claes Ahlund (ed.), *Scandinavia in the First World War: Studies in the War Experience of the Northern Neutrals*, Lund, 2012

Richard R. Brettell and Joachim Pissarro, *Pissarro à Éragny: la nature retrouvée*, exh. cat., Musée du Luxembourg, Paris, 2017

Norma Broude and Mary D. Garrard (eds), *The Expanding Discourse: Feminism and Art History*, New York, 1992

Norma Broude (ed.), *Gauguin's Challenge: New Perspectives After Postmodernism*, New York, 2018

Caroline Corbeau-Parsons, *Impressionists in London: French Artists in Exile, 1870–1904*, exh. cat., Tate Britain, London; Petit Palais, Paris, 2017–18

Anne Distel, *Impressionism: The First Collectors*, New York, 1990

Anne Distel, *Les Collectionneurs des impressionnistes: amateurs et marchands*, Paris, 1989

Douglas W. Druick and Peter Kort Zegers, *Van Gogh and Gauguin: The Studio of the South*, exh. cat., Art Institute of Chicago; Van Gogh Museum, Amsterdam, 2002

Ann Dumas et al., *The Private Collection of Edgar Degas*, exh. cat., The Metropolitan Museum of Art, New York, 1997–98

Ann Dumas and Michael E. Shapiro (eds), *Impressionism: Paintings Collected by European Museums*, exh. cat., High Museum of Art, Atlanta; Seattle Art Museum; Denver Art Museum, 1999

Ann Dumas et al., *Alfred Sisley: poète de l'impressionnisme*, exh. cat., Musée des Beaux-Arts, Lyon, 2002–03

Théodore Duret, *Les Peintres impressionnistes: Claude Monet, Sisley, C. Pissarro, Renoir, Berthe Morisot*, Paris, 1878

Théodore Duret, *Histoire des peintres impressionnistes: Pissarro, Claude Monet, Sisley, Renoir, Berthe Morisot, Cézanne, Guillaumin*, Paris, 1906

Gail Feigenbaum (ed.), *Degas and New Orleans: A French Impressionist in America*, exh. cat., New Orleans Museum of Art, 2000

Dominique de Font-Réaulx et al., *Gustave Courbet*, exh. cat., The Metropolitan Museum of Art, New York, 2008

Flemming Friborg et al., *Ancient Art to Post-Impressionism: Masterpieces from the Ny Carlsberg Glyptotek, Copenhagen*, exh. cat., Royal Academy of Arts, London, 2004

Chantal Georgel, *La Forêt de Fontainebleau: un atelier grandeur nature*, exh. cat., Musée d'Orsay, Paris, 2007

Kristof Glamann, *Beer and Marble: Carl Jacobsen of New Carlsberg*, Copenhagen, 1996

Robert L. Herbert, *Impressionism: Art, Leisure and Parisian Society*, New Haven, 1988

Sarah Herring, *Corot to Monet: French Landscape Painting*, exh. cat., National Gallery, London, 2009

Johan den Hertog and Samuël Kruizinga (eds), *Caught in the Middle: Neutrals, Neutrality and the First World War*, Amsterdam, 2011

Cornelia Homburg and Christopher Riopelle, *Gauguin: Portraits*, exh. cat., National Gallery of Canada, Ottawa; National Gallery, London, 2019–20

Rasmus Kjærboe, 'Collecting the Modern: Ordrupgaard and the Collection Museums of Modernist Art', PhD thesis, Aarhus University, 2016

Karl Madsen (intr.), *Fransk malerkunst fra det nittende aarhundrede*, exh. cat., Statens Museum for Kunst, Copenhagen, 1914

Kasper Monrad (ed.), *Henri Matisse: Four Great Collectors*, exh. cat., Statens Museum for Kunst, Copenhagen, 1999

Sylvie Patry (ed.), *Inventing Impressionism: Paul Durand-Ruel and the Modern Art Market*, exh. cat., Musée du Luxembourg, Paris; National Gallery, London; Philadelphia Museum of Art, 2014–15

Sylvie Patry et al., *Berthe Morisot: Woman Impressionist*, exh. cat., Musée national des beaux-arts de Québec; Barnes Foundation, Philadelphia; Dallas Museum of Art; Musée d'Orsay, Paris, 2018–19

Ingrid Pfeiffer and Max Hollein (eds), *Women Impressionists: Berthe Morisot, Mary Cassatt, Eva Gonzalès, Marie Bracquemond*, exh. cat., Schirn Kunsthalle Frankfurt, 2008

Eliza E. Rathbone (ed.), *Impressionists on the Seine: A Celebration of Renoir's Luncheon of the Boating Party*, exh. cat., Phillips Collection, Washington, D.C., 1996–97

Abigail Solomon-Godeau, 'Going Native: Paul Gauguin and the Invention of Primitivist Modernism', in Norma Broude and Mary D. Garrard (eds), *The Expanding Discourse: Feminism and Art History*, New York, 1992, reprinted from *Art in America*, no. 77, July 1989

Belinda Thomson (ed), *Gauguin: Maker of Myth*, exh. cat., Tate Modern, London; National Gallery of Art, Washington, D.C., 2010–11

Gary Tinterow, Michael Pantazzi and Vincent Pomarède, *Corot*, exh. cat., Galeries Nationales du Grand Palais, Paris; National Gallery of Canada, Ottawa; The Metropolitan Museum of Art, New York, 1996–97

Mary Tompkins Lewis (ed.), *Critical Readings in Impressionism and Post-Impressionism: An Anthology*, Oakland, 2007

Catalogues Raisonnés
Refer to the bibliography listed in Fonsmark et al. 2011 when no catalogue raisonné exists for a particular artist.

BOUDIN
Schmit 1973
Robert Schmit, *Eugène Boudin*, Paris, 1973

CÉZANNE
Rewald et al. 1996
John Rewald, with Walter Feilchenfeldt and Jayne Warman, *The Paintings of Paul Cézanne: A Catalogue Raisonné*, New York, 1996

COROT
Robaut and Moreau-Nélaton 1905
Alfred Robaut and Étienne Moreau-Nélaton, *L'Oeuvre de Corot*, 4 vols, Paris, 1905

COURBET
Courthion 1985
Pierre Courthion, *L'Opera completa di Courbet*, Milan, 1985

Fernier 1978
Robert Fernier, *La Vie et l'oeuvre de Gustave Courbet: catalogue raisonné*, Lausanne and Paris, 1978

C.-F. DAUBIGNY
Hellebranth 1976
Robert Hellebranth, *Charles-François Daubigny*, Morges, 1976

DAUMIER
Fuchs 1927
Eduard Fuchs, *Der Maler Daumier*, Munich, 1927

Fuchs 1930
Eduard Fuchs, *Der Maler Daumier, Nachtrag-Supplement*, Munich, 1930

Klossowski 1908
Erich Klossowski, *Honoré Daumier*, Munich, 1908

Maison 1996
K. E. Maison, *Honoré Daumier: Catalogue Raisonné of the Paintings, Watercolours and Drawings*, second edition, San Francisco, 1996

Mandel 1972
Gabriel Mandel, *Tout l'oeuvre peint de Daumier*, Paris, 1972

DEGAS
Lemoisne 1946
Paul-André Lemoisne, *Degas et son oeuvre*, 4 vols, Paris, 1946

Minervino 1970
Fiorella Minervino, *L'Opera completa di Degas*, Franco Russoli (ed.), Milan, 1970

DELACROIX
Bortolatto 1972
Luigina Rossi Bortolatto, *L'Opera pittorica completa di Delacroix*, Milan, 1972

Hureaux 1993
Alain Daguerre de Hureaux, *Delacroix*, Paris, 1993

Johnson 1981–89
Lee Johnson, *The Paintings of Eugène Delacroix: A Critical Catalogue*, 6 vols, Oxford, 1981–89

Robaut 1885
Alfred Robaut, *L'Oeuvre complet d'Eugène Delacroix: peintures, dessins, gravures, lithographies*, Paris, 1885

DUPRÉ
Aubrun 1974
Marie-Madeleine Aubrun, *Jules Dupré: catalogue raisonné de l'oeuvre peint, dessiné et gravé*, Paris, 1974

Aubrun 1982
Marie-Madeleine Aubrun, *Jules Dupré: catalogue raisonné de l'oeuvre, supplement*, Paris, 1982

GAUGUIN
Sugana 1972
G. M. Sugana, *L'Opera completa di Gauguin*, Milan, 1972

Wildenstein et al. 1964
Georges Wildenstein, Daniel Wildenstein and Raymond Cogniat (eds), *Gauguin*, 2 vols, Paris, 1964

Wildenstein 2001
Daniel Wildenstein, *Gauguin, premier itinéraire d'un sauvage: catalogue de l'oeuvre peint*, Paris, 2001

GONZALÈS
Sainsaulieu and Mons 1990
Marie-Caroline Sainsaulieu and Jacques de Mons, *Eva Gonzalès: étude critique et catalogue raisonné*, Paris, 1990

GUILLAUMIN
Gray 1991
Christopher Gray, *Armand Guillaumin*, Chester, C.T., 1991

INGRES
Camesasca 1971
Ettore Camesasca, *Tout l'oeuvre peint d'Ingres*, Paris, 1971

Ternois 1980
Daniel Ternois, *Ingres*, Paris, 1980

Wildenstein 1954
Georges Wildenstein, *Ingres*, London, 1954

MANET
Duret 1902
Théodore Duret, *Histoire d'Édouard Manet et de son oeuvre, avec un catalogue des peintures et des pastels*, Paris, 1902

Jamot and Wildenstein 1932
Paul Jamot and Georges Wildenstein, *Manet*, 2 vols, Paris, 1932

Orienti and Venturi 1967
Sandra Orienti and Marcello Venturi (eds), *L'Opera pittorica di Édouard Manet*, Milan, 1967

Orienti 1970
Sandra Orienti, *Tout l'oeuvre peint d'Édouard Manet*, Paris, 1970

Orienti and Pool 1985
Sandra Orienti and Phoebe Pool,
The Complete Paintings of Manet,
Harmondsworth, 1985

Rouart and Wildenstein 1975
Denis Rouart and Daniel Wildenstein,
Édouard Manet: catalogue raisonné,
2 vols, Geneva, 1975

Tabarant 1931
Adolphe Tabarant, *Manet, histoire
catalographique*, Paris, 1931

MATISSE
Carrà 1982
Massimo Carrà, *Tout l'oeuvre peint de
Matisse, 1904–28*, Paris, 1982

MONET
Wildenstein 1996
Daniel Wildenstein, *Monet: catalogue
raisonné / Werkverzeichnis*, 4 vols,
Cologne, 1996

MORISOT
Angoulvent 1933
Monique Angoulvent, *Berthe Morisot*,
Paris, 1933

Bataille and Wildenstein 1961
Marie-Louise Bataille and Georges
Wildenstein, *Berthe Morisot: catalogue
des peintures, pastels et aquarelles*,
Paris, 1961

Clairet et al. 1997
Alain Clairet, with Delphine Montalant
and Yves Rouart, *Berthe Morisot: catalogue
raisonné de l'oeuvre peint*, Montolivet, 1997

PISSARRO
Pissarro and Venturi 1939
Ludovic-Rodo Pissarro and Lionello
Venturi, *Camille Pissarro: son art, son
oeuvre*, Paris, 1939

REDON
Berger 1964
Klaus Berger, *Odilon Redon,
Phantasie und Farbe*, Cologne, 1964

Wildenstein and Lacau St Guily 1996
Alec Wildenstein, with Agnès Lacau
St Guily, *Odilon Redon: catalogue
raisonné de l'oeuvre peint et dessiné*,
Paris, 1996

RENOIR
Daulte 1971
François Daulte, *Auguste Renoir:
catalogue raisonné de l'oeuvre peint*,
5 vols, Lausanne, 1971

Fezzi 1972
Elda Fezzi, *L'Opera completa di Renoir
nel periodo impressionista, 1869–83*,
Milan, 1972

SISLEY
Daulte 1959
François Daulte, *Alfred Sisley:
catalogue raisonné de l'oeuvre peint*,
Lausanne, 1959

Photographic Acknowledgements

All works are reproduced by kind permission of the owners. Every attempt has been made to trace the rights holders of works reproduced. Specific acknowledgements are as follows:

Unless otherwise stated, images of all works are © Ordrupgaard, Copenhagen. Photo: Anders Sune Berg

Additional photographic credits:
Copenhagen, Ny Carlsberg Glyptotek: figs 4, 14
Copenhagen, © Ordrupgaard. Photo: Adam Mørk: figs 10, 11
Florence, photo Fine Art Images/ Heritage Images/Scala © 2019: fig. 6
Philadelphia, The Barnes Foundation © 2020: fig. 15
New York, The Metropolitan Museum of Art: fig. 13
Washington, National Gallery of Art: fig. 2
Winterthur, Oskar Reinhart Collection 'Am Römerholz': fig. 5

Additional copyright:
Henri Matisse, © Succession H. Matisse / DACS 2020: cat. 60, fig. 15

Supporters of the Royal Academy of Arts

THE PRESIDENT'S CIRCLE

Blavatnik Family Foundation
The Clore Duffield Foundation
Mervyn and Jeanne Davies
The Dorfman Foundation
Dunard Fund
Mrs Drue Heinz Hon. DBE
Heritage Lottery Fund
Mrs Gabrielle Jungels-Winkler
Ronald and Rita McAulay
The McLennan Family
Sir John Madejski OBE DL
The Mead Family Foundation
Mr and Mrs Robert Miller
The Monument Trust
Julia and Hans Rausing
Simon and Virginia Robertson
The Rothschild Foundation
Dame Jillian Sackler DBE
The Garfield Weston Foundation
The Maurice Wohl Charitable
    Foundation
The Wolfson Foundation

MAJOR BENEFACTORS OF THE
REDEVELOPMENT PROJECT

The 29th May 1961 Charitable Trust
Ambassador Matthew Barzun and
    Brooke Brown Barzun
Aryeh and Elana Bourkoff, LionTree
Sir Francis and the Hon. Lady Brooke
The Cadogan Charity
Sir Richard and Lady Carew Pole
Adrian Cheng
Jeremy Coller Foundation
John and Gail Coombe
Lady Alison Deighton
The Eranda Foundation
The Fidelity UK Foundation
The Foyle Foundation
J. Paul Getty Jr Charitable Trust
Horace W. Goldsmith Foundation
Mr and Mrs Jim Grover
The Alexis and Anne-Marie Habib
    Foundation
Charles and Kaaren Hale
Nicolette and Frederick Kwok
The Kirby Laing Foundation
Lord Leverhulme's Charitable Trust
Christian Levett and Mougins Museum
    of Classical Art
The Linbury Trust
Miss Rosemary Lomax Simpson
The Lord Mayor's Appeal
Mr William Loschert
Philip and Valerie Marsden
The Paul Mellon Estate
Milner Educational Trust
Christina Ong
P. F. Charitable Trust
The Porter Foundation
John Porter Charitable Trust
The Schroder Foundation
Mr Sean Scully RA
Jake and Hélène Marie Shafran
Mr Richard S. Sharp
Dasha Shenkman

William and Maureen Shenkman
The estate of the late Mrs Pauline
    Sitwell
David and Deborah Stileman
The Swire Charitable Trust
The late Sir Anthony Tennant and Lady
    Tennant
The Thompson Family Charitable Trust
Sir Siegmund Warburg's Voluntary
    Settlement
The Welton Foundation
Mr W. Galen Weston and the Hon. Mrs
    Hilary Weston

BENEFACTORS OF THE
REDEVELOPMENT PROJECT

Aldama Foundation
Lord and Lady Aldington
Mrs Allen-Huxley
Joan and Robin Alvarez
The Anson Charitable Trust
The Band Trust
Sir David and Lady Bell
Ms Linda Bennett and Mr Philip Harley
The Deborah Loeb Brice Foundation
The Consuelo and Anthony Brooke
    Charitable Trust
Garvin and Steffanie Brown
Mr and Mrs John Burns
Peter and Sally Cadbury
Carew Pole Charitable Trust
Dr Edmund Carter
Mr Richard Chang
Sir Trevor and Lady Susan Chinn
Mr and Mrs Jonathan Clarke
Mr Andrés Clase
The John S. Cohen Foundation
Ina De and James Spicer
Sir Harry Djanogly
The John Ellerman Foundation
Mr Richard Elman
The Lord Farringdon Charitable Trust
Mr and Mrs Stephen Fitzgerald
Mr Thomas Gibson
The Golden Bottle Trust
Nicholas and Judith Goodison's
    Charitable Settlement
Antony Gormley and Vicken Parsons
Sir Nicholas Grimshaw CBE PPRA
The Roger De Haan Charitable Trust
The late Sir Ronald Grierson
Fiona and Peter Hare
Mr and Mrs Julian Heslop
Mr and Mrs Jeremy Hosking
Harry Hyman and family
The Inchcape Foundation
Japanese Committee of Honour of
    the Royal Academy of Arts
Alistair D. K. Johnston CMG FCA
The David Lean Foundation
Christopher Le Brun PPRA and
    Charlotte Verity
The Lennox and Wyfold Foundation
Mr Nelson Leong
Mr and Mrs Mark Loveday
Molly Lowell and David Borthwick
Dr Lee MacCormick Edwards
    Charitable Foundation

Mr and Mrs Donald Main
Mr Javad and Mrs Narmina Marandi
HRH Princess Marie-Chantal of Greece
J. P. Marland Charitable Trust
The late Mr Minoru Mori Hon. KBE and
    Mrs Mori
Mr Charles Outhwaite
Simon and Midge Palley
John H. Pattisson
The Pilgrim Trust
Mr and Mrs Maurice Pinto
Mrs Tineke Pugh
Sir Simon and Victoria, Lady Robey
    OBE
Richard and Ruth Rogers
Sir Paul and Lady Ruddock
Mr Wafic Rida Saïd
Mrs Coral Samuel CBE
The Basil Samuel Charitable Trust
Edwina Sassoon
Guy Senior, in memory of Brian and
    Mary Senior, Friends of the RA
Louisa Service OBE
David and Sophie Shalit
Mr Brian Smith
Mr Christopher Smith
Mr and Mrs Roger Staton
Sir Hugh and Lady Stevenson
The late Sir David Tang KBE
Julian and Louisa Treger
Martin and Anja Weiss
Sian and Matthew Westerman
Chris Wilkinson OBE RA and Diana
    Wilkinson
Mr Peter Williams
Ivor and Caroline Windsor
Manuela and Iwan Wirth
Mr Yuzo Yagi

MAJOR BENEFACTORS TOWARDS
REDEVELOPING THE RA SCHOOLS

Julia and Hans Rausing
Dunard Fund

The Band Trust
Adrian Cheng
Lady Alison Deighton
The Garfield Weston Foundation
Mrs Gabrielle Jungels-Winkler
Nicolette and Frederick Kwok
The Mead Family Foundation
Milner Educational Trust
The estate of the late Miss Constance-
    Anne Parker
Jake and Hélène Marie Shafran
Sir Siegmund Warburg's Voluntary
    Settlement

MAJOR BENEFACTORS OF THE RA
SCHOOLS ENDOWMENT FUND

Dunard Fund
Ronald and Rita McAulay

Chenevière Travel Award
The Eranda Rothschild Foundation
Peter Greenham Fund
Sir Roger de Grey Memorial Fund

E. Vincent Harris Fund
J. Heritage Peters Maintenance Fund
Ivor Rey Scholarship Fund
Schools Portfolio Fund
The estate of the late Mrs Pauline
    Sitwell
Starr Fund
Patricia Turner Award Vandaleur

BENEFACTORS OF THE RA SCHOOLS

Artists Collecting Society
Charlotte Bonham-Carter Charitable
    Trust
William Brake Trust
John S. Cohen Foundation
Dreamchasing
The Gilbert and Eileen Edgar
    Foundation
Epson
The Eranda Rothschild Foundation
Holbeck Charitable Trust
The Charles Michael Holloway
    Charitable Trust
Intrinsic Value Investors
Leverhulme Trust
Mr and Mrs Mark Loveday
Mr Nelson Leong
The Maccabaeans
The Machin Foundation
Batia and Idan Ofer
Andrés Olow Clase
Christina Ong
Stanley Picker Charitable Trust
Red Butterfly Foundation
The estate of the late Mr Ivor Rey
Peter Rippon
The Rose Foundation
Archie Sherman Charitable Trust
Sir Paul and Lady Smith
The South Square Trust
The Nina and Roger Stewart
    Charitable Trust
Tileyard Studios
Celia Walker Art Foundation
Mr W. Galen Weston and the Hon. Mrs
    Hilary Weston
The Harold Hyam Wingate Foundation
*and those who wish to remain
anonymous*

PATRONS

Chair of RA Patrons
Mr Matthew Langton

International Circle
Mrs Niloufar Bakhtiar-Bakhtiar
Mr Lars Bane
Lady Alison Deighton
Jacques and Valentina Drouin
Victoria Gelfand-Magalhaes
Mr Alexander Green
Mrs Ellen Hanson
Mrs Stella Kesaeva
Nelson Leong
Mr Christian Levett
Mrs Aarti Lohia
Mr Nick Loup

Mrs Fatima Maleki
Mr and Mrs Scott Mead
Mrs Christina Ong
Mr Hideyuki Osawa
Maya Rasamny
Frances Reynolds
Mr Thaddaeus Ropac
Negin Rostami
Mrs Sabine Sarikhani
Yukiko and Anders U. Schroeder
Petri and Jolana Vainio
Yvonne Winkler
Ms Chizuko Yashiro
Mercedes Zobel
*and those who wish to remain
anonymous*

Platinum Patrons
Celia and Edward Atkin CBE
Paul Baines
Mr Christopher Bake
Alex Beard and Emma Vernetti
The Deborah Loeb Brice Foundation
Mr and Mrs Frank Destribats
Hugo Eddis
Tatiana Fokina
Mr Stephen Gosztony
Mr Jim Grover
Charles and Kaaren Hale
Mr Yan Huo
Mrs Elizabeth Lenz
David and Sophie Shalit
*and those who wish to remain
anonymous*

Gold Patrons
Joan and Robin Alvarez
Tom and Diane Berger
Sam and Rosie Berwick
Molly Lowell Borthwick
Richard Bram and Monika Machon
Sir Francis Brooke Bt
Mrs Diana Carney
Ms Lisa Carrodus
Mr Andres Clase
Christopher and Alex Courage
Nicoletta Fiorucci
Mrs Patricia Franks
Swag and Nupur Ganguly
Jonathon Gill
Mrs Robin Hambro
Rosalyn and Hugo Henderson
Mrs Elizabeth Hosking
Mr Christopher Kneale
Ms Maxine Kohn
Sir Sydney Lipworth QC and Lady
    Lipworth
Natalie Livingstone
Mr William Loschert
Scott and Laura Malkin
Federico Marchetti
Mr Stephen Marquardt
Mr Michael Marx
Sir Keith and Lady Mills
Lady Myners
Simon and Sabi North
Mr and Mrs Simon Oliver
Yana and Stephen Peel
Paulo and Caroline Pereira

Melanie Rademacher
Lady Rayne Lacey
Jean and Geoffrey Redman-Brown
The Lady Renwick of Clifton
Dasha Shenkman OBE
Mr Richard Simmons CBE
Mr Kevin Sneader and Ms Amy
    Muntner
David and Alison Sola
Jane Spack
Raksha Sriram
Mr Michael Stiff
David Stileman
Robert and Simone Suss
Kathryn Uhde
Erica Wax
Mr Peter Williams
Manuela and Iwan Wirth
Mr Robert John Yerbury
Alex Zadah
*and those who wish to remain
anonymous*

Silver Patrons
Lady J. Lloyd Adamson
Mrs Spindrift Al Swaidi
Mrs Susie Allen-Huxley
Ghalia and Omar Al-Qattan
Mrs Jacqueline Appel
Marco and Francesca Assetto
Mr John Attree
Mrs Leslie Bacon
Mrs Enfys Bagguley
Mr Richard Baldwin
Mrs Jane Barker
Lorna Anne Barker
Constance and Boris Baroudel
Ms Martina Batovic
Mr David Baty
Juliet de Baubigny
Catherine Baxendale
Mr and Mrs Jonathan and Sarah
    Bayliss
Francesca Bellini Joseph
Mrs J. K. M. Bentley, Liveinart
Ms Miel de Botton
Jean and John Botts
Eleanor E. Brass
Viscountess Bridgeman
Mr and Mrs Richard Briggs OBE
Mrs Elizabeth Bristow
Mrs Marcia Brocklebank
Mrs Charles Brown
Jeremy Brown
Mr and Mrs Zak Brown
Lord Browne of Madingley
Ms Debra Burt
Ms Pauline Cacucciolo
Mr F. A. A. Carnwath CBE
Brian and Melinda Carroll
Ursula Casamonti
Diana Cawdell Trew
Mrs Ann Chapman-Daniel
Sir Trevor and Lady Chinn
Mr Philip Chitty
Jenny Christensson
Damian and Anastasia Chunilal
Rosalind Clayton
Mrs Alyce Faye Cleese

Mr Richard Clothier
Mr and Mrs George Coelho
Denise Cohen Charitable Trust
Vanessa Colomar de Enserro
Mrs Jennifer Coombs
Andrew M. Coppel CBE and
    June Coppel
Mark and Cathy Corbett
Anne Cortazzi
Mrs Caroline Cullinan
Mrs Georgina David
Mr Daniel Davies
Mrs Dominic Dowley
Mr and Mrs Jim Downing
Ms Noreen Doyle
Mrs Janet Dwek
Mrs Samira El Hachioui
Mr and Mrs Jeff Eldredge
Susan Elliott
Nigel and Christine Evans
Mrs Catherine Farquharson
Catherine Ferguson
Mrs Stroma Finston
Commander P. Fletcher
Mrs Jocelyn Fox
Virginia Gabbertas
Mrs Jill Garcia
Mr Stephen Garrett
Mr Mark Garthwaite
Joanna George
Mrs Mina Gerowin Herrmann
Jacqueline and Jonathan Gestetner
Caroline and Alan Gillespie
Mr Mark Glatman
Stephen and Margarita Grant
Mrs Michael Green
Mrs Margaret Guitar
Mrs Selima Gürtler
Roger Hall
Mr Lindsay Hamilton
Alex Haidas and Thalia Chryssikou
Mr Christopher Harrison
Mrs Sarah Harvey-Collicott
The Hayden Family Foundation
Sir John Hegarty and Miss Philippa
    Crane
Sir Michael and Lady Heller
Lady Heseltine
Mrs Michele Hillgarth
Mr and Mrs Jonathan Hindle
Mary Hobart
Anne Holmes-Drewry
Professor and Mrs Ken Howard RA
Mr Philip Hudson
Mr and Mrs Jon Hunt
Mark and Fiona Hutchinson
S. Isern-Feliu
Mrs Caroline Jackson
Sir Martin and Lady Jacomb
Mrs Raymonde Jay
Mrs Cathy Jeffrey
Fiona Johnstone
Mrs Marcelle Joseph
Mr and Mrs S. Kahan
Dr Elisabeth Kehoe
Paul and Susie Kempe
Miss Rebecca Kemsley
Mrs Emma Keswick
Shareen Khattar

Princess Jeet Khemka
Mr Gerald Kidd
Mr D. H. Killick
Mrs Anna Kirrage
Mrs Aboudi Kosta
Mrs Alkistis Koukouliou
Mr and Mrs Herbert Kretzmer
Nicolette Kwok
Fawzi Kyriakos-Saad
Kathryn Langridge
Mr Matthew Langton
Jessica Lavooy
Patricia Lawrie
Mrs Anna Lee
Alan Leibowitz and Barbara Weiss
Lady Lever of Manchester
Dr Julie Llewelyn
Mrs Susanne Lobel
Miss R. Lomax-Simpson
Mr Guido Lombardo
Mr and Mrs Robin Lough
The Loveday Charitable Trust
Charles G. Lubar
Mr and Mrs Henry Lumley
Gillian McIntosh
Andrew and Judith McKinna
Sir John Mactaggart
Mr George Maher
Olivier and Priscilla Malingue
Mr Richard Mansell-Jones
Philip and Val Marsden
Mr Charles Martin
Mr and Mrs Richard C. Martin
Tessa Maxwell
Itxaso Mediavilla-Murray
The Anthony and Elizabeth Mellows
Mrs Victoria Mills
Victoria Miro
Mr Daniel Mitchell
Ms Bona Montagu
Ms Alessandra Morra
Simon Morris and Annalisa Burello
Jim Moyes
Mr Eli Muraidekh
Mr Stephen Musgrave
Mr James Nicholls
Mrs Tessa Nicholson
Patrick and Benedicte de Nonneville
Ms Emma Norden
Emma O'Donoghue
Ms L. C. O'Hara
Mr Richard Orders
Neil Osborn and Holly Smith
Roderick and Maria Peacock
Mr and Mrs D. J. Peacock
David Pike
Mr Basil Postan
Susan Prevezer
Lady Purves
John and Anne Raisman
Ms Mouna Rebeiz
Mrs Catherine Rees
David Remfry RA and Caroline
    Hansberry
Peter Rice Esq.
Mrs Kate de Rothschild
Miss Elaine Rowley
Sir Paul and Lady Ruddock
Sarah Ryan

Mrs Janice Sacher
Richard Saltoun
Mr Paul Sandilands
Christina Countess of Shaftesbury
Mr Robert N. Shapiro
Mr James B. Sherwood
Mrs Veronica Simmons
Mr and Mrs Alan K. Simpson
Brian D. Smith
Mr Stuart Southall
The Lady Henrietta St George
Miss Sarah Straight
Mrs Ziona Strelitz
Sir Hugh and Lady Sykes
Mr Matt Symonds
Anne Elizabeth Tasca
Nick Thexton
Mr Anthony J. Todd
Mrs Kirsten Tofte Jensen
Mr Ray Treen
Mrs Arabella Tullo
Miss M. L. Ulfane
John and Carol Wates
Mr Craig D. Weaver
The Duke and Duchess of Wellington
Mrs Juliana Wheeler
Mrs Diana Wilkinson
Mrs Janet Winslow
Marek and Penny Wojciechowski
Mr and Mrs Maurice Wolridge
David Zwirner
*and those who wish to remain
anonymous*

Young Patrons
Kalita Al Swaidi
Sophie Ashby
Ms Vanessa Aubry
Mr Gergely Battha-Pajor
Cy Bernheim
Mr Nicholas Bonsall
Mr Alexander Bradford
Ariana Brighenti
Jacqueline Chan
Mr Matthew Charlton
XiaoMeng Cheng
Frederike von Cranach
Christopher Eaton
Erola Farre Sola
Dr Brian Fu
Pierre-Antoine Godefroy
Adam Gordon
Miss Lemara Grant
Dr Irem Gunay
Merrilee Harbinson
Litian He
Mr Sidney Hiscox
Miss Amelia Hunton
Mr Phoebus Istavrioglu
Peter Jones
Ms Huma Kabakci
Rasika Kajaria
Miss Min Kemp
Miss Petra Kwan
Miss Carolina Lane
Han Lo
Mrs Victoria Luxem
Christina Makris
Mr Jean-David Malat

Patrick McCrae
Elaine MacDermot
Mr Joe Phelan
Mr Sebastian Plantin
Sophia Robert Kacacinskas
Ziba Sarikhani
Manon Elise Sel
Lily Stone
Sharon Strom
The Hon. Clarence Tan
Mr Milan Tomic
Mr Vassili Tsarenkov
Miss Navann Ty
Ms Zeynep Ugan
Miss Anna Wallington
Ms Cynthia Wu
Miss Burcu Yuksel
Alma Zevi
*and those who wish to remain
anonymous*

Patron Donors
Geoffrey and Johanna Ainsworth
William Brake Charitable Trust
Maryam Eisler
Mr and Mrs James Kirkman
Jacqueline and Marc Leland
Ms Ida Levine
Mrs Alexandra Nash
Cate Olson and Nash Robbins
Sir Michael Palin
The Michael and Nicola Sacher
    Charitable Trust
H. M. Sassoon Charitable Trust
Jake and Hélène Marie Shafran
Anthony and Rachel Williams
*and those who wish to remain
anonymous*

TRUSTEES OF THE ROYAL ACADEMY
TRUST
Registered Charity No. 1067270

Honorary President
HRH The Prince of Wales KG KT GCB
OM AK QSO ADC

Trustees
Lady Alison Myners (Chair)
Rob Suss (Deputy Chair)
President of the Royal Academy
    (ex officio)
Secretary and Chief Executive of
    the Royal Academy (ex officio)
Treasurer of the Royal Academy
    (ex officio)
Mr Petr Aven
Mr Aryeh Bourkoff
Mr Richard Chang
Dr Adrian Cheng
Ms Melanie Clore
Lady Deighton
Sir Lloyd Dorfman CBE
Mr Stephen Fry
Lady Heywood
Mr Clive Humby
Dame Carolyn McCall
Mr Philip Marsden
Mr Scott Mead